MAGICAL/
REALISM

ALSO BY VANESSA ANGÉLICA VILLARREAL

Beast Meridian

MAGICAL/ REALISM

Essays on Music, Memory, Fantasy, and Borders

VANESSA ANGÉLICA VILLARREAL

Tiny
Reparations
Books

An imprint of Penguin Random House LLC
penguinrandomhouse.com

Tiny Reparations and Tiny Reparations Books with colophon are registered trademarks of YQY, Inc.

All photographs courtesy of the author.

"Le Canción de la Nena" originally published in the *Oxford American*. "The Fantasy of Healing" originally published by *The Cut* and Vox Media, LLC, on December 10, 2021. "Memory, a Lacuna" was previously published in *The Seventh Wave*. Parts of "En Útero," "My Boyfriend's Maid," and "After the World-Breaking, World-Building" originally published in *Harper's Bazaar*, Hearst Magazine Media, Inc. "In the Shadow of the Wolf" was previously published by Graywolf Press. Parts of "Volver, Volver" originally published by Haymarket Books.

Excerpt from "Ditat Deus," from Eduardo C. Corral's *Slow Lightning* (2012), reprinted by permission of Yale University Press.

LIBRARY OF CONGRESS CATALOGING-IN-PUBLICATION DATA
Names: Villarreal, Vanessa Angélica, author.
Title: Magical/realism: essays on music, memory, fantasy, and borders / Vanessa Angélica Villarreal.
Description: [New York]: Tiny Reparations Books, [2024] | Includes bibliographical references.
Identifiers: LCCN 2024006002 (print) | LCCN 2024006003 (ebook) | ISBN 9780593187142 (hardcover) | ISBN 9780593187159 (ebook)
Subjects: LCSH: Villarreal, Vanessa Angélica. | Mexican American women authors—Biography. | Children of immigrants—United States—Social conditions. | Popular culture—United States. | American essays—Mexican American authors. | American essays—21st century.
Classification: LCC PS3622.I4939855 M34 2024 (print) | LCC PS3622.I4939855 (ebook) | DDC 813/.6—dc23/eng/20240311
LC record available at https://lccn.loc.gov/2024006002
LC ebook record available at https://lccn.loc.gov/2024006003

Printed in the United States of America
1st Printing

BOOK DESIGN BY DANIEL BROUNT

For Joaquín and Gilbert,
and for
every dream deferred, and every dreamer denied

I came to theory young, when I was still a child. . . .
I was desperately trying to discover the place of my
belonging. I was desperately trying to find my way
home.

—BELL HOOKS

Imagination like all living things lives *now*, and it
lives with, from, on true change. . . . The land out-
lasts the empires. The conquerors may leave desert
where there was forest and meadow, but the rain
will fall, the rivers will run to the sea. The unstable,
mutable, untruthful realms of Once-upon-a-time
are as much a part of human history and thought as
the nations in our kaleidoscopic atlases, and some
are more enduring.

—URSULA K. LE GUIN

CONTENTS

CONTENTS

CONTENTS

THE MIGRANT'S JOURNEY

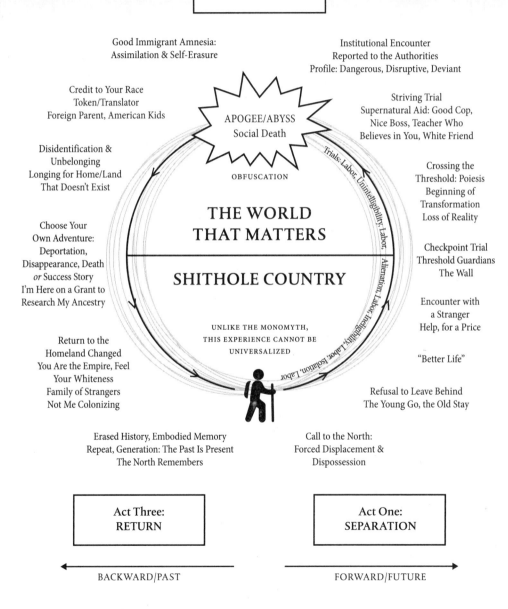

Act Two:
SUPREME ORDEAL

Good Immigrant Amnesia:
Assimilation & Self-Erasure

Institutional Encounter
Reported to the Authorities
Profile: Dangerous, Disruptive, Deviant

Credit to Your Race
Token/Translator
Foreign Parent, American Kids

Striving Trial
Supernatural Aid: Good Cop,
Nice Boss, Teacher Who
Believes in You, White Friend

Disidentification &
Unbelonging
Longing for Home/Land
That Doesn't Exist

APOGEE/ABYSS
Social Death

OBFUSCATION

Crossing the
Threshold: Poiesis
Beginning of
Transformation
Loss of Reality

Choose Your
Own Adventure:
Deportation,
Disappearance, Death
or Success Story
I'm Here on a Grant to
Research My Ancestry

THE WORLD
THAT MATTERS

SHITHOLE COUNTRY

Checkpoint Trial
Threshold Guardians
The Wall

Trials: Labor, Unintelligibility, Labor, Alienation, Labor, Illegibility, Labor, Isolation, Labor

Encounter with
a Stranger
Help, for a Price

UNLIKE THE MONOMYTH,
THIS EXPERIENCE CANNOT BE
UNIVERSALIZED

"Better Life"

Return to the
Homeland Changed
You Are the Empire, Feel
Your Whiteness
Family of Strangers
Not Me Colonizing

Refusal to Leave Behind
The Young Go, the Old Stay

Erased History, Embodied Memory
Repeat, Generation: The Past Is Present
The North Remembers

Call to the North:
Forced Displacement &
Dispossession

Act Three:
RETURN

Act One:
SEPARATION

← BACKWARD/PAST

FORWARD/FUTURE →

ABOUT A GIRL

*T*HAT NEVER HAPPENED. *12345678X*

---

1. In the end, this is the phrase I remember most from my marriage: a phrase that echoes through time, tying my marriage to my fore-mothers' marriages, my story to their stories, their stories a missing record in history, a history I can never reclaim. What is memory but a battleground, a bordered terrain between two versions of the truth?

2. SELF-ERASURE: And before that, there was the word Papi said to me at fourteen: *compónete. Compónete ya, por favor.* Fix yourself now, please, said in defeat. It was no longer the *pórtate bien* from my childhood. *Puros pinches problemas,* he would say, wishing for a more

obedient, feminine, respectable daughter. Fast-forward to me at thirty-seven, standing in someone else's dream: on the rim of the Pacific Ocean with a baby in my arms, married to a stranger who despised me, about to start a doctoral program. All surreal outcomes for the troubled teen with a past; at last I had *fixed myself, me compuse*. I'd become *una mujer recta, casada*, a mother, a college graduate, living the so-called American Dream.

It was a life I created in apology to my parents, the dream that I would live a decent life and never know struggle, a trap I rebelled against. *Para que nunca tengas que batallar.* I'd only ever repaid their sacrifices with sabotage, so to make it up to them, I erased the problems, the color, the wildness, and created the *buen hija* they could be proud of, living out the grand narratives of what a "better life" meant to them: assimilation to whiteness, cis-heteronormativity, bootstraps individualism, mestizaje, Manifest Destiny, and the earliest one little girls are taught to believe, Happily Ever After. These too are fantasies, the grand narratives that execute inside us without much thought until at midlife, something inevitably begins to fail.

3. MEMORY LOSS: When we moved to Los Angeles in 2016, the final year of my marriage, I was a new mother in the first year of my PhD program, and writing my first book. But my mind was in pieces, and time slipped through some enormous, yawning wound I could not close. One of the more concerning symptoms I reported before receiving a PTSD and ADHD diagnosis was the feeling that, since having the baby, I was living in a state of unreality, or chirality—as if my home, my body, and my life only existed on the other side of the mirror. Derealization and depersonalization, the nurse called it. It was the same unreality of my adolescence, but now I was the mother, facing much higher stakes. My brain had erected a barrier

between me and the profound loneliness of my marriage, a reality that was always shifting on unstable, unknowable ground.

4. When I visualize my memory, I imagine the defrag screen in Windows 95—rows of little blue squares punctured with missing data, the corrupted files speckled throughout in pink and yellow. I loved to defrag my Compaq computer and watch the teal squares turn blue and rearrange themselves. The pink and yellow files were errors, places the file structure was broken, or duplicated, overwritten, deleted. Odd little squares that recorded nothing, invited speculation.

5. My father has cut off all contact with his family, for good reason; on my mother's side, borders and elders with old grudges have made us all strangers. *El árbol empieza aquí,* or, the tree starts here, Papi says. As far as he's concerned, our line begins in 1980, the year he and my mother were married in Reynosa. The family who came before would become unknown and unremembered, and over time, cease to exist.

Another word for starting over is *shame,* and when shame is combined with the immigrant dream of a "better life," it's easy to see how mestizes erase themselves by "starting over," how entire lineages are lost, disowned, renamed, hidden, disappeared. If I am expected to be the repository of cultural and ancestral memory, the recipe librarian, the secret keeper, what lineage will my child inherit? Not family, not language, not stories, not traditions, nor any sense of a homeland—just absence. Whiteness. To heal the present, I must recover the past.

I try to piece our narrative back together from photos, documents, stories, songs—portals into my childhood, my parents' childhoods, our dead, to the land and their migrations, a line I trace

5

back that ends at a cotton hacienda. Then, *No records found.* The same result I get from the Demand for Production and Discovery in my divorce proceedings: *February through May are missing. Therefore, that never happened.* As the ancestral memory I was trying to recover disappeared, my memory was also being erased in the present. I was stranded in time, a field of cotton, a whiteness that covers the land.

6. Perhaps memory loss is the intended result of America. I am a mestiza, a race defined by erasure and negation—*not* Indigenous, *not* white, but a national construct of mixedness, one that, according to the casta system, is the halfway point on the way to whiteness. The hacienda is where our indigeneity ends and "Mexican" begins—an identity born in the field between nations, a ghost in the marrow, trying to remember its name. I grieve this loss. Memory itself is a *terra nullius,* a land emptied by language and law, laid bare for a man to plant his flag.

7. OVERWRITE: Theory, not therapy, is what helped me begin to make sense of it all. As I studied for exams and raised my child while embroiled in divorce litigation and the world under Trump burned, I encountered the concepts of hauntology, post-humanism, critical fabulation, queer phenomenology, disidentification, the rhizome, racial cartographies, the subaltern, the production of space—language and frameworks that allowed me to remap and reworld my broken reality. But it was the loss of the real, Jean Baudrillard's concept of the simulacra that shape our reality, that finally separated the layers— the grand narrative, and my real life. He begins *Simulacra and Simulation* by citing "On the Exactitude of Science," a short Jorge Luis Borges story about cartographers who draw a map so detailed, the map itself is the size of the empire, an exact replica reproducing the territory point for point, until the map itself covers the land,

then *becomes* the land. "The territory no longer precedes the map, nor does it survive it. It is nevertheless the map that precedes the territory . . ."

Baudrillard used the fabulation and allegory of magical realism to clarify the fiction and violence of borders, the simulation of different nations on either side as a panting black bear paces its length; how the land does not produce borders, but borders themselves produce the land; how empire draws the map until its signifiers replace the land itself. Borders are sites of race-making, nation-building, temporal dislocation—the loss of the real, derealization, and depersonalization. In other words, trauma as I understood it: the moment you lose your reality to someone else's story.

8. A dark thread pulls behind my navel; the nerve-ghost of my umbilical cord connected to a black, starry pool in my center, the nebula I was connected to before I was born. It is a knowing beyond language. I light candles for my dead, listen for their voices. I write from this starry center; I write what they say until it's true.

9. Once, a friend invited me over for dinner and put on a vinyl record as background music. In the first nanosecond, the breath the audience takes before the cheers and applause begin, I asked, "Is this *Unplugged?*" They teased me mercilessly about it—how could I recognize the album from *silence*, when the song hadn't even started yet? It was because as a kid, I played those first few seconds over and over to hear Kurt's voice introduce "About a Girl": "Good evening. This is off our first record, most people don't own it." It stuck with me; something about it radiated truth.

10. Magic and trauma are inextricable; both begin in the language of disbelief; *This can't be real. I can't believe it.* I look out at the wall that

extends an imaginary border beyond the land and into the sea, as if it could split the ocean in half. How do you make sense of an incomprehensible world? Baudrillard turned to magical realism to expose the absurdity of empire through fabulist allegory. If trauma is a state of unreality, and grief is a site of magical thinking, then magical realism is both its narrative and interpretive mode.

11. *¡Toma el llavero abuelita*
     Y enséñame tu ropero!
     Con cosas maravillosas
     Y tan hermosas que guardas tú

     It is a given that the adult often sings the lullaby to the child. But in the 1934 song "El Ropero," by Mexican composer Francisco Gabilondo Soler, also known as the singing cricket Cri-Cri, the lullaby is sung from the perspective of the child *to* the grandmother, asking her to open her wardrobe so that they might see all of her old, wonderful things: their grandfather's sword, their mother's old doll, an old book of stamps. It is a singular song with a singular sentiment, culturally specific to Latin American grandmothers, their relationships to their grandchildren, their histories. Perhaps the child's desire to see objects of the past is a primal, tender force; a need to know a disappearing history; a desire to remember a past lost to colonization. My mother and my son have this tender relationship, as I did with my own grandmother and the stories she told me about her things—pañuelos, castañetas, perfumes. I still have an old rosary of hers I've draped over the edge of her photo on my altar. I think often of her ghost. There is no English equivalent to this song.

12. What if, through objects, I could time-travel through family history, precolonial history, return to the scene of the crime and

examine the evidence; reinscribe family silences with the truth. This is probably my most persistent magical thought—using objects my elders touched as portals. To see my grandmother again, right the wrongs in her life, know who my ancestors were, reconnect with their persistent presence, absence. But reality doesn't permit time travel or ripping portals into space-time; it insists on moving forward, a linear flow between the seen and unseen, the real and the imagined. Until I found out about New Materialism and Object-Oriented Ontology, a theory of speculative realism, the raw tools of world-building. I imagine a history reclaimed from the mnemonic void of colonization—the history itself an elaborate invention I conceived in the realm of the fantastic.

13. Fantasy is an act of imagination; to recall a memory activates the imagination; history is a collective imagination. Where is the line between fantasy, memory, and history if each is set in an imagined past? What demarcates their borders? Every act of remembering corrodes the memory itself, warps its details, pushes it toward fantasy.

14. History is one man speaking over a vast silence. For historically silenced voices, truth, Dian Million writes, is "an elaborate edifice of memory and emotion." The only proof we have of the past is the trauma it produces in the present—an enigma, a narrative position of silence.

15. If all written history is colonial, then the past is irretrievable. Stories, myths, folktales—these are the echoes of a past before history.

16. In 2018, author Lionel Shriver wrote in the *Spectator* that "from now until 2025, literary excellence will be secondary to ticking all those ethnicity, gender, disability, sexual preference and crap-education boxes . . . If an agent submits a manuscript written by a

gay transgender Caribbean who dropped out of school at seven and powers around town on a mobility scooter, it will be published whether or not said manuscript is an incoherent, tedious, meandering and insensible pile of mixed-paper recycling." Two years earlier, she gave a similar speech protesting accusations of cultural appropriation in a sombrero.

17. In the drafting of this book, I frame this quote from Melissa Febos's *Bodywork* above my desk: "Listen to me: It is not gauche to write about trauma. It is subversive. . . . By convincing us to police our own and one another's stories, they have enlisted us in the project of our own continued disempowerment."

18. Scarcity tells me, *you only have one shot*. This book cannot simply be an essay collection on immigrant daughterhood, motherhood, divorce, or institutional violence. The vast silence from borderlands voices across the literary landscape, especially in creative nonfiction, cultural criticism, and memoir, makes the responsibility to represent overwhelming. As I wring my hands about not misrepresenting or exploiting my mother's and grandmother's immigration stories, *American Dirt*, a novel about a Mexican mother and son who are forced to illegally cross the border due to cartel violence, written by Jeanine Cummins, a white American woman, received a seven-figure advance, was an Oprah's Book Club selection, and remained on the *New York Times* Best Seller list for thirty-six weeks, selling over three million copies. While fully capitalizing on immigrant trauma as a plot, it remains apolitical in its assessment so that the Middle American reader never has to confront the stickier moral territory that drives displacement and migration. In her afterword, Cummins attempts to humanize "the faceless brown mass" at the

center of American anti-immigrant debates, and cites her undocumented husband, an Irish immigrant who lived in the United States for ten years with no legal consequences, being pulled over by police as inspiration. "I wish someone slightly browner than me would write it," she says. "But then I thought, *if you're the person who has the capacity to be a bridge, why not be a bridge.*" Many people slightly browner than her have written that story, for a lot less money and exposure—people who have crossed that bridge to get here.

19. How can one write from the narrative position of silence? In "The Site of Memory," Toni Morrison writes about the importance of writing as a Black woman, and as marginalized people, about things that are "too terrible to relate" after centuries of intentional forgetting and self-silencing. Black women and marginalized writers, in the act of writing, she argues, have historically self-silenced and omitted upsetting details to keep the comfort of the white reader in mind. White writers have never had to self-censor for a more powerful race this way. But marginalized people's writing—enslaved, Indigenous, immigrant, queer—is full of these silences. Silence registers the presence of power.

20. In an op-ed titled "The Long Shadow of *American Dirt*," critic Pamela Paul argues that since the publication of *American Dirt*, writers of color have silenced white writers and bullied their way into publishing via cancel culture, and now white writers are self-silencing so as not to offend the angry mob. But I see it differently—the long shadow of *American Dirt* is not the "self-censorship" of white writers but the absences that writers like Jeanine Cummins are allowed to fill. Her version of the immigrant narrative is a profound failure of imagination, and yet nothing has eclipsed it in the popular

imagination. Paul argues that the value of *American Dirt* as a novel is that it creates "empathy," a useless feeling that never creates material change for undocumented people. Would Paul have that same praise for a book that *challenges* Americans and, rather than appeal to their empathy, turns its gaze back on the reader? A book that, instead of having the reader gaze across the border in pity from the comfort of a gated community, in the Brechtian tradition, holds up a mirror, and turns the reader's gaze back on itself? Isn't that what cancel culture is? The reversal of the gaze?

21. Cancel culture is the practice of collective memory. *This you?* If history is a carefully curated public narrative, then collective memory is its counterpublic—the insubordinate publics that form in opposition to a dominant narrative. Counterpublics can be social constructions, like "women of color"; I also like to use the term for other kinds of groups, like "redwood trees." The point is insubordination and the subversion of power—that's a counterpublic. For the working class, women, people of color—the intended recipients of carefully curated histories—to refuse a narrative and crowdsource a new one is a radical act. Remembering against the accepted account is a radical act.

22. *Radical*, meaning "of, relating to, or proceeding from a root," derives from the Latin *radix* (as does *radish*, a root vegetable). The word evolved between the seventeenth and nineteenth centuries to take on the sense of reform—"change from the roots." How that evolution came about, though, is less clear. The etymological history of *radical* doesn't point beyond England, but the period in which it came to mean extreme political ideology, or challenge to institutions, coincides with the height of American colonization and the transatlantic slave trade. That semantic shift has been credited to the

reforms of the British liberal party, but I think its true source was the people closest to the land, the people who worked the land—the enslaved, Indigenous peoples, migrant workers—and the challenges their rhizomatic communities represented to Empire. The land itself is a perfect record, and the root of every plant is exquisitely conscious. The body is an extension of the land; remembering is its radical act.

23. The best toy to get at the tiendita was the magic slate board: a black cardboard rectangle with two sheets—gray carbon paper in the middle and a clear plastic sheet on top—paired with a plastic pen, like an Etch A Sketch. You could write something on top of the clear surface, and when you lifted the sheets up, it was erased, but everything you had written before remained impressed onto the surfaces beneath, every stroke a trace impression that would be recorded forever. Thirty years later, in graduate school, I would read about Freud's notion of the unconscious as the Mystic Writing Pad, a surface that can be endlessly inscribed upon and erased, or renewed, but each renewal leaves a trace of the previous inscription. Then I would read Edward Said on how Antonio Gramsci said you are a product of all of history depositing its traces in you, in your body. It is the colonized person's imperative to create an inventory of those traces, Said wrote. Through writing.

24. If the past is embodied, what has left its trace in me?

25. I've always been fascinated by tree rings, ice cores, and sedimentary rock, and the idea that these long earth processes are the most accurate records of deep time—the reversal of poles, sea levels, climate, animal life. The earth also holds memory in the form of energy, from the radiation that lingers at bomb sites to the psychic imprint

violence leaves behind, the tension you can feel in a room after a fight. I remember reading somewhere that ancient pots, in the way they were made—this act of spinning in the hands—accidentally "recorded" the sounds of life around them in the clay grooves, much like a blank disc of vinyl records music into its grooves. Archaeologists were able to "play" the grooves in the pots and hear voices, children, animals, for twenty to sixty seconds. Imagine hearing these lost voices, held inside the grooves of a pot. Imagine all the other textures in the world that hold voices in ways we don't know how to "play" yet. Everything that has happened is recorded in the matter around us.

26. My favorite line from *Game of Thrones* has always been "The North remembers." On the show, it means that the North's history is stored as collective memory, which is the kind of memory that, no matter what forces attempt to erase it, will live on in the memories and stories of its people. And even if all the people of the North are eradicated, the Weirwood trees—white-trunked, red-leaved trees that weep blood from the faces formed in their whorls—are both witness to and recorders of all history, stored in the body of the tree, and felt in the roots in the land. That resonated with me—that a people on the farthest margin of a country, the people of a borderlands, a conquered people who maintain the "blood of the First Men," would protect their collective memory. It always meant something different to me, the daughter of norteños: jornaleros, hacendados, braceros, campesinos. "El norte recuerda."

27. CORRUPTED FILE: Once upon a time, this book was going to be about a girl, a restored record of my grandmother's childhood on a hacienda in San Alberto, Durango, as the eldest daughter of cotton laborers; about how she was sold off as a child bride at fourteen to

14

a man over twice her age; about having a child as a child; about being cut open over and over, only to ever deliver stillborns; about men who hit; about running away from those men, over and over, even if it means leaving your children behind and crossing a border alone; about how my mother and uncle crossed the border as children, unaccompanied, to join her; about their undocumented lives in the Rio Grande Valley; about cancer; about the borders cut into our mothers' bodies; about patterns, and how they repeat when our mothers insist on silence.

28. All the best stories are about a girl. (I say this only as a provocation— Joseph Campbell is rolling in his grave.) Odysseus, Luke Skywalker, Aragorn, Jesus? Amateurs. Look no further than the fairy-tale princess, shining daughter of impossible beauty, object of desire and chivalric love, her story told over and over, an inescapable cycle: Helen of Troy, Psyche, Isolde, Stephanie Seymour in "November Rain," Buttercup, Pretty Woman, Maid in Manhattan.

29. BIT ROT: My earliest memories are of borders and fairy tales. Like most girls, I was raised on cuentos my elders told me in Spanish. When Mami would drive me across the Brownsville border to spend a few days in Matamoros with my padrinos while she worked, my tía Lupe would let me listen to *Walt Disney Presenta Cuentos en Español* on vinyl. On long, slow afternoons I watched bright-green lizards crawl up the windows and blow pink bubbles in and out of their throats as the black disc spun tales of Cenicienta, rescued from a life of endless domestic labor; La Bella Durmiente, doted on by three magical tías; Blanca Nieves, a refugee who despite her beauty and whiteness still had to cook, clean, and take care of seven grown men to earn love.

30. This core memory is mostly fantasy now. All of the individual facts are true, but I've called it up so many times, I've strung its images and fragments together into a kind of fiction. It feels true. My padrinos, Tío Mario and Tía Lupe, are gone now, and this is what little I have left of them. *Mi reina.* My queen, they'd say.

31. Grief is how fantasy fuses with the memory of Mexico, and how the land of the Rio Grande Valley becomes an enchanted kingdom. And when we moved away, home became a place imagined in memory, peopled with our dead.

32. Princesses I have been for Halloween, in chronological order: She-Ra Princess of Power, 1986; Snow White, 1987; Pocahontas, 1995.

33. In my family, the women are made powerless through the denial of their language, in which the story of a life becomes a silence, a shame withheld. Information is passed in pláticas between comadres, spoken softly so the children can't hear. The refusal to speak against a violent husband, the withholding of cancer screening results—these are the silences that took my grandmother's life at fifty.

34. In September 2017 I flew to Chetumal to visit my dear tía Mela, my grandmother's last living sister, to ask for the details of my grandmother's and mother's life. I took a video camera to Chetumal to record our pláticas, conduct an interview. She agreed, wanted to help. But as soon as I hit record, my tía lowered her voice to barely above a whisper. She skimmed over details, omitted critique, spoke well of everyone. Upon playback, over half of what she said was inaudible.

35. And as in so many immigrant families, the story becomes a silence refusing its forgetting, doomed to repeat itself inside every daughter until one becomes so haunted with nerve data, it surfaces in the

body—a diagnosis will coincide with animal apparitions, synchronicities, memories that aren't hers, irrational terror, a nameless grief that holds the place a memory once was. Once, the language of "breaking generational curses" and "epigenetics" appealed to me because it captured this kind of deep, inherited memory, able to show the effect of food deserts, poverty, stress. But the idea has dangerous implications, especially for people with mental illness, so I use a different framing: the daughter who remembers for everyone. To write her story is to begin with the testimony from when an unprecious life had no listener, when to speak was to be unheard, unacknowledged, unbelieved.

36. Navigating a silence is different from being kept from a secret. One is a ghost, the other is a locked door.

37. If there's one thing men know how to do, it's cover their tracks. A man's most enduring harm is the manipulation of memory, history wiped clean of evidence and told on his terms. To this day, I can't find any records of my grandmother's life in Mexico, or prove she existed at all. Instead, my filing cabinet is full of doctored, redacted, and missing records from my ex-husband's incomplete discovery. I have no documents proving the existence of the woman who loved me the most, and an excess of documents proving that of the man who didn't. How should I write her history as anything but a fiction? Maybe I don't even know her real name.

38. Philosopher Jacques Derrida said that any attempt to trace our origin is subject to the limitations of the archive, which is subject to the limitations of language.

39. On FaceTime, I ask:
    "Mami, really, what's your real name?"

"Ay, Vanessa, por favor."

Teasing, Papi points at her with his tongue in his cheek. "Yo digo que se llama Alma."

"Ay cállate, Gilberto."

Some deeper mystery was locked behind my mother's silence, a line she could not cross.

40. Is the hero's journey about a girl? Is the fairy-tale princess even on the hero's journey? Or is the true hero on a journey despite her? Perhaps her journey is inverted, going backward. Heroes yearn to leave home, princesses yearn to end up in a castle. She's not *called* to adventure, she's *chased* through the forest; she doesn't make decisions, things happen *to* her; she doesn't transform through trials and tribulations, she's put to sleep while the prince fights for her, her fate dependent on whether she stays the same—beautiful, moral, good. (Is she well liked?)

41. Are migrants on the hero's journey? The American Dream is a fairy tale, after all. Migrants, like heroes, are forced to leave home, but their journey is not into the underworld—it's to the overworld, the global north, into empire.

42. On the hero's journey, the threshold between the known and unknown is marked by a border. From this point forward, there's no going back home. The hero can freely cross this border, this threshold. The migrant cannot.

43. Is the migrant woman on the hero's journey? Migrant men journey toward work; migrant children journey toward the future. Migrant women journey for many reasons, all related to survival: to raise their children, to support their families, to flee violence. Does the hero's journey imagine a migrant woman at its center? Does the fairy

tale? Migrant women are not princesses; no one is coming to save them. What do you call the journey where the migrant woman must save herself? America loves a survivor story.

44. Another night on FaceTime, I ask Mami too many questions, get too many names from ancestry.com wrong. I know I'm on the brink of something, but nothing is surfacing in my research. And that's when she says, *Enough*. For her, this is not some genealogy project. I am awakening a lineage of monsters, their names forever linked to horrific childhood memories. Not my story to write. I don't understand. She's witnessed how writing saved my life, turned me from at-risk youth and near dropout to being the first in our family to graduate high school, go to college, write a book. Doesn't she trust me? But my writing has broken some deep foundation of trust, just as I did as a teenager. She calls me a liar, says I exaggerate in my writing, says she watches my maudlin readings and interviews on YouTube. And just like that I am fourteen again, a girl accused, just trying to tell the truth.

45. My mother used to share my poems and essays with pride until I started identifying as the daughter of formerly undocumented immigrants. Whatever legitimacy that purchased me as a writer, it stole something from her. There is such deep shame about her formerly undocumented status, and what I have made that mean, that she no longer shares my work.

46. I think of writers I admire who write about their mothers, who write radically against shame, against silence, write erased people back into the public record, repair generational harm. Isn't this also my work? But I hadn't considered how immigrant sons are allowed to write about their mothers in a way daughters cannot. *Varones.*

Mijitos. When immigrant sons write about their abused mothers, it is an act of love. When daughters write about their abused mothers, it is an act of betrayal. Immigrant sons inherit their fathers' authority, and whether they know it or not, they wield it on the public stage by virtue of being men. What they can write that we cannot, that too is a silence.

47. And for the first time, I saw my mother as a daughter, a survivor, a scared little girl watching her mother beaten unconscious, over and over again. When they fled and crossed over, her silence *protected* her mother from those men, even long after everyone was dead. As long as she holds that silence, they will all be safe.

48. As immigrants' daughters, we have different relationships to our mothers. Different relationships to violence. Different roles as witnesses than sons. Our mothers remain authorities over us into adulthood, command obedience and respect even in death. We know what it means to keep their secrets. What few memories my mother has shared with me in moments of trust and vulnerability were not for anyone else but me. She shares less with me now; so much of it reappears in my writing. I never know if this is right.

49. And so for immigrant daughters, our telling is not brave, or beautiful. It is a betrayal. It is a speaking for, and speaking over, the living and the dead.

50. If I have a question, the answer is "Cómo chingas."

51. Once upon a time, I was tempted to write a legible Mexican American girlhood: kind-eyed grandmothers and cumbieros, immigration trauma, a poor childhood, assimilation and in-betweenness, broken-down pickup trucks and undocumented family members, a

harrowing tale of survival and resilience, just enough authenticity to claim the identity while being respectable enough to join the middle class.

52. But these stories are not mine to tell. What I can do: tell our stories through the stories and storytellers that are most legible in America. *Star Wars, Game of Thrones*, Nirvana, *The Witcher*. Popular music, video games, films, and television have always been sites of cross-cultural recognition, representing us in the shadows long before representation mattered, reading ourselves into the world and its metaphors. Will you recognize us in public texts if we show ourselves to you in them?

53. Working-class immigrants are experts in pop culture, theory, the arts. They are nuanced critics with endlessly obscure pop culture references and wild connections, having studied American pop culture inside and out to connect, learn English and social norms, survive. Migrant children deserve to lose themselves in fantasy too. Because they shouldn't have to be exceptional survivors to be heroes or princesses, writers or critics. Because we deserve not to be triggered every time we read our stories.

54. DEFRAGMENTED: Once upon a time, all I had was the present. I am proof enough of the past.

ALL THE ATREYUS
AT THE SPHINX GATE

TWO ENORMOUS SPHINXES STAND ASLEEP FACING EACH OTHER, forming a mystic gate against a starry desert sky. Despite their slumber, their magnificent wings are spread in aggressive arches toward each other, forming two crescent moons, sharp as blades. Each sphinx wears a usekh, a broad jeweled collar that lies just above its bare breasts. This is the Sphinx Gate, one of two gates one must pass to reach the Southern Oracle. In order to pass, the seeker must be brave, and sure of themselves, with pure intentions. Those who try to pass through the gate to seek glory, or who doubt themselves, or whose hearts reveal darker intentions will awaken the sphinxes, a terrible fate—caught between their gaze as their eyes open to cast white-hot beams of judgment, fiery and lethal. No one has ever passed the gate.

Atreyu—a dark-haired, dark-eyed child, and great warrior of his people—approaches cautiously, having already seen a brave armored knight try to pass on horseback, only to fail. Atreyu has already suffered great losses on this journey, but his intentions to pass through the gate are pure, and selfless, and for the survival of his people. He makes it halfway through the gate without disturbing the sphinxes, but then a stray wind blows open the helm of the knight, revealing the incinerated flesh that was once his face. Atreyu becomes fearful, aware of his vulnerability between the sphinxes' gaze, doubtful that he is any better than the dead knight. And it is here that the sphinxes begin to open their eyes, roused by Atreyu's self-doubt. *Be confident. Be confident!* Bastian, the reader, pleads. And so Atreyu runs, and survives the blast.

This is a scene from *The NeverEnding Story*, a 1984 family film adapted from the novel by the same name. It remains one of the most formative scenes of my life—so strange, thrilling, terrifying, complex. As a little Mexican girl, I couldn't help but imprint on Atreyu, who was racialized as American Indigenous from the Grassland People of Fantasia. And what Atreyu was fighting—The Nothing, an inky-black cloud spreading across the land, swallowing all of Fantasia's creatures into its abyss—was not some great evil, or monster, or army. Atreyu was fighting the loss of memory, the erasure of Fantasia, of being forgotten.

This is a metaphor for the colonial encounter, a force that must empty the land in order to settle it. A metaphysical genocide, or an epistemicide, which not only annihilates a population but obliterates all memory of it.

One of my earliest memories is crossing the puente, the US-Mexico border bridge between Brownsville and Matamoros. As Mami and I waited in line to be cleared in dense, standstill traffic, young boys between six and ten years old would walk up and down the lanes selling light-up roses, marzipan, chicles—tiles of candied gum that came four to a package. I was maybe three or four, and I remember feeling sorry that I was in a bochito and they were outside, on a bridge, in the sun, working, their voices lilting in the air.

I've always wondered why the Sphinx Gate scene from *NeverEnding Story* made such an impression that it continues to live rent-free in my head today. Only now do I realize that it depicts a brown child crossing a threshold with two terrifying guardians on either side, a scene I first watched when I was crossing the Brownsville/Matamoros puente regularly. It is a scene whose symbols are tied to a core memory, still informing my aesthetic choices—how can I make writing feel like this passage, full of tension and difficulty and risk? —*The NeverEnding Story*, like other fantasy films of the time, trusted children to handle the strangeness of sphinxes' bare breasts. Their nudity was never contextualized as erotic but as an encounter with something ancient, arcane, powerful, and mysterious.

Perhaps I was so moved by these small moments in 1980s fantasy because I never identified as an American child. Growing up in a mixed-status immigrant family, I had to negotiate two layers of meaning as I watched something as simple as *Rainbow Brite and the Star Stealer*, understanding about half of the language, unsure of the meanings of basic idioms like "up and at 'em." ("Upen Adam?") The feeling of English films was not one of foreignness but rather of a standard I should live up to, and often failed to meet or understand. Like most children, I watched the same films over and over from a stack of Kodak VHS tapes, but for slightly different reasons: as I learned English language and culture, I was also indulging in the fantasy of being an American girl.

The fantasy films of the 1980s weren't afraid to be androgynous (Gozer), seductive (Gareth the Goblin King), bizarre (*Moonwalker, Return to Oz*), terrifying (*Legend*), witty (*Ghostbusters*), sexy (*Labyrinth*).

They were made not necessarily with the family in mind but rather on their own terms, with complicated themes, terrifying imagery, and strong language, an open invitation for children to rise to the occasion. Perhaps this is a relic from the baby boomer era, when there was only one TV and content was made primarily for parents, who had control of the remote.

Now my son is in charge of the family content. As I sit down to watch Disney+ with him today, my attention wanders after fifteen minutes, my brain turned into soup as it's bombarded with zero-stakes special effects. And it is indeed a marvel how the heroes of today's family films are better-looking than ever, but somehow sexless, empty, anodyne, safe, lost in the spectacle and speed of capital. Something has been lost in all that precision—the heart of the fantasy itself.

———

When I talk to fellow migrants and first-generation friends, we all share this common history: an obsessive consumption of American pop culture and media as children. Little is written about first-generation children as translators for their elders, parentified early, with the critical pressure of needing to be fluent enough to perform American normativity in order to navigate institutions and authority. But even less is written about the formative media that translated us into, and for, Americans. (We don't really have a Chuck Klosterman of immigrants, but I will happily fill that role.)

But this responsibility for first-gen kids to be keepers of memory, language, culture, obligated to maintain ties to a home country and distant family we barely know—that kind of cultural recordkeeping, when combined with an obsessive love of pop culture, throws familiar titles into new light, casts different shadows. It's more than just code-switching and double-consciousness—that's just the surface, interacting with the outside. Within, there is a deep split in consciousness, a rift between two identities, two lands growing ever apart as time goes on. The more American I become, the farther away my Mexican identity feels. So what emerges between the two selves is a secret self, a third self—one allowed to live without the burden of either identity. This is the self that fantasy engages.

For culturally alienated children, this secret third self—the fantasy self, the displaced self, the forbidden self, the self not identified by others from the outside—is the avatar self, the self free from outside projection. This is not to say that we don't bring our identity contexts into the realms of fantasy, either by projecting our identity onto a character or by creating an avatar with our features and skin color; instead, the rift itself becomes a world, immersed in the distant fantasy of belonging.

Nothing liberated me from my identity when I was growing up more than the earthy realms of fantasy, the biome planets of science fiction, the thrill of seeing the world through the eyes of adventure—portals into a world of belonging in a land of alienation. At times, more than the characters and story, I marveled at the land, having never seen such pristine landscapes. My craving for fantasy was also connected to some deeper longing for a relationship to the land. And as I grew up, somehow the line between fantasy and reality began to get blurrier and blurrier—clinically known as disassociation, derealization, and depersonalization.

I was born in McAllen, Texas, on the US-Mexico border, and grew up in Houston, an ever-sprawling, drowning city under construction where nature proper, the same nature preserve where they built the state prison, is at least an hour's drive away. I've always lived in places where environmental racism and infrastructure disrupt nature—trailer homes, apartments, our little pink house in Houston next to the municipal water plant. White flight is constantly pushing north, felling trees to make room for neighborhoods unironically named the Woodlands, endless strip malls, and megachurches, while other areas of Houston get frequent boil-water notices and heavy petroleum fumes in the air. Race and class are spatialized, established geographically in Houston as in any city, but racial geographies, rather than forming distinct districts, are disorganized. The way you can tell if an area is rich and white is if it has mature trees: wealthy areas have access to the precious little nature Houston has left.

Growing up in Texas, my identity informed every traumatic encounter with authority figures, institutions, teachers, peers, even family. Nowhere was safe—not school, not home, not friends' houses—so I would end up wandering the swampy young pines behind our house, or jump the fence to walk Greens Bayou, the long drainage ditch dividing our neighborhood from the trailer park. It wasn't nature, and it wasn't a forest, but a curtain of saplings covering municipal tanks, and it was the closest thing I had to the ancient forests and waterfalls of fantasy. Those pines, like fantasy, were a place of safety where I could escape the confines of gender, compulsory heterosexuality, and race. I could pretend to be an elf princess with a stick for a bow, jump my bike over ditches with boys, smoke cigarettes and listen to music with the bad girls, escape angry parents to read *The Bell Jar* under honeysuckle, tag anarchy symbols under bridges, explore flooded creeks and catch crawfish when the power was out after hurricanes, kiss and undress a little with every gender.

After I got caught sneaking out at thirteen, my parents took my bedroom door off its hinges permanently, opening my room to constant disciplinary surveillance, so throughout my adolescence the little forest was the only place I had any privacy. It was also the place where I became brave, the place that held my forbidden self, a sanctuary of desire that made safe my secrets, the moonlit clearing where young love blossomed in my body, a haven for a young girl in trouble to hide.

The nature of my youth was not the normative Nature of national parks or nature preserves or fantasy films—it was a nameless, neglected half acre of undeveloped land between cheap starter houses and mobile homes. The only way to open a portal to our world was to be disobedient, daring to break a rule, stay out after hours, trespass, damage property, jump the fence. It was a liminal site of fantasy, disobedience, rebellion, and provocation where I could fully express my most subversive, vulnerable, provocative, brave self. When I moved to Boulder, Colorado, at thirty, I would see a version of nature, and whiteness, that humbled me, enough to haunt my memories of the woods behind our house and imagine the inner nightlands of my first book of poetry, *Beast Meridian*.

Perhaps this is how I developed magical thinking early on as a coping mechanism. *The Baby-Sitters Club* was just as improbable a reality to my child self as *Legend*, both worlds made inaccessible through the opacity of whiteness. I survived my difference by observing American life from a great distance, projecting myself into films, music, and shows and then performing what I'd learned with peers. I anchored my identity in mirroring their speech, mannerisms, hair, and dress.

As pop culture became a means of socialization and survival, everything entered the realm of fantasy. *The Cosby Show* was just as fantastical a reality as *Willow; Full House* was a story of princesses and their magic guardians, *Fresh Prince*, one of a real-life prince in his castle.

And every threshold is a sphinx gate, holding me in its gaze. Will I be worthy to cross? *Be confident, be confident!* Sebastian yells into the pages of his book at Atreyu, at me.

In the rift between countries and identities, what lies beyond the threshold is fantasy. A threshold is a site of possibility, transformation, the passage from one reality to another. Fantasy is formed by the presence of a border, what we believe will emerge beyond the bordered terrain. Borders are where one side imagines the other, where one side imagines itself. Fantasy is the imagination crossing a border; it is the practice of immigrant dreaming, where if we love American music, films, and television enough, America may love us back.

Encyclopedia of All the Daughters I Couldn't Be

Buen Niña

This is the phrase you remember most from childhood: *Pórtate bien*. Or: Be good, said as a warning. Be good, or I will [punishment].

And by all accounts, you were good when you were young—quiet, obedient, sweet. Eager to please, early reader, excellent grades and behavior marks. Like every Mexican daughter, you learn early: to be good is to be worthy of love. The firstborn daughter in America must be good if she is to live out her family's dreams and be worthy of their sacrifices.

Now you know the fear behind it: Be good so men can't hurt you. Be so good, America can't deny you. Be so good, you remain invisible, and that's how you can stay.

Me singing into my Michael Jackson microphone, age 2

Americana

Citizenship binds you to a nation as it estranges you from the land. You scarcely remember the Rio Grande Valley, an ecotone of coastland to arid desert and subtropical landing place for migratory birds and people. You almost remember the flat gray ocean of the Gulf of Mexico, its warm, slow waves, the bronze sand, the chickens in the yard and cows in the field between rows of lush oranges, the scent-memory of salt and earth that fades as you move north.

You are five when your family moves to Houston, pinethick city of the future tangled up in highways, with diamond-sharp skyscrapers, state-of-the-art hospitals, NASA, the Astrodome its crown jewel. Space City. Your mother's promotion and your grandmother's cancer meet in time: Houston is where the best cancer hospital is, where your grandmother can receive care pro bono, where your mother can strive and achieve a better life.

You move into the Prestonwood apartments, and when your grandmother is hospitalized, your mother enrolls you in the Honey Tree, a day care two blocks away. You have never stayed in a place where no one spoke Spanish, or spent time with white children. You know some English phrases, like "You are pretty" and "You are cool" and yes and please and no. This should do fine. When you arrive, you are told to place your things in a cubby. You do not know what a cubby is. You hold on to your things. Cheerios or Frosted Flakes? You do not understand. You only know "Postoses," Spanglish for Post Toasties, the cheapest cereal in the store. A boy named something like Josh or Brian asks if you are afraid of the bogeyman. *You are cool!* They ask you more questions. *You are pretty* has also stopped working, so you say nothing. The boy leads you to a closet, then closes the door. You are in the dark. You stay there, afraid of getting in trouble.

On the first day of kindergarten, you stand in a dark denim dress, bien peinada con trensitas by a row of maple trees with your grandmother, waiting for the bus. Your mother has pinned a yellow paper bus to your dress with your name written on it. "Vila Reel?" the bus driver asks. You nod, but you don't understand what he is asking. You arrive at the building, and your mind goes blank. Although you and your mother know TV English, it has never really been spoken to you by an American white person, or an authority figure. Your tongue binds itself to your old language. You do not know how to answer questions. You do not understand the children. You are sent to the office to figure out which classroom you belong in. You are escorted there late. You do not understand what to do. It is safer to read, so you read every book. This is what saves you.

AFTER THE
WORLD-BREAKING,
WORLD-BUILDING

N THE FIRST WEEK OF MY DOCTORAL PROGRAM AT THE UNIVERSITY of Southern California, a senior professor greeted me by name. I was relieved, until he complimented my work: "I really loved the poems in your application, they have a real *Latin American, magic realism feel.*" The poems were about cultural alienation, mental illness, and childhood racial and institutional trauma—poems that would end up in my first book—and as a PhD, I'd planned to research state and medical archives to write about the mass sterilization of women of color in the United States. My work was concerned with colonialism, race, and institutions, not magic. But it wasn't the first time I'd heard my work described this way—as Silvia Moreno-Garcia wrote in an op-ed for the *New York Times*, most Latine writers' work is labeled "magic realism" no matter its genre, because that is the space carved out for us in the American imagination, the label often a reductive essentialization of Latine (and global south) writing as imaginatively excessive, exotic, and primitive, from the mysterious expanse beyond the border to an older time, full of dark, magical people.

It's easy to assume the worst about this professor's compliment, but in hindsight, perhaps he *was* picking up on some other vein of language pulsing through my work—a vein of magical thinking, written in the mythic language of fantasy, the language I used to access my intuition, my subconscious, articulate buried feelings, forgotten memories, bodily data. Because in the year that followed, my life would fall spectacularly apart.

FOR THE PAST FEW YEARS, I'VE BEEN OBSESSED WITH FANTASY. I don't just love it—I exist on a different plane because of it, far above the ravines of a deadly lifelong depression. It began with bingeing *Game of Thrones* every day during my four-year divorce, then falling back in love with reading after my doctoral exams, revisiting old fantasy books, then fantasy role-playing video games. In my doctoral studies I was researching state and medical archives to write about the links between colonial science, mass incarceration, medical violence, and the involuntary sterilization of Latinas and other women of color in the United States. But doing that kind of work in the midst of grief, single parenthood, and the Trump presidency, family separations at the border, migrant detention, uprisings for racial justice, white supremacist mass shootings, climate catastrophes, and finally the COVID-19 pandemic made it difficult to face my work. Reality had broken down into a series of world-shattering emergencies, both personal and global, and I was powerless to stop any of it.

I felt broken, unable to trust, and unwilling to try again. Once an avid film buff and reader of fiction, now I found the psychological surgery of realism nauseating. My life was unbearable, and I didn't need to relive infidelity, conflict, or domestic misery—I needed a way to imagine myself out of it. Fantasy was the only kind of story that felt safe; it zoomed out, was about the powerless reclaiming power, made heroes out of regular people. It was a conduit to the imagination. Fantasy RPGs also filled the social gaps after trauma. My traveling companions felt like real friends when I had none; fantasy romances fulfilled me emotionally; immersive stories relieved obsessive over-thinking and hypervigilance. And the block I was experiencing be-tween myself and my academic work began to lift. For all its flaws as a genre rooted in Western European colonial history, fantasy became a productive space to stage questions of race, gender, colonialism, prison abolition, and political revolution. In games based on Dun-geons & Dragons such as *Dragon Age Inquisition* and *Baldur's Gate 3*, your traveling party is a coalition, made up of a group of fighters who are often from rival peoples and races (like the elves and dwarves in *Lord of the Rings*), each with a specialized power, who must join forces and become allies to fight overwhelming oppression against impossible odds. At first it felt immature and unserious to draw these compari-sons, but I desperately needed to reconnect with a sense of hope.

IN THE LAST DECADE, AMERICAN WRITING AND STORYTELLING HAS been marked by the "speculative turn," most excitingly in works of nonfiction and memoir. From the rise of Black horror and surrealist fiction to speculative memoirs and imagined histories, such as Carmen Maria Machado's *In the Dream House* and Ingrid Rojas Contreras's *The Man Who Could Move Clouds*, the speculative differs from fantasy—rather than make up a history, or tell it in allegory, it is the reparative imagination in constant discourse with the silences of the past, addressing gaps in archival and collective memory, where the imagination is a mode of time travel that can excavate silenced accounts, reanimate erased histories, and even imagine radical futures. Rooted in Black feminist thought, Saidiya Hartman's seminal essay "Venus in Two Acts" is often cited in these works, where she describes the encounter with the sparse records of enslaved girls' lives as vast silences in the archive. The failure of the archive to ever provide an accurate account of history leads Hartman to theorize the practice of "critical fabulation," the attempt to tell impossible stories by writing with and against the archive to "illuminate the contested character of history . . . engulf authorized speech in the clash of voices . . . which weaves present, past, and future in retelling the girl's story and in narrating the time of slavery as our present." She identifies fabula as her guiding narrative mode—a speculative mode, the root of fables, myths, and fairy tales—the connective tissue able to bind documented historical events into a narrative. Through fabulation, the specter that haunts the archive becomes animated, embodied, the document now a site for what we can never know interacting with what we do know.

This, to me, is something like world-building, and the imagined specter coming back to life is a practice of magical thinking. Writers like Joan Didion have explored magical thinking as the grief-consciousness of loss, but I'm interested in that grief-consciousness shared on a mass scale. What if that grief is an ancient, generational, epigenetic scar that is wounded and re-wounded by state violence? What does the constant state of loss after colonization, enslavement, and dispossession do to the collective imagination? How does it affect our stories? This, to me, is the root of magical realism: fabulation—the fable, the myth, the fantasy—as the radical, reparative speech of the counterpublic, for whom documents are often an absence, and records an echoing

36

silence. It is the story that emerges from the scant evidence left at the scene of the crime, adding layers of context to what we can never know, so that we might know. It is no wonder that critical fabulation and the speculative make up the narrative mode that most lends itself to writers contending with trauma, personal and generational, remembered and felt, believed and unbelieved.

Alongside this turn to the speculative in the literary world, in popular culture, we're in a bit of a radical speculative moment. Aside from the copycat fantasy television franchises that came after *Game of Thrones,* the genres of Black and Indigenous surrealisms (like *Atlanta* and *Reservation Dogs*), comic-book adaptations (not just Marvel movies but *The Watchmen* and *Wandavision*), and most recently *Barbie,* the speculative mode has become a site of political rigor, where radical discourses about our ongoing oppressions are staged in allegory, symbolism, and the absurd.

IT MAY SEEM LIKE I'M USING THE TERMS *MAGICAL REALISM, MAGICAL thinking, speculative,* and *fantasy* interchangeably, but I'm not—I've agonized over the differences. There is a very real border between magical realism and fantasy as similar but distinct genres. We learn in literature classes that magical realism is set in *our* world, where the supernatural is a part of everyday life and magical happenings are treated as normal, while fantasy is set in a *constructed* world, where magic is a logic of world-building, subject to rules and limitations. In both, magic is a site of memory, something from the past; but in fantasy, magic is also the language of history, an archive of power written and practiced by masters who have extracted arcane knowledges from forgotten peoples who once shared a mind with the land. Both genres are metaphors of history, just from opposite poles, and opposite definitions of what it means to remember.

A closer look at the geographies of magical realism versus fantasy paints a clear hemispheric picture. Magic is present in both, but how it is used separates the genres further. Magical realism is best known as the genre of the twentieth-century Latin Boom; stories labeled thus are largely from the global south, or by diasporic writers living through postcolonial realities. Magical realist stories often focus on families, towns, and communities, where the local is forced to reckon with a violent unknown. Magic is a manifestation of memory, an externalized feeling, an irrational occurrence that *happens to* the characters, often without intention or control. By contrast, traditional fantasy is primarily by first-world writers from the global north, set in the metaphors of European history, continental in scope, a hero's journey encountering unknown lands and races through conflict. In fantasy, magic is memory wielded as power, either by kingdoms or against them, a glorification of the past with saviors fighting for the future. Magic (memory) is a thing to be controlled or used to control, a weapon that can be learned, wielded, or willed.

In *The Art of Fiction*, David Lodge further contextualizes the use of magic in magical realism as "when marvelous and impossible events occur in what otherwise purports to be a realistic narrative . . . associated with contemporary Latin-American fiction . . . [by writers who] have lived through great historical convulsions and wrenching personal upheavals, which they feel cannot be adequately represented in a discourse of undisturbed realism." Those "great historical convulsions" Lodge refers to are the afterlives of colonialism, slavery, and political subjugation—the realism of a place and people who have experienced a loss of cultural memory, the unreality of collective trauma.

In short, both genres look to history, but from opposite positions.

Fantasy discovers the New World, whereas magical realism is the world invaded by violence. If fantasy is a literature of world-building, then magical realism is the literature that results from world-breaking.

Take Netflix's wildly popular 2017 show *Narcos*. In the opening credits, this prologue ominously appears in white letters: "Magical Realism is defined as what happens when a highly detailed, realistic setting is invaded by something too strange to believe." Then "too strange to believe" turns red, like blood, and remains on the screen as the rest of the words fade out. Enter a spicy acoustic guitar melody: "There is a reason magical realism was born in Colombia," now *all* in red. Sure, why not. This is not factually true—*magical realism* was coined as an art term in 1920s Germany, and then, when it came to Latin America, Mexican writer Juan Rulfo's *Pedro Páramo* and the work of Jorge Luis Borges, an Argentine writer, would go on to greatly influence Gabriel García Márquez—the point of the prologue is not accuracy. It is so that clear associations are made: *Latin America, Escobar, cocaine, violence, drug wars = magical realism.*

Narcos is not a work of magical realism, though. It is part crime drama like *Breaking Bad*, and part neo-noir police procedural like *The Wire*, but it is rarely mentioned in the same breath as those shows, or thought of as prestige television. Yet it was an incredibly popular show. When my mom posted an old photo of my dad holding me as a newborn to Facebook for Father's Day, a white coworker of hers commented, "Wow, he looks like a narco guy!" It was nominated for three Emmys, but only in technical categories like editing and design. This is just one example of how Latine stories are not considered entries into mainstream genres on their own terms. They are "Latino" first, defined not by their story but by their alterity. It would be absurd to describe *Breaking Bad* or *The Wire* as magical realism, but it is invoked at the beginning of *Narcos* to emphasize its "Latino" themes: drugs, organized crime, and ultraviolence, politically decontextualized, which only underscores American anti-immigrant sentiment and "secure our borders" rhetoric. The narcodrama is little more than American propaganda, ahistorically omitting all traces of CIA interventions responsible for destabilizing the region, and therefore, as the site of a cover-up, is rarely considered part of Hollywood's universal human narratives with relatable or significant characters, but rather a hyperlocal spectacle of the wretched and the damned, far away from here, and therefore easy to ignore.

The blanket "magic realism" label is an industry standard that persists despite the fact that few write it anymore. It is a generalizing force that overlooks writers who don't fit its mold, and "subtly erases the efforts of an emerging group of horror writers, such as V. Castro and Gabino Iglesias, whose work cannot be neatly encompassed by that term," writes speculative novelist Silvia Moreno-Garcia in the *New York Times*. Perhaps this isn't an accident.

Magical realism's popularity in the United States was funded and supported by the CIA to soften Latin American leftism during the Cold War. Following the Cuban Revolution, the US was faced with a growing Communist anti-imperialist movement in its backyard. So the CIA enlisted the help of respected leftist writers, including García Márquez in Latin America, James Baldwin on the civil rights front, and Ernest Hemingway in Cuba, to move the political needle toward the center. While magical realist authors were leftists, their work was not primarily concerned with political critique. Since then, it has become a reductive essentialization of Latine writing as imaginatively excessive, exotic, and primitive. Magical realism is a genre that operates within a much larger Western narrative, the same one that drives the fear of Latin America as a poor, dangerous continent full of violent, uneducated people, a narrative that manifests as anti-immigration policy as a consequence. I can't help but wonder if that aspect of the genre continues to serve political ends—to categorize Latine horror as "magical realism" is to decontextualize and defang its critique.

If Latine books about the horrors of colonialism, US imperialism, and the political destabilization of the region were treated like mainstream horror, that would require the mainstream reader to engage with an ugly, buried history that directly contradicts US history and immigration narratives—in the vein of *Get Out* or the Tulsa Race Massacre history finally exposed in *Watchmen* (2019). But if it's magical realism, it shrinks the audience and marginalizes the book. And the failure to even properly categorize Latine books points to an even bigger silence—the failure of criticism to truly and thoughtfully engage Latine work and interpret its cultural urgency or relevance with the rigor it deserves.

Still, I am curious as to why magical realism is invoked at the start of *Narcos*—why that connection? My guess is that in the American imagination, magical realism *includes* the narcodrama. Take into account its stereotypes—even the richest, most glamorous narcotraficantes are guided by magical Indigenous mystics; characters are tattooed or named after Mesoamerican gods and symbols; gang members perform bloody "savage" rituals; La Virgen and Santa Muerte imagery watch over the business; and every aspect of the world—from the language to the otherworldliness of the landscape to the ultraviolence to the altered states—creates the sense of an altered reality. Latin America is both mystical paradise and the heart of darkness in America's backyard.

Magical realism is not a neutral literary genre but a marginal one. It is racialized, connected to colonial ideas of primitive mysticism and magical people of color with an Indigenous connection to the supernatural. It is an exoticized, backward world, the global south of stories.

And if magical realism is the global south of stories, then what is the global north? Fantasy.

Salman Rushdie said as much in 1982 in a tribute to García

Márquez for the *London Review of Books*, writing, "*El realismo magical*, 'magic realism,' at least as practised by García Márquez, is a development of Surrealism that expresses a genuinely 'Third World' consciousness. It deals with what Naipaul has called 'half-made' societies, in which the impossibly old struggles against the appallingly new, in which public corruptions and private anguishes are more garish and extreme than they ever get in the so-called 'North,' where centuries of wealth and power have formed thick layers over the surface of what's really going on.... It would be a mistake to think of Márquez's literary universe as an invented, self-referential, closed system. He is not writing about Middle Earth, but about the one we all inhabit. Macondo exists. That is its magic."

Rushdie is showing us the fracture in hemispheric consciousness here, or how the stories and magics of the global north and south differ—how magical realism is set in the fallout zones of the colonized world and the afterlives of imperial power, while fantasy and the idealized natural world of Tolkien are products of a first-world colonial imaginary. Magical realism and the Latin Boom were articulations of a postcolonial consciousness in the twentieth century—not a production of the real but a production of *truth*. In an interview published in the *Atlantic* in 1973, García Márquez said of magical realism, "In Mexico, surrealism runs through the streets.... Surrealism comes from the reality of Latin America."

Both are fabulation; what separates the two is power.

FANTASY, SCI-FI, AND SPECULATIVE FICTION IN THE WEST EMPHASIZE the importance of world-building in order for the story to "work." The writer plays god, mapping the land, territories, and histories of their characters' respective cultures and races as sites of discovery and conflict. World-building is an inherently colonial narrative position, which gives the author full omnipotence and control, not only as a god who creates the world in his image but as the single source of the story, the mind of the universe, and therefore the arbiter of what is "universal." Fantasy, sci-fi, and speculative fiction satisfy the imperial urge for full control of a world narrative and its interpretation, making the text the sole source of accurate lore and the devout reader the ultimate authority on the world's "canon." This empowers the phallogocentric reading we see in (often white, male) fans who self-deputize as authorities and police the laws of the world by restricting its interpretations as canon, non-canon, retcon, and headcanon. The last is sometimes also called fanon, as in "fan canon," not Frantz Fanon, but the coincidence is kind of apt: fanon is validated in fanfiction.

As a teacher of beginning writers, I see fanfiction as an early form of critical intervention, allowing young writers to explore feminist retellings, queering, and critical race interpretations within the structure of an accessible text they love with a built-in community discourse to provide feedback. Fanfiction is largely looked down upon, though: according to a census of Archive of Our Own user demographics, its participants overwhelmingly identify as women (80 to 90 percent) between the ages of sixteen and thirty, beginning writers whose work is dismissed as wish fulfillment—alternate ships (romantic relationships, many queer or poly), character erotica, gender-swapped or race-bent retellings, and alternate endings. It's Barthes's Death of the Author in practice; the authority of the text or intentions of the author no longer matter—the death of the author is the birth of the reader, who gets to interpret its biases by reading the text against itself, against the grain, contextualizing it based on its history, its writer's structural position in society, the cultural and political forces that shaped the story. This is why fanfiction exists, and also what criticism does—to expand their relevance so that beloved stories can continue beyond the time they're written in, to expand the audiences they're written for, for fans to see themselves in them. If the world-building of Western fantasy and the Hero's Journey is a phallogocentric storytelling modality, centering the narrative structures of white Western European male thought, then fanfiction begins the journey of reworlding, a coming back to feminine, nonlinear, critical, rhizomatic, intuitive forms of storytelling with no end in mind, which is also the project of this book. I am chronicling a life in which details were kept from me and I did not have control of the narrative, or the world; therefore, attempting to tell it with linear storytelling will fail. I am a detective putting the story together.

WHILE THE LINK BETWEEN THE SPECULATIVE MODE AND TRAUMA IS clear, fantasy as a site of the revolutionary imagination and collective world-building requires a bit more exploration. This summer I came across an article called "Dungeons & Dragons Players of Death Row," written by Keri Blakinger for the Marshall Project and published in the *New York Times*, which illustrates the link between trauma and mass incarceration, and D&D not just as a therapeutic modality for processing trauma but also as a critique of the carceral state. Blakinger profiles two death row players who used the character creation, world-building, and collective storytelling of D&D as a form of narrative therapy, processing their histories of abuse and abandonment through the metaphors of magic. It was a narrative mode that finally allowed them to access their imaginations, form bonds, and work out their own stories. Prison abolition is an inherently speculative project, one that imagines a world without prisons and police—political ends that are often dismissed as pure fantasy. But a deeper dive into its ideas reveals abolition to be a world-building project—one that values every human life. The liberation of every prisoner requires the dismantling of carceral logics, from addressing the root causes of crime like food and housing instability toward one of accountability and rehabilitation. The article uses D&D as a site of the abolitionist imagination—a place where death row prisoners can imagine themselves free in a world that makes rehabilitation and restorative justice possible through allegory and role-playing.

After reading about the D&D death row prisoners, whose acts of character creation and world-building were only enriched by their backstory, I came back to Parul Sehgal's "The Case Against the Trauma Plot," particularly her observation of the tyranny of backstory, and how trauma in recent American storytelling has made stories feel reductive and moralistic. "The prevalence of the trauma plot cannot come as a surprise at a time when the notion of trauma has proved all-engulfing," she writes. "Its customary clinical incarnation, P.T.S.D., is the fourth most commonly diagnosed psychiatric disorder in America, and one with a vast remit." I am one of those people; in the nineties, the era of teenage angst, *Prozac Nation*, and Kurt Cobain's suicide, troubled teens like me were being diagnosed with manic depression and bipolar disorder; and in the aughts, after 9/11, millennials were being diagnosed with anxiety in droves. Those "Internet writing mills" coming out of the "first-person industrial complex," a natural evolution from Live-Journal and MySpace, commodified trauma and made it lucrative. But I'm less interested in that analysis—critics such as Jia Tolentino and Laura Bennett have already explored this. Instead, I'm more interested in trauma shared on a mass scale and what that does to stories. For example, Trump's "alternative facts," internet conspiracy theories, and the January 6 insurrection have already resulted in the splintering of alternate realities as seen in the prevalence of the multiverse. How will

COVID lockdowns, the loneliness epidemic, mass incarceration, and increasing strikes and uprisings change our stories?

And what if there is no "post" to trauma? Once referred to as "shell shock," PTSD, coined in 1980 and first appearing in the *DSM-III*, was initially diagnosed in veterans of (Western) wars. "PTSD better describes the experiences of an American soldier who goes to Iraq to bomb and go back to the safety of the United States. He's having nightmares and fears related to the battlefield and his fears are imaginary. Whereas for a Palestinian in Gaza whose home was bombarded, the threat of having another bombardment is a very real one. It's not imaginary," says Dr. Samah Jabr, chair of the mental health unit at the Palestinian Ministry of Health. "There is no 'post' because the trauma is repetitive and ongoing and continuous." If the trauma is generational, ongoing, and likely to happen in the future, PTSD is an insufficient diagnosis that fails to take into account the social, cultural, and political forces of trauma, nor its collective experience. Like most psychiatric diagnoses, which limit mental health disorders to the individual, and treatment as individual responsibility, PTSD is a diagnosis that assumes peacetime, and can be shared by the soldier who did the bombing as well as his victim. In a tweet from October 26, 2023, and widely quoted across the internet since, disability advocate, abolitionist, and writer Stefanie Lyn Kaufman-Mthimkhulu writes, "PTSD is a white, western, colonial concept that locates the source of trauma in the linear past and requires a 'non-traumatic baseline' to compare us to ('you're safe now, it's no longer happening'). What the Palestinian people have experienced, and are continuing to experience, as a result of genocide cannot be accurately described as PTSD. It is not a comparable framework. The trauma is enduring, colonial, intergenerational." Many of the trauma stories Sehgal cites as examples, such as Art Spiegelman's *Maus*, television's *Reservation Dogs*, and even *Sula*, draw from collective intergenerational trauma resulting from slavery, colonization, and genocide. Trauma shapes the imagination, and curiously, all of these works also have speculative, magical realist elements central to their telling. "Modern life is inherently traumatic," Sehgal offers, but perhaps it's more complex than that. In a time when millennials—consumers of the "personal essay industrial complex" and participants of "writing mills"—the poorest, most highly educated generation, are nearing middle age and reflecting on their lives, and Black, Indigenous, and immigrant writers of color who have inherited their family's experiences of atrocity are finally getting published, perhaps that is the reason for the tyranny of trauma narratives—the recording and recognition of erased histories. And perhaps we, too, are tired of the world-breaking, reality-altering events that have defined our generation, from 9/11 to Ferguson to COVID; perhaps once we acknowledge one another's multiple histories, repair our multiple realities, we can begin to rebuild our "backstory" as many collective pasts, which is the first step to world-building for our collective futures.

I DON'T KNOW MUCH LATIN AMERICAN HISTORY AT ALL—IT JUST ISN'T taught here. I'm embarrassed to admit I only learned of El Halconazo, the massacre of student protesters in Mexico City in 1971, after seeing the film *Roma* and asking my mother about it; nor did I know the Chiquita Banana Massacre in Colombia, the history García Márquez's *One Hundred Years of Solitude* is based on, until a few years ago. I didn't know about Che Guevara or Pinochet or any US interventions in Latin America until well into my thirties upon reading *The Open Veins of Latin America*. It is no wonder why Latine writers have been shut out of the mainstream for so long—our histories are suppressed, and if you dig too deep, they implicate the United States. Perhaps magical realism relieved that narrative pressure. Now, Latine writers are expected to fulfill the task of "representation," which develops another layer of narrative pressure, and a different kind of silencing. I have been kept from my own history and denied a history here; everything, from the education system to the Western canon to even my immigrant parents, has made sure that my history begins *here*, in the United States, and so the data that fills the space of history and memory is my fanatic love of American pop culture. But my writing is illegible to American audiences, no matter how much I love *Star Wars* or Michael Jackson or *The Great Gatsby*; in return, my life is invisible, unintelligible to the only culture I know. Despite our exclusion from mainstream media, immigrant Latines identify with TV shows, films, and music that have never had us in mind; through these are translated our pain, our grief, our joy, our love, our heartbreak. We learn American culture inside and out, learn to speak its intricate languages, but are rarely entrusted, or imagined, in its stories. Our contributions have their little corner, an elective in the curriculum of American imaginaries, with the expectation that we translate ourselves through trauma, interpreting our painful family secrets to indulge the American reader's need to empathize. The historic absence of our voices creates a double bind once we do get that shot. For white writers, it's show, don't tell; for writers of color, it's *represent* as you *tell*. And to represent is to be bound to trauma, not imagination.

Both trauma and fantasy are portals into the past; both are sites of memory. If magical realism results from world-breaking, fabulation then is *world-building*, the imagination working alongside the past to make something whole from the embodied traces of history, an echo through time. In *Beloved*, Toni Morrison calls this "rememory," where memory itself is a supernatural phenomenon that connects time to time in the body. By relieving our ghosts of the burden of their stories through *fabulation*, we are liberated to imagine the fantasy of possible futures.

Encyclopedia of All the Daughters I Couldn't Be

Inteligente

Brownsville, 1985. One summer night, you are sitting at the round laminate dining room table drawing pictures on your mother's legal pad. She has drawn a smiling flower for you in blue ballpoint pen and is cooking spaghetti Mexican-style with Knorr consommé and Ragu mushroom sauce in the white vinyl apartment kitchen. When you are finished drawing, you want to write something for the first time below it: V A N E S S A. Your father passes by, glances over at your paper, and sees that you, a three-year-old, have written your name without being taught how to.

"Silvia! Mira que hija de su . . . la nena escribió su nombre! ¿Tú le enseñaste esto?" Your mother pops her head out, then sways over. V A N E S S A. He figures out that you have copied the letters from the VHS tapes he has recorded for you. "A ver, ¿qué dice?" he asks. "Vanessa," you say. You point to yourself. Impressed, he lets out a "Ha!" sits down, and begins to write little words to see if you can read other things. CAT. "Cat." MOM. "Mom." Mira que hija de su . . . He

laughs. He is ecstatic, writing the next word, and the next. You can't tell if he's mad, but you play along. Did you do something wrong? It doesn't matter. You are just so glad he is playing with you.

The next night, while grocery shopping, your mother buys a few beginner workbooks for children from the magazine aisle. All of the covers have a photorealistic pencil sketch of a little blond boy in the corner. When you come home, she starts working with you on reading and writing while your father is at gigs. You are about to start kindergarten in Houston in a few months, and although you can read and write and speak English, she is concerned that they will still put you in the English as a Second Language classes that neglected her, just because you're brown and Mexican and your household primarily speaks Spanish. She knows from experience that in Texas, ESL students are taught below grade level and rarely transition into advanced classes. So every night when she gets home, while your grandmother watches *Cuna de lobos* and your father rehearses another Prince song in the bedroom, your mother will ask you to sit at the table and write over and over again: *Jill kicks the ball, Jill kicked the ball, Jill will kick the ball.*

Home was always where our whole family did homework for America. My grandmother and mother practicing their English lessons in Mead spiral notebooks for the evening classes at the Prince of Peace Catholic church. My father practicing Top 40 pop songs in English for hours in the bedroom. My mom watching floral arrangement courses and motivational speakers on VHS tapes. "Find Your Niche or Stay in a Ditch," she'd repeat. My uncle calling the 800 number to order *Inglés sin barreras,* only for his credit card to be declined. Me studying the Encarta CD-ROM every night in high school once we got our first Compaq computer at Best Buy in 1997, five years behind everyone else, listening to the poetry of the James Joyce entry over and over, the reader saying in an Irish accent, "And then he asked me would I yes to say yes my mountain flower and first I put my arms around him yes and drew him down to me so he could feel my breasts all perfume yes and his heart was going like mad and yes I said yes I will Yes."

LA CANCIÓN DE LA NENA

Side One

HAVE ONLY THE FAINTEST RECOLLECTION OF THE BORDERS Apartments on Media Luna Street in Brownsville, Texas. The landscape itself is more feeling than memory: the clay soil, the stubborn grass and tangle of palm trees, the wet, heavy air, the common brown ducks crossing and uncrossing la resaca behind the complex, the flatness of the Texas horizon, endless land upon which to labor. And within all that ordinary was us: my mother, father, and grandmother. A little knot in a nondescript apartment complex. It was designed for working-class transborder immigrants, the people I loved—day laborers; truck drivers; domestic, food, and grocery workers—and among them my father, Gilberto Villarreal, a twenty-nine-year-old musical prodigy at the foot of this country, in a place no one ever expects to find someone extraordinary. It was in that little one-bedroom

My father and me before my second or third birthday party at Chuck E. Cheese in Brownsville, Texas, 1984 or 1985. He was always very fashion-forward, shown here in a wine-colored velvet blazer, a white dress shirt, full beard, and jeans. I am miserable in a lacy white dress, but with Papi, so it's okay.

apartment where my first memories formed while observing the life of the artist: the grind, the study, the promise, the obsessive repetition over inconsequential details, hours spent grappling with an invisible problem, interior and gigantic. Later, I would learn too of invisibility, of illegibility, of unsustainable years full of almosts, the quiet, volatile aftermath of failure.

I always come back to the same scene in that apartment. He sits on the edge of the bed to compose and work through songs, facing an amp, while I curl into his velvet-lined guitar case and listen. He cycles through a milk crate of felt-edged records, playing along, adding expressive flourishes to the lead. *Purple Rain*, by Prince. "Cause We've Ended as Lovers," Jeff Beck. The entirety of *Breezin'* by George Benson. I have called up this memory so many times I feel the gauze of fiction starting to overlay its details. But it is a memory so dear, I reanimate it against the heaviness of the present—my father, full of promise and possibility, years before the shell he would become, now shut away in my childhood bedroom in the graying light of ever-closed blinds.

I'm often asked to name the first poem or poet I ever loved, and the question always leaves me kind of stumped. Nothing ever comes to mind—I didn't have many books growing up, and so to this day I have some anxiety around being well-read enough. I consider possibilities for the real answers: *In Utero*? "Amor Eterno"? The *Nuyorican Poets Café Anthology*? And then it becomes clear: my literacy began in my family's extensive catalogs of music, constantly playing in every household, from every genre on either side of the border. From Donna Summer to Juan Gabriel to Janet Jackson to Rocío Dúrcal to the Charlie Daniels Band to George Strait to Queen to Little Joe y La Familia to Led Zeppelin to Grupo Mazz to Prince to Vicente Fernández, my childhood was steeped in music, populated by musicians. And what I experienced as poetry came first through the song my father wrote for me when I was two years old, a song whose melody is a turning helix in my blood, another way of speaking my name. Do you have a song like that, written for you? It is the rarest gift I have ever received. It created me.

I WAS BORN IN MCALLEN, TEXAS, A BORDER CITY IN THE RIO GRANDE Valley recently in the news as the site of Trump's migrant child separations, where ICE's tent cities turned to tent hospitals in the era of COVID. The Valley, or El Valle to locals, is the subtropical stretch of land between Brownsville and Eagle Pass at the southernmost tip of Texas where everything has two names: Rio Grande/Río Bravo; Laredo/Nuevo Laredo; McAllen/Reynosa; Brownsville/Matamoros. The cities along the river are not distinct cities but transborder metroplexes, split by language. And the people begin to develop dual identities as well, not just the English and Spanish versions of their names like my tío Javier/Xavier, but half alter egos, like my tío Joel who now goes by "George," or migrants who change their names entirely upon arrival, untethering themselves from a certain fate.

Although much of what Chicana scholar Gloria Anzaldúa wrote has been rightfully subject to critique, her observation of the US-Mexico border as an open wound "where the Third World grates against the first and bleeds" persists because to this day, her work gives us the language to describe the psychic ruptures of the border, the "emotional residue of an unnatural boundary [. . .] in a constant state of transition [where] the prohibited and forbidden are its inhabitants." What Anzaldúa wrote about best was this in-between, how the border produces a racial terrain every day, and how the wound of the border is a spiritual wound that becomes embodied as a psychic rupture of displacement, dispossession, of many selves at inner war. For me, however, the border is an eraser, a haunted site of constant loss, swallowing a deep history that is disappearing, existing only in the memory of elders who leave us too soon.

El Valle is also a place of family, tradition passed down in tiny trailer-home kitchens and yards with miraculously resurrected trucks and flourishing chile bushes. Its people are overwhelmingly generous; hilariously witty; constantly reinventing language, food, fashion, music. The borderlands are, by design, a subculture difficult to explain to outsiders, partly because it is a subaltern, a region totally invisible to the rest of the United States. That said, the Rio Grande Valley has more than kept up with every era of American pop culture, all while developing its own ignored cultural giants and contributions in response: *The Johnny Canales Show*, Freddy Fender, rock ácido, Tejano, Chicano punk, and conjunto norteño, to name just a few.

Mostly, it is a land of forgetting and the forgotten—like all south-ernmost places, a site of invisible labors done by invisible people, of colonial erasure and self-erasure, where historical bodies refuse to disappear from their children and the dead have a way of sticking around. A place of joy and split and striving, it isn't a valley in the geographic sense; rather than land between mountains, it is a place between myths, each country a reflection and metaphor of the other.

THIS IS THE LANGUAGE MY FATHER USES: *I WAS WAITING TO BE discovered.*

His is a story I've never seen on VH1's *Behind the Music*: 1966, Reynosa, Tamaulipas, Gilberto Villarreal, an eleven-year-old son of migrant laborers, learns guitar on his own, practices day and night, far surpassing his ten thousand hours before he turns fifteen. While his parents are far away working las pixcas, or the fields, through sheer will, he manages to find Beatles and Cream albums, distortion and wah-wah pedals. He was not a rare mind dreaming in a place that suppresses dreams with debt and labor. What is rare is that he almost made it. Steeped in the corrido tradition—songs farmworkers would invent to pass on information, stories, and warnings about plantation life—he would let that texture inform his craft and make yet another contribution to American music from those who work the cotton fields, one that would go unheard.

Before SoundCloud and online demo submissions, "getting discovered" was the story musicians told one another about how to get a foot in the door. The most famous acts of the day were plucked from obscurity on the basis of their talent. But mostly that was a lie—the way into the music industry was either to be white and fit a formula or to be part of a zeitgeist, a momentarily electric subculture that could be co-opted to reinvigorate the charts. Faithfully playing the clubs, booking small tours, and making a demo in the hopes a suit would show up to discover you was a far-fetched fantasy that everyone told my dad would happen to him—if anyone could make it, it was him. But no one, not even local labels, sent scouts to the Rio Grande Valley borderlands to seek out talent. And so he gave his all in obscurity, hoping destiny would walk in. In the 1970s and '80s, if scouts went beyond New York or LA, they mostly sought out new rock talent in America's postindustrial nerve centers, cities like Detroit, Minneapolis, Chicago, Nashville, and the deep South—places with a thriving Black culture and white, English-speaking acts to reap the benefits.

Could the eldest son of migrant farm laborers, with only a secondary education from Reynosa, Tamaulipas, self-taught on a Sears Roebuck classical guitar, playing rock and pop in Mexico and the transborder region, ever be what a major label scout had in mind?

Part of finding the next rock star, the next pop star, the next big thing, is sex appeal, usually determined by the desirability politics of race and class, which are not neutral factors. So-called refined facial features, light skin, cishetero performance, height, and weight are just some factors that signal which bodies can accrue wealth and which bodies are made abject and assigned labor. This has consequences, not only on the lives of laborers but in how they see themselves depicted in a dominant culture. If the Rio Grande Valley is historically a site for laboring bodies, it is not a site Hollywood has any interest in, not even when the region gets the rare opportunity to represent itself. (See: actresses from New York or Los Angeles cast as Selena.)

I often wonder how America envisions the US-Mexico border and its people, what desirability means when mapped onto the migrant body. My best guess is that the Rio Grande Valley and its people are not thought of at all, and if they are, it is as an *undesirable* region filled with *undesirable* people, a place of poverty, criminality, violence, detention centers, "border surges." Desire, desirability, and undesirability are libidinal impulses, and if desire is the underside of belonging, it is central to the fate of the migrant. Headlines insisting that there's a "surge at the border" exist only in the realms of colonial fantasy, where our fears, biases, and racial imaginaries determine the reality on display. The realm of fantasy informs not just laws and borders, who is defined as citizen, prisoner, or alien, but also popular culture, music, film—what we value reflected back as desire.

I'm reminded of a scene in *Game of Thrones* when Oberyn and his paramour Ellaria, visitors from the hot southern kingdom of Dorne, are introduced in the main brothel in King's Landing, city of the royal seat, to underscore their foreignness via their deviant and insatiable sexual appetite. As they consider the women on offer, Oberyn, a handsome olive-skinned bisexual prince in his forties, is coded as the Latino lover archetype: a gallant masculine sexuality defined by excess, eroticism, exoticism, and danger. As he contemplates a slender, nervous, fair-skinned young sex worker, he smiles and says, heavily accented, "Look at this one. How lovely is she?" The sex worker is visibly anxious at his attention, the unspoken tension of the scene underscoring Oberyn's aberrant sexuality, too much for even the brothel to accommodate. Ellaria, curly haired and bronze-skinned, leans back with a wine goblet, unthreatened. She nods in agreement and says, "Beautiful. But *pale*." As he slides the young girl's dress down, Oberyn replies, "They like them pale in the capital, it shows they don't work the fields."

This scene emphasizes Oberyn and Ellaria's ethnic markings via their accents, skin color, and pansexual appetites as something aggressive, to be feared. But the scene also shows a shift in social station in the presence of whiteness. The prince comes from a far southern place of fields, whose desire becomes a menace in the presence of whiteness in a city that produces nothing but culture, politics, ideas, and status. The fields are far from King's Landing, and we only imagine the laborers. Desire is mapped onto the delicate, slender white body that has not darkened working the fields, and whiteness is mapped onto first-world cities where things *happen* because the beautiful white people are there. So if the Rio Grande Valley and the transborder region is a land of fields—an area populated mostly by primarily Spanish-speaking non-white migrant laborers living in cities routinely named as the "fattest," poorest, least-educated cities in the United States, who by virtue of their abjection scare white girls—why would any record company send a record executive looking for talent there?

The people who live in the Texas borderlands navigate a terrain of overlapping colonial systems, reality pushed and pulled across the border's blade so much that it creates a rupture in time itself. On one side modernity, and the "developed," "fast-paced" United States creating the future; on the other the "undeveloped" Latin America, always a decade behind, with its "primitive" housing and "low-tech" manual laborers anchored in the past. Time runs differently on either side of the line, making the borderlands themselves a site of temporal dislocation, where even the people are excluded from modernity itself, as they are thought to be incapable of the skills needed for the future. This is the condition of borderlands Indigenous descendants, whose tribal ties have been long obliterated by colonization: stranded in space and time, with no memory of the past, they are also denied access to the future.

Futurelessness is a deliberate racialized condition, and necessary to produce invisible workers—*temporary visa, seasonal labor, guest worker.* Temporal dislocation and futurelessness create the ideal conditions for exploitable labor, a never-ending shift in an endless strawberry field, with no guarantee you can stay. Like "working the fields" in the scene above, "Strawberry Fields Forever" means something different for the people at the border—an invisible life sung by the most famous band in the world.

My father says of his youth, "I was born in the wrong place," speaking of the invisibility and remoteness of the Valley and its culture. Could the music industry, looking ever forward into the future, looking to make a star, ever consider a place that's not even part of modernity, or the future at all?

My father—swarthy, afroed, primarily Spanish-speaking—was never going to be what they were looking for, despite his good looks, talent, and carefully curated wardrobe. As the darkest-skinned child of five, and the eldest son, he was the least loved, and given so few clothes when he was growing up that as an adult he made up for it in elegance and stage presence, taking great care to dress well and in the latest fashions. Photos from this era show his studious but friendly nature, accented by a sharp personal style in bell bottoms and ascots, velvet four-piece suits, tweed blazers, all the way to the white chinos and statement pastels of the 1980s. He's just one example of how chic and sophisticated Rio Grande Valley youth culture could be, despite humble origins. But no matter how beautiful he was, or how deserving his talent, he was on the wrong edge of the country. And perhaps it is this geographic, cultural, racial, and linguistic remoteness that developed my father's rare gift into the expressive, but difficult, thing it became.

Side Two

According to the community, it was only a matter of time before Beto Villarreal, the heaviest and most technical guitar player in Reynosa, would "get discovered." Not only did he have the looks, the sex appeal, and an ineffable cool, he was absolutely sick with natural talent. He began playing in multiple bands professionally in La Zona Rosa, a strip of nightclubs, bars, and other nightlife in Reynosa, starting at age fifteen with his first rock trio, La Máquina. Soon the band came to be known *as* him—"Beto Máquina," a signifier of how hard he worked, how untouchable and singular he was. As his star grew, he joined the Reynosa acid rock group Canela India, a band that would be honored in 2015 by the Reynosa Institute of Culture and Art and inducted into its museum as an important contributor to rock en español in Mexico and El Valle.

He'd always been the black sheep of the family, and music began to strain his relationship with his mother. One night, when she didn't let him go out for a gig, he stuffed the only clothes he had—two pairs of jeans and a few shirts—in a backpack and ran away from home. And not just to crash with a friend, of which he had many. He bought a one-way ticket and got on a bus to Mexico City to follow his dream.

Once he arrived in Mexico City, his star shone bright. He hooked up with friends and musicians and almost immediately gained notoriety as the heaviest rock player on the scene. The music magazine *México Canta*, the equivalent of *Rolling Stone* in Mexico, ran a full-page profile on him, highlighting the exciting new talent who, at only seventeen, was already being compared to prominent rock guitarists like Eric Clapton and Jimmy Page. At the time, he resisted the comparisons; he didn't think he was on their level. But now, after a life of playing jazz and learning music theory, he resists them for another reason:

Esos guitarristas eran como dioses, famosos, con unas guitarrotas hermosas. Eran lo máximo en ese tiempo. Pero ahora ya que sé más de la música y la guitarra, me he dado cuenta que no servían, casi no tocaban, no tanto como decían. Lo único que eran de Europa, eran blancos.

Those guitarists were like gods, ultra-famous, with these gorgeous expensive guitars. They were the pinnacle of rock back then. But now that I know so much more about music and playing guitar, I've come to find out that they weren't all they were cracked up to be. They didn't play as well as everyone said. They were just white, and from Europe.

The much more technical, melodically richer, and more inventive guitarists, he says, were the Black funk and soul players in bands like Sly and the Family Stone, Ohio Players, Earth, Wind & Fire, and Funkadelic—artists who never got their "guitar god" flowers. As rock gentrified in the 1960s, it became associated with the avant-garde, elevated as the genre of artistic genius and experimentation, associated with glamour and wealth, or country-fried in the South—claimed by the realms of whiteness. As rock guitarists gained individual notoriety and prestige, Black rock, soul, funk, and R&B bands of the 1960s and '70s were not as solo-driven as rock & roll, nor were their guitarists often recognized as virtuosos. (That is, not until one of my dad's favorites, Prince, came along.)

The week Prince died, I texted my dad to see how he was doing with the news, and to tell him I'd gone to see *Purple Rain* in the theater. He of course was sad, and as we talked through it, I told him about an interview Eric Clapton had done where the journalist asked him what it felt like to be the best guitarist in the world, to which Clapton responded, "I don't know, you'll have to ask Prince." My dad texts back, "Correctamondo."

I never realized that while my father was young and playing rock throughout Mexico and in Mexico City, not just in small clubs but at big events like the Jazz & Rock Benefit, the Mexican government had banned rock & roll following the 1968 Tlatelolco massacre in Mexico City (recently portrayed in the film *Roma*), where the US-backed authoritarian PRI regime massacred more than three hundred student demonstrators. Even before the massacre, in 1965, the Beatles were banned from playing in Mexico, and later the Doors and other big acts were too. The Mexican government heavily censored all music and media, advancing a rhetoric of rock & roll as "immoral and not correct." But the true fear was of how rock gathered and organized youth, its rebellious nature, and its ability to encourage radical politics, people power, and protest. Bands that did manage to put on shows faced shutdowns and police brutality—even the US band Chicago was forced offstage by police and the military in 1975. So rock musicians and youth retaliated by creating venues called "hoyos fonkis," or funky holes—abandoned buildings, parking lots, warehouses—where rock music could go underground (sometimes literally), and a counterculture flourished under violent state repression and censorship. In the past, when he told me about his time with Canela India from 1971 to 1973, touring major cities in Mexico such as Acapulco, Cuernavaca, Jojutla, Mexico City, and Tampico, he never made it sound like he was part of a counterculture engaging in acts of antiauthoritarian resistance. A life of humility and almosts has warped his memory into thinking he was never really part of anything big or culturally significant, but ever in the margins somewhere.

Perhaps the violent, oppressive environment of Mexico and Latin America at large never permitted rock & roll bands to become massive superstars like those from England or the United States. Xenophobia, First World–Third World relations, American racism, language barriers, and white supremacy made rock en español a hard sell to Middle American audiences. And there was certainly no Mexican equivalent to the star-making apparatus of the US entertainment industry.

US-Mexico cultural exchange is very one-sided, extractive of resources, culture, food, and labor but never people, whereas Canada is a superstar and celebrity factory. So, like many talented and beloved Mexican rock bands of the era, with no future in sight, Canela India broke up.

Still convinced he was a hot commodity destined for big things, with a magazine profile under his belt, after an explosive year in Mexico City my father decided to try his luck in Chicago. He arrived in 1974, when Chicago's Mexican American and Latino immigrant communities were growing and working "unskilled" factory jobs. Despite big dreams of finding his way into the funk and soul music circuit, he found it difficult to secure his footing in the everyday world, much less the music world or the nightlife. Talent and originality alone don't get you far in a new town, especially if that town is severely segregated by race and class like Chicago was, and continues to be. He got by working in a paint factory and made decent money, visiting clubs and attending shows when he could to try to connect to musicians. But after one year of no luck, it was time to come back to El Valle, to the river that calls back all its unwanted children.

MY FATHER EMPHASIZES HOW CLOSED ENGLISH-SPEAKING MUSIC scenes were to him. Looking back at his photos, I wonder how. I see a fashionable, elegant, handsome man, but with dark, ethnically ambiguous features and tightly curled hair—definitely not white, but not quite mestizo. He was an outcast in the land of outcasts, his unreal talent amplifying his already racialized otherness. I have asked and asked about Blackness in our family, and constantly come up against a hard blank wall of forgetting, of absence, only trace evidence and rumor combined with a history of the region that never produces a name—the mixedness of colonial subjecthood in the Valley.

Something about the combination of his features, his accent, and his lack of connections made auditioning for English-speaking rock and pop bands an exercise in constant alienation and rejection. He couldn't simply arrive in any American city and start networking like he could in Mexico. And this negation began a seismic shift in his life, and a new pattern: a fiery spark of endless potential, and a letting go of the dream. He wanted nothing more than to play rock, but by 1975 the rock en español trend was waning, and disco was heating up every dance floor in the Valley. Las discotecas del Valle are near-legendary in the region, sources of urban legends such as Devil in the Disco, a cautionary tale about a girl who went out on Good Friday and met a handsome man who made her dance all night to her death. Throughout the 1970s, Valley folks bragged about sightings of legendary celebrities stopping at local restaurants and bars for one last night in the United States before crossing the border, and McAllen and Brownsville occasionally got big names to come through, like War, Santana, Javier Bátiz (a legendary rock player from Mexico), and AC/DC.

One of those encounters could have been life-changing for my dad. In the late 1970s he was playing with a band named Mister, or Etc., depending on which side of the line. This is another instance of the two-name problem in the borderlands: three of the band members didn't have papers, so in the United States they were Mister, and in Mexico they were Etc. After a number of years establishing their reputation, the opportunity of a lifetime came knocking on the unlikeliest of doors: Chic, one of disco's greatest bands, was coming to McAllen, Texas, and Mister would open for them. My father remembers few details from the night, which was both a typical worknight and an extraordinary occurrence. He remembers Nile Rodgers's clear Stratocaster,

and he remembers the band coming out to watch Mister open—
something Chic ordinarily didn't do. I asked if he stuck around to talk
to the band, and he said no, Mister had to go to another hotel gig
right afterward at the Hilton. But opportunity would seek Mister out
again—while they were playing their set at the Hilton, Chic and their
management came to watch them play. They offered Mister a perma-
nent opening gig for the rest of the tour after the show, but Mister's
manager (a white Cuban, my dad points out) wanted too much money,
and in the end, no deal was made.

The reality of the music scene in South Texas in the 1970s and '80s
is one of hybridity, where the discoteca is also a taquería and conve-
nience store, and performances are also often family affairs, bailes organized around a quinceañera, or wedding, or child's birthday. Those
kinds of events lack the cool and cultural capital of a CBGB, which
strips legitimacy from serious performances, and anchors upward tra-
jectories. It was at one of these restaurant/nightclub-and-bar combos,
Lalo's, where one of my dad's bands played steady gigs and my mother
worked as a waitress, that my parents met. After they married in 1980
they lived in a small trailer house in McAllen, but eventually, with a
child to support, circumstances would pull my mother away to work
for a grocery store chain in Corpus Christi, and then away again to
work in Houston, where my grandmother could receive cancer treatment. And the cycle would repeat again—opportunity to the north,
labor pulling families apart, legacies of migration replicating themselves in new contexts.

My father would continue to live in the apartment in Brownsville
alone from 1984 to 1989 as my mother and I moved farther and farther north; he needed to stay there to maintain his weekly club and
hotel rotation with his band Memories, and his bands were doing well,
making money—they would soon "be discovered," and we wouldn't

My father in a wicker peacock chair looking extremely eighties— somewhere between Miami Vice *and* Billy Ocean—*in a white blazer, white pants, and white sneakers, with Ray-Ban Wayfarers hanging from his neck and a healthy mustache. This photo was likely taken as a band promo, probably around 1986.*

have to worry about money anymore. I think, deep down, he believed another opportunity like Chic would come along again, so long as he kept working. He came up to visit on weekends until finally, when it was clear that no one from Hollywood was coming, he could no longer stand the distance and came to live in Houston with us.

MY FATHER SOMETIMES SAYS THAT IF HE WEREN'T TIED DOWN TO a family, if he hadn't moved to Houston, he would have "made it." Mostly that's wishful thinking, because it was the move to Houston that pulled him out of obscurity and put him right in the nucleus of La Onda Grupera, a busy hub for major Tejano and cumbia acts like Selena, and home to the legendary sax player Fito Olivares and his band. After working in roofing for a week or so, he auditioned for a new cumbia band, Los Super Villahnos, and got the position right away. They soon signed to Gil Records, an independent Latino music label, and began touring heavily, playing the baile circuit all along the southern states. It was their 1992 appearance on *Johnny Canales*, however, that got them on the radio with their most famous single, "Vete." Having a family was not a burden so much as a landing place between tours, major concerts, television, and radio spots—but to him this was his last shot.

And yes, he played with Selena: once on *Johnny Canales* when she was still a child, and once in 1992 in Laredo, Texas. And of his touring tales, he says this one is true: my father's signature guitar, a white Fender Stratocaster, is a relic from the end of his Top 40 pop and rock days in the Valley. It was the most versatile, working for heavy rock solos as well as light pop rhythm guitar, and he brought it with him into the cumbia scene. When he met Chris Pérez, Selena's guitarist and husband, who would go on to blend cumbia and rock in Selena's music and famously play a white Fender Stratocaster, Pérez wasn't yet playing a Stratocaster, nor was he playing any solos. Hair metal had little organic audience in the Valley, so many rock musicians played in cumbia and Tejano bands to pay the bills. At that Laredo show, Chris saw in my dad a rock player incorporating solos, distortion, and rock flourishes into cumbia on his white Stratocaster. From then on Chris Pérez would be associated with blending rock solos with cumbia, and with a white Fender Stratocaster. There are many stories my father tells me to hold back on—maybe they can't be verified, or someone will have a different take on the same event. But about Chris Pérez and the Strat, he says I can print this one: it's true.

My father, third from right, stands embraced by Los Super Villahnos band members and roadies in front of their tour bus. This photo was taken somewhere far from home on a winter night between 1990 and 1992. I don't know their names, except Cristóbal, the bassist, far left, and Chevo, the man kneeling in the front, a jack-of-all-trades and a good friend to my dad.

In my father's three years with the Villahnos, the band soared to great heights in the cumbia scene, opening for major acts like Bronco, Los Tigres del Norte, Selena, and Fito Olivares all across the United States and Mexico. He remembers playing shows with more than twenty thousand people—the biggest crowd he ever played. Eventually they caught the attention of Sony Records' Spanish division in Chicago and recorded their last album, *Entrégate*, in 1993. Los Super Villahnos broke up due to circumstances beyond my father's control, and to this day they get airplay on the radio in Texas here and there, with fans still wondering what became of this great band and that one rola, "Vete."

In 1993, the legendary cumbia sax player Fito Olivares had seen firsthand how my father ran sound for the Villahnos while playing the show. He'd been the band's sound engineer, roadie, and guitarist all in the same night, and not only did Fito admire his hustle, he ran excellent sound. So the same week the Villahnos broke up, my father began working for Fito Olivares as a sound engineer, his first ever W-2 job.

It is from here that my father's luck would take a downward turn. With the death of my grandmother and the birth of my brother, he was under tremendous pressure to earn. As sound engineer for the renowned and successful Fito Olivares band, with the promise of a position as a guitarist in the band, he described himself as "having it made," but that promise never panned out. He began running sound for other bands on the bill for extra money, using Fito's equipment. He would play jazz guitar at sound check instead of Fito's recorded music. People at Fito's concerts would recognize him from Los Super Villahnos or from his other bands in the Valley, and when he played guitar on the bus between gigs, it was clear he could run circles around any of the musicians in Fito's band. Resentment began to build, and by 1998, five years later, he was out. No formal firing, they just never called him back.

Throughout the years he would scrape together gigs here and there, and ended up playing bajo sexto for a Tejano/conjunto band called Sabiduría Norteña. The switch from guitar to a more traditional acoustic instrument was aesthetically very far from where he wanted to be, which was playing jazz and really showing his technical gifts, if even just to a tiny, intimate audience. But Sabiduría Norteña signed with Univision and recorded three popular albums. By then, in my twenties, I perceived my father as an adult rather than a child, could better understand the pressure he faced, the money he needed to make, the dreams he never fulfilled. I could tell he wasn't happy—he never discussed his work or invited us to performances, and he kept all of his stage costumes in the trunk of the car.

YOU MIGHT THINK FROM MY TONE THAT THIS IS A SAD STORY. AND maybe it is, but it is also a tribute to an unseen life, a long-overdue recognition of ordinary genius worn down by circumstance.

When I FaceTime my father one summer night to ask him the music theory behind the song he wrote for me back in 1984, he shrugs and says, "No sé." No explanation, although I know there's a meticulous understanding of every expression, a reason behind every note. Thirty-five years later, he still doesn't understand how he wrote the song—he will only come to understand how complex it was later. The song speaks to an innate refinement in his musical ear at a young age, developed solely by instinct—a complexity people ascribe to Wes Montgomery or John Coltrane or Prince. He can explain the theory, the scales, the modes, but how he wrote it? That part is simply forged from the mystery of creation.

When I ask him about his writing process, he says only that one day he became so overwhelmed with emotion upon seeing me, his infant daughter, that the song just poured out of him, fully formed— very unusual for my dad, who is a meticulous tinkerer and perfectionist when it comes to songwriting. The song remains untitled, referred to in my family only as la canción de la nena, "the baby's song," a shorthand that betrays its tenderness and complexity.

The song itself is, from a music theory standpoint, technically intricate. Using jazz chords with shifting root positions to underlie a lead melody played at the same time, my father composed a song at twenty-nine that impresses even elder jazz musicians, a song that would become our intimate musical language, able to communicate tenderness, regret, pride, absence, or forgiveness over the course of my life. Because I've listened to him play since my first day on earth,

I've developed a sensitive ear. I can describe the slight difference in mood between an F-minor 7th and a half-diminished chord, pentatonic versus blues scales, Aeolian versus Phrygian modes. And while melody, rhythm, and harmony come easily to me (I sing and taught myself guitar), growing up bilingual and lonely attuned my ear to the mood, rhythm, and music of language. Just as I have dozens of notebooks of old drawings and poetry, my father has decades of staff notebooks, cataloging experiments in jazz guitar and music theory in light, precise pencil. He never had the means to go to school for music. It hurts to see those notebooks now, the sole record of a life of dedicated study, stacked somewhere beneath boxes and cables in the garage—artifacts of an extraordinary mind to be forgotten along with every poster, promo, and album since he lost his vision.

I have only one recording of the song: a phone video recording a friend was able to capture from my wedding. It's not as agile as the versions from my childhood, but it still captures the inventive chord structure, the deft lead, before my dad's fingers would atrophy and make it hard for him to play. I barely remember the performance, and even though it's mostly a happy memory, something about the document of that moment makes it too hard to watch.

MY FATHER BEGAN TO DEVELOP TYPE 2 DIABETES IN HIS FORTIES after a life of touring, and since then it's caused significant nerve damage in his extremities and macular degeneration and glaucoma, which has made him almost totally blind. Diabetes is strongly linked to Latine communities, but it is more a disease of poverty, food deserts, and the demands of capitalism. His fingers and hands have atrophied, joints permanently bent, which, over time, slowly made playing guitar painful, sometimes impossible. Today, he cannot play at all—while home alone, he fractured his arm from a fall and, since then, has not recovered his mobility or finger dexterity.

These days, I try to lift his spirits by calling him on FaceTime. "¿Has visto la nueva serie de Selena, Papi?" *No.* "¿Cómo te sientes, pa?" *Bien.* "Aver, tócame una de Wes Montgomery." *No, más tarde.* Sometimes when I ask him about his work or his past, he'll get a spark of energy, and his old self will shine through with a story. But mostly he stays in my childhood bedroom, door closed, lights off, surrounded by diabetes and blood pressure medications, pain pills he gets from a tío in Pasadena, and the tablet he holds inches from his face to watch YouTube jazz performances, stand-up specials, and, lately, conspiracy videos.

I feel an aesthetic kinship with other poets and writers who are also the daughters of musicians. I wonder about our shared preoccupation with documents, sound, obscurity, and the artifacts of the past, ephemera and recordings and photos that are not to be cataloged or listened to but stacked away in storage, under cables, motor oil, old towels, and broken appliances. Every corner in my home is filled with relics like this, containing unknown histories—ranch life, Tampico high society, survival stories, family sagas—every artifact charged with haunting.

I think often of the CDs, tapes, promo posters, notes, sketches, and newspaper clippings from my father's past as a professional musician, and the way in which these objects form an archive of failure and obscurity, never to be inducted into the Rock & Roll Hall of Fame. The objects make me want to show the world what it missed out on, how invisible my dad was as a Mexican immigrant, either playing rock and jazz because it was his passion, or playing cumbias and conjunto as part of an invisible community, rich with laughter

Papi playing lead guitar and harmonizing during a gig, the band all in white suits with black dress shirts, likely late 1970s, with his band Etc./Mister.

and culture and drama. I've been able to recover some documents from the forgetting: his first televised performance on *Johnny Canales*, his album covers, his first band Canela India's induction into Reynosa's cultural museum, artifacts I show in the short documentary film I made about his life. I think of Harmony Holiday's collection *Hollywood Forever*, her own father's similar obscurity, the enduring hit "Put a Little Love in Your Heart," and how the documents of his career weave themselves into the fabric of her work, how she lets the historical contexts of those documents tell on themselves, reveal the pernicious racism and obscurity he lived through.

The body is a haunted terrain—a living record of personal, familial, social, and epigenetic memory. To look at my father's body now—the way he shuffles when he walks, the atrophy in his once-nimble fingers, the nerve pain in his feet, the cloudiness in his eyes as he loses his sight—it too is a record of both his splendor and his decline, his once dazzling beauty and potential and the systems that failed him. I have to carry the memory of him in his splendor and his decline. And what I carry of him is also connected to the land, its seam connecting memory, legacy, into the future. Memory is a kind of map, linked to textures, smells, songs, place, the act of remembering in and of itself a kind of haunting. Music is one of the few portals I have into my fragmented memory, and writing is the only way I know to recover my people from the nothing of forgetting, to resist the eraser of the border and its constant overwriting of history, to salvage what is disappearing.

But already this essay is engaged in the act of omission, forming itself into something to be archived, a thing of the past that, like the Valley, cannot imagine a future. So I will imagine this: Papi, you are on a stage, a sturdy stage with expensive lights and a roaring crowd. Your band, undefined by genre, is holding a note for you, the drums rumbling, and it's up to you to deliver the solo that will take us home. Your body is not bent, or sick, or tired, but limber and alive. Your contributions to jazz, funk, disco, pop, rock, and cumbia are now legendary—the man who could do it all, who could cross geographic, racial, language, and genre boundaries and deliver solos as memorable as those of Prince or Billy Preston—this immigrant, son of migrant laborers, not yet a citizen, captivating thousands. The show is an anniversary perhaps, or an induction. And you take it all in, give that smile everyone loves, and rip into a fiery solo, one that defines a career, and finally you are legible, visible, heard.

Encyclopedia of All the Daughters I Couldn't Be

Bonita

"No hagas esa cara."

"What do you mean?" I ask.

"This face." She pushes her lips out. "You look like a fish when you put lipstick on." There are three things Mami is an expert on: flowers, fashion, and makeup. I am not going to win.

"I do not."

She starts to mock me in her mirror, pushing her lips out grotesquely at the reflection, putting too much on. "That's what you look like."

She rolls back the tube of lipstick and drops it in her bag, takes out her drugstore eyeshadow palette, and expertly closes the lid of one eye to apply it.

Her sense of fashion is from the Donna Summer, Studio 54, Halston era, updated for the 1990s. Ever a modern, glamorous woman in chic structured dresses and thick leather belts, she is hypercritical of my grungy, androgynous aesthetic in flannels, Chucks, and overdone eye makeup. We have always been opposites like this—she is drop-dead beautiful and trying to enchant, I am awkward and intense and trying to provoke. While she scours the clearance racks at Foley's, I shoplift band T-shirts and find used flannel shirts in the gym lost and found. When the school counselor recommends that I start going to therapy, I take one of Papi's white T-shirts and write "I WENT TO THE RAPIST" in Sharpie, wear it to school, and don't even last through first period. My dress code violations are so frequent that every few weeks, Mami has to leave work, pick me up, make me change clothes, and take me back to school. But I did wear perfume, when I had it.

Our ideas of beauty will forever be at odds, but on one thing we agree: whatever your look, it must make a statement, and convey a strength of character. Everything about her is bold—her red lipstick, her violet eyeshadow, her lined eyes, her high walnut cheekbones, her graceful posture, her cigarette balanced between shapely fingers, her signature scent.

For my mother, perfume, like daily bread, is a nonnegotiable necessity. The woman wore full makeup and perfume to give birth to me, and to this day she has not gone a single day without wearing it. She keeps an extra bottle in her car, and even on weekend mornings will spritz it on her décolletage just to clean the house in her leopard-print bata. *El glamour*, my tía Mela teases. Her signature scent is Estée Lauder's Knowing, a chypre-floral aurum from 1988, very of-its-time with a strong character of oakmoss, rose, and amber—refined, elegant, sophisticated.

I absolutely hate it. It has a searing metallic quality from aldehyde, an alcohol in synthetic fragrances. To me, it smells like Melanie Griffith's *Working Girl* makeover preserved in paint thinner, and no, I will not elaborate. But I love it on my mother, how it captures the strength of her character—described by Estée Lauder as "intensely feminine," it's also a strong masculine scent, a good marriage of woody and floral that is assertive, bold, resilient, never fades, like the brave, loving, take-no-shit breadwinner and chingona she is. (Yes, she's an Aries.) Her scent is a sensory roadmap of my own identity too, connected to concepts of womanhood and work, poise and femininity. Although her perfume might conjure up curly bobs and erotic thrillers and Madonna's "Vogue" on cassette, for her, and for all the women in my family before her, the practice of personal beauty and style

is culturally Mexican, and a much older, more sacred inheritance.

Born in Torreón in the 1950s, my mother is from a generation of Mexican women that considered a signature scent to be the height of elegance and a significant part of one's identity, like María Félix famously using Joy by Jean Patou, or Marilyn Monroe sleeping in nothing but Chanel No. 5. Perfume is a luxury that, even at their most pobrecitos, they found a way to afford—more than a statement or a calling card, being clean and smelling good is a show of dignity and self-respect. But it goes much deeper than that.

Beauty is the only thing my mother's mother left her, her only inheritance, her only source of generational wealth. Anytime anyone talks about Angélica, my abuela, it begins and ends with how rare and astonishing her beauty was. The daughter of hacienda farmworkers, she was both very poor and very privileged in her lifetime, upper middle class for a few years but only through marriage, and died a penniless immigrant. Her wealth was earned, conditional, and temporary, so when she escaped both of those brutalizing bastards, she left as a migrant with nothing but the clothes on her back. But throughout her life, no matter the circumstance, even with cancer, she was always clean, beautiful, composed, arreglada, smelling of Estée Lauder Youth-Dew oil. It was how she took back her power—no one, not a rich man nor a poor man nor a white man, could determine her class or her worth but her.

Perfume is also how my mother imposes gender on me when she gives it to me every Christmas. Listen, I know I'm hard to shop for. I love books, but not bestsellers; I love makeup, but not her colors; she's a lady, I'm a tomboy. Every year, she gets me a new variation of Estée Lauder Beautiful, or Clinique Happy, perfumes that were popular when I was in high school. At a loss, she wants to give me something personal—my own signature scent, a passing on of a generational tradition.

But I think I've maybe always had a signature scent—CK One. I was rebelling against everything and everyone, and one of those things was gender. While every other girl in eighth grade was trying to look pretty and get boys' attention, I was wearing red lipliner as eyeliner and black lipstick, earning me afterschool detention. When a teacher told me to wash it off, I'd respond with "Sir, yes sir!" and a military salute with a stomp. I was restless, distracted, angry, fire-raw, and hungry for something real. To be seen, understood, held.

Today I am wearing brown lipstick and Sharpie eyeliner in the inner and outer corners of my eyes. Looking at myself, then at my mother, I decide my face is a mess. My eyes are lined with too much black, and my lipstick is caked over the soft skin of my fourteen-year-old lips.

"At least I don't look like an evil stepmother." I'm always challenging my mother, especially when I most need her. I always go too far. She's just had a baby and is working eighty hours a week at a grocery store, the sole provider for our family, now two payments behind on a predatory starter-home mortgage, supposedly cheaper than renting an apartment. The bank needs immigrants to take out loans, and lured us in. We are broke, and my weekly therapy sessions are not covered by insurance. In a few months, I will need to be hospitalized.

"Okay. Let everyone make fun of you, then."

She blots her lipstick on a fold of toilet paper, expertly sealing the hue. She sucks in her cheeks, exposing her cheekbones, and presses in the blush brush, blending burnt bronze onto the ridges. The woman has incredible bone structure, I'll give her that. I catch myself admiring her, the plump bow of her lips, the doe-like set of her eyes.

"OK, give me a kiss." She always kisses me goodbye after she's applied her lipstick. Many a Saturday morning, I've woken up to a bright fuchsia kiss mark on my cheek, lips, forehead.

"Show me how."

"What do you mean?"

"Show me how to put makeup on."

She sighs, tries very hard not to smile. "Okay, but really quick, because I'm going to be late. Wash your face."

She begins with a dash of lotion on my nose, blending the moisture in. "You don't need base, you have such beautiful skin," she comments. She applies the slightest touch of blush to the apple of my cheek. I notice that where she contoured her face, she merely adds a flush to mine.

"Stand still. Close your eyes." I do as she asks. I feel the lightest brush on my eyelid. When I open my eyes, I am delighted to see a light beige highlight on my browbone. My eyes are hooded, like my father's, and dark with curiosity. She lifts something out in them, an innocence she sees that no one else can. "Stand still. Okay, you do the mascara."

I curl the wand upward into my lashes as she decides what lipsticks to try on me. She decides on a light plum-pink shade. "This will look very nice with your dark hair."

"Let me do it." The lipstick is my favorite part.

"Okay. But don't do this." Fish face. "Así bonita, like a boy you like is watching. Because he might be." She doesn't know that right now, my crush is a girl named Mandy, a Goth girl in NIN T-shirts and black JNCOs who smokes in PE and writes me poems.

She relaxes her face and shows me how to run the tube across my lips softly, slowly, accentuating the suppleness of the flesh, pouting out slightly. I understand. I understand exactly.

"Okay, done," I say.

"Let me look at you." I feel her gaze sweeping across me, finally proud. "So beautiful. Okay, ya me voy a trabajar. Give me a kiss."

I do. And when I see myself, I see myself through her eyes, then a boy's eyes, then Mandy's eyes, then white American eyes, and from then on, always, always, from the outside.

CURANDERISMO

Plant. *Lactuca serriola.* Prickly lettuce, also known as milk thistle. Weed. Soporific; milk and leaves can be used in tinctures to treat pain.

Literary Device: *The Ordinary World, the Call to Adventure*

N THE YEAR OF DISBELIEF, THE YEAR TEN HURRICANES DRAGGED walls of water from the Caribbean to the Gulf Coast and drowning cities drowned again; the year Puerto Rico, an island already without power, went dark for 181 days; the year the deadliest mass shooting in US history was followed by the deadliest mass shooting in US history; the year Donald Trump took office and broke the illusion of the Obama years and Middle America found itself in an unrecognizable country— that year was the year reality seemed to finally break for everyone along the cracks forming since Ferguson in 2014; since Trayvon in 2012; since Obama in 2008; since Bush in 2000; since Columbine; since on and on. Violence after violence, betrayal after national betrayal, disaster after emergency after disaster. This was all happening in the fall of 2017, when my marriage ended, and the story I'd been telling myself shattered too. A couple of weeks later, on October 7, 2017, I posted a selfie to Instagram with the caption: "Just making sure I'm still here."

For days I'd been outside my body, unrecognizing of all the surfaces of my life. How had I gotten here, to California, in this house, alone with this stranger? Stranded in the West, far from home, I felt my surroundings strange, unfamiliar, like I was living in a mirror world, not the real one. Time stopped until it reminded me of its passing: *pick up the baby, eat something, sunrise.* Was I ever real, or did I imagine myself? Even the mirror could not corroborate my reality; I didn't know who that was.

After ten years of losing myself to him, I'd become unrecognizable to myself. My face, once dark, mercurial, and angular, had become swollen and wide; my hair, once long and black, was cut short after falling out in handfuls; a size seven my whole life, I was now over two hundred pounds, with a hugely distended and scarred lower abdomen, despite working out every day; once sharp and organized, with tons of ideas and an exceptional memory, now I had no sense of time and could no longer trust my mind. And although I could see my reflection, I could not locate myself in my postpartum body. I hadn't felt beautiful in years, or desired, and still don't as a result of his comments. I had died and been reborn a "wife" and "mother" in service of someone else, the kind of woman who is ignored by the world—no longer attractive, no longer visible, no longer valuable. I was also completely lost as a mother, an impostor among other mothers, and so terrified of being alone that I was willing to accept any level of disrespect from this man so long as it meant I was safe, financially secure, would never be poor again. I chose not to see how my relationship was becoming dangerously volatile as time went on. I let a man "break me with my own love," as the poet Khadijah Queen writes, over and over, until I was a shell of a person, slowly killing myself with banal but brutal self-neglect.

The day I took that selfie, I did my makeup in a way I knew my husband would like. He was finally coming home after days of not telling me where he was. I was hoping the promise that I could be beautiful again would prevent him from abandoning me. And in preparation for his arrival, on my father's advice, I put a piece of folded paper in my shoe.

Loss is the condition needed for the suspension of disbelief. To truly believe in magic—to believe that words, actions, and intentions can manifest a desire into reality—one must first know the experience of profound, instantaneous, irreversible loss. Death thins the veil and suspends disbelief; an animal appears, and you recognize its presence, or the ordinary world begins speaking in signs. Accidents are another way to feel that loss: totaling a car on a freeway, or dropping a valuable ring into the sea. By the age of fourteen, I'd already had many losses, losses it took me ten years to repair. When I moved in with him at twenty-five, having a partner with a stable job finally gave me the foundation I needed to start the life I should have started at eighteen: to go back to college, get my degree, apply to graduate school. Now thirty-five, a new mother, and a doctoral student on a limited income, I could not do this life alone. I wasn't just losing my marriage, I was losing the person I'd built over twenty years as proof I'd gotten better, and now I was losing the chance at a life I'd never had a shot at, that I could never have built on my own—the dream of being a writer, an artist, a professor, a dream I'd only been able to pursue while with him. He kept me grounded, focused, realistic, disciplined, on a routine. I could not survive in this world without him.

Plant. *Salvia rosmarinus*. Rosemary. One of the oldest sacred plants; first recorded use by Egyptians, to embalm corpses. Symbol of remembrance, memory and cognition, cleansing, purification.
Literary Device. *The Hero's Journey Is a Circle, the Heroine's Journey Is a Spiral*

Toward the end of our marriage, in 2016, I was put on no fewer than five medications nearly all at once, each one endlessly switched out for another on loop—Abilify, Adderall, Lamictal, Inderal (a beta-blocker), Prozac, Seroquel, Trileptal, Trintellix, Vyvanse, Wellbutrin, and Xanax, to name a few. These medications followed a formal PTSD/c-PTSD, ADHD, postpartum depression, and generalized anxiety disorder diagnosis. My already unstable reality shifted just a little bit every time I adjusted to a new medication.

Motherhood is a constant state of emergency, a siren wailing in every cell of your body every minute of the day. Fold the stroller, take the stroller down the stairs, check the stroller at the gate, take the stroller up the stairs with one hand, baby in another; poopy diaper in public, neighbors complaining about being woken up by crying at 2:00, 3:00, 4:00 a.m., spill water on laptop, no, don't eat that. When I started my doctoral program, my son had just turned one, forcing me to do all of my work in the wee hours after everyone had gone to bed. And after a long day of classes, hot gridlock commutes, endless domestic labor, dinners, shopping, mothering, I just couldn't do it anymore. I couldn't concentrate on anything for more than thirty seconds, couldn't remember enough to make a to-do list, couldn't organize myself, couldn't assimilate new information. It was more than absent-mindedness—it was something deeper that I couldn't fix by just trying harder, applying myself. This felt life-threatening. I couldn't do basic things like make appointments, keep track of time, much less be on time. I couldn't follow a schedule, meet a deadline, respond to an email, remember a task, get organized, or be with others without dis-associating. I routinely missed important dates, lost entire days of time, forgot names I'd known for years, blanked out on common words. I was constantly embarrassing myself.

In my first therapy session since my teens, the doctor asked me to describe what was going on in my life and my marriage. When I was done, she asked if she could record our session, gave me papers to sign, and said, "Tell me everything again, as close to exactly what you just said, for the camera." Afterward she handed me the card of her friend, a real estate agent, and urged me to call her, to find a new apartment and start making an exit plan. She said it sounded like PTSD burnout—a condition I thought was only for veterans, or survivors of extreme violence. She described it like trying to do a pirouette on the deck of a sinking *Titanic:* "Your brain is 90 percent occupied with keeping you safe and alive right now. All the little connections that help you concentrate and remember things and organize information, that neural structure has just kinda . . . pfft . . . collapsed."

As the life I was building fell apart, my mind shielded me from what was happening in my marriage with long periods of derealization and disassociation. This had happened before in my adolescence, following the events that led to my hospitalization—to survive it, I retreated deep into fantasy, until the boundary between fantasy and reality became porous, and then finally broke.

Post-traumatic stress disorder and *complex trauma* are scientific terms for a narrative called *again*. PTSD isn't just flashbacks and triggers of painful memories, or being so sad and anxious you can't function. It's a different relationship to reality, to time, to memory. In a recent study, researchers found that with PTSD, traumatic memory isn't experienced like sad autobiographical memories are in the hippocampus, the part of the brain that processes and contextualizes events and structures time; instead, traumatic memories aren't experienced as memory at all, but rather as events happening in the present. This defies how time is structured in the brain and experienced in memory—there are certain events that always stay in the present. PTSD was once described to me as drawing a spiral, and then drawing a slash through one side.

As the spiral grows outward, or inward, your pen hits that line again and again, even though you're at different stages in the spiral's progression. Like a scratch in a skipping record, or tree rings cut by a scar that connects a fire in 1600 to rising temperatures today. If time is linear, trauma is a problem, an aberration that disorganizes the sequence, something you're expected to move past; in cyclical time, tree time, trauma is the memory of the land, a mark that records an event and changes its growth, a point in the story that radiates outward and must be acknowledged by every cycle.

In the absence and erasure of record, magic is the memory of violence.

> **Plant. Yerba buena,** *Mentha spicata,* or garden mint, common
> mint, hairy mint. Uses range from purification to exorcism;
> commonly used in energy-sweeping rituals. Antiemetic. Bundles
> are placed under the bed to absorb illness and bring good spirits,
> and interpreted for diagnosis the next morning.
> **Literary Device.** *Penelope Weaving and Unweaving as a Metaphor of*
> *Time: The Unweaving Is the Taking Back of Narrative Control*

My ex is a militant atheist, the kind who hates it when people say "Bless you" after a sneeze because God doesn't exist and blessings are bullshit. So it really aggravated him when I began, very earnestly, to believe in magic.

Actually, let me not frame it like he would. In Colorado, while I was pregnant and alone and far from family, I felt a deep need to come back to my foremothers' spiritual practices, which in times of deep grief and personal disaster connected me to the memory of my bisabuela's hands, conduits to ancestral knowledges, the embodied memory of plants, our connection to the land—curanderismo.

In the ten years we were together, our life was completely devoid of all spirituality. Where I once wore a scapular and had a collection of old rosaries from Mexico, over time, I toned it all down so as not to offend him. When I started to come back to it after we were married, I knew he would lose respect for me, so I kept it a secret.

First, it was because I left the candles lit—a safety concern. Then it was because I gave the baby a bendición. It's something our families do as an act of love and protection, but it didn't matter. He simply said, "We're not doing that."

Later, when my mom came to visit, she gave the baby a barrida with an egg—a spiritual cleansing that removes colic, molestia, ojo. That made him furious. "It's more than a little weird," he said. When my tía Mela gave my mom tips over the phone for how to make my suegra cut her visit short and leave early, he rolled his eyes when he found out later why the broom was upside down against the door halfway through her visit.

In Los Angeles, city of botánicas, when I was finally able to build a real altar for Día de los Muertos, complete with marigolds, pan dulce, Miller Lite cans, and Benson & Hedges cigarettes for my grandmother, his reaction was, "Uhhhh, you bought *cigarettes* for this?" He made me ashamed of something that connected me to my family so far from home.

Upon hearing news of my marriage ending, queer and trans friends, BIPOC friends, and poet witches sent me care packages of magic objects: a white PODER novena candle from Brooklyn Brujeria, a pretty box of crystals and a note listing their powers, spearmint oil, tarot cards, offers to read my tarot on Skype. My dad told me to write his name three times on a piece of brown paper, write my name over his, fold it three times, and put it in the bottom of my right shoe to walk on all day. I still wonder if it worked—the day he came back, the day of the selfie, he did agree to at least try one session of couples therapy. But his mind was made up. The paper trabajo might have bought me time, but in the end it could not change his will.

After I moved out, living alone gave me the privacy I needed to explore my spiritual practice without fear of mockery or derision. At first I didn't trust my abilities and sought magic-adjacent energy experiences with experts. I tried reiki first, upon a friend's recommendation, and during my session, cried big, silent, uncontrollable tears. When I got home, I threw up. To this day, I still don't know what happened, but I do believe in the energies of the subtle body, and that I released something painful and heavy. Los Angeles has many new age options for spiritual cleansing, but I sought its curanderes. I got a tarot reading and energetic diagnosis by a Mexican vidente who said that I needed twenty-one limpias. Later, I saw a Mexican Yaqui chamán who owned a botánica in Echo Park and cleansed me by blowing tobacco smoke from a hand-rolled cigar all over my body, praying as he said "ay mi niña" over and over. He was the one who reminded me most of my bisabuela. At the end of the limpia, he pushed his thumbs into my brow ridge and said I had a snake wrapped around my head like a blindfold that trapped me in my thoughts and hid the true intentions and identities of others. He gave me a large white candle free of charge and hugged me. Usually I could get everything I needed for my rituals at Vallarta Supermarket or various botánicas around town, but when I did occasionally wander over to the pagan side when I needed herbs or special candles, I'd go to a shop in Burbank called the Crooked Path, owned by a grumpy male witch and devotee of Hekate, where I got a bone reading from an old Creole psychic.

I went to Olympic Spa in Koreatown a few times and sat naked in the mugwort bath, dipped my body in icy pools, lay in pink rock salt, rooms of red light. When it was time for my body scrub, the woman assigned to me was about my mom's age, working in humid conditions all day. She was stern, efficient, wordlessly telling me to turn over, and when I turned face-up, she saw my ragged c-section scar and examined it. She tsked, then began to scour the scar, dragging the abrasive cloth back and forth over the suture, a wound I could never touch, much less look at. When I began to cry, not from the pain but from the stored emotion, she stopped, put her hand on my forehead, nodded, and said, "You okay now." Can you love a stranger? I was overwhelmed with love and gratitude for her.

These were all inadequate substitutes for the rituals my bisabuela Carmen did for us when she was alive. When our abue and tías would get permiso to visit us in Houston, my mother would bring home bunches of ramas, or leaves, for barridas—spiritual cleansing rituals my great-grandmother Carmen (whom we lovingly called Abue) performed on my grandmother to try and cure her cancer. Barridas, literally "sweepings," usually performed with bunches of albahaca, yerba santa, or yerba buena, sometimes also with eggs, were long, solemn, meditative rituals where Abue would go into a kind of trance, remote and inaccessible, as she prayed silently over us, the words only audible when she inhaled. Every once in a while, she would locate stuck energy and press her hands to it. From here on, I cannot share more about these rituals, only that they were intense and sacred, followed by lighting a candle and praying a rosario.

But only children believe in magic. Only lonely women call psychic hotlines; all tarot readers are scammers. Astrology is fake; only crazy girls go through a pagan witch phase; and witch doctors, voodoo priests, and brujería are primitive folk superstitions. This is the dominant narrative of "magic"—a feminized, infantilized, racialized practice done by primitive or unwell people, despite its history in the healing arts. Ancestral knowledge is reduced to "magic" to strip it of legitimacy, shamed, ridiculed, or framed as dangerous because it is how disempowered people—women, the enslaved, the colonized, the unwell—have historically healed, rebelled, and reclaimed their narratives.

———————————

It was when I started reconnecting with my foremothers' ancestral practices that I understood what "magic" truly was. It was a language of metaphors, a way of externalizing feelings, problems, desires, representing them, changing them, visualizing a new story. It was a narrative-making tool, spoken in symbols, archetypes, cycles, seasons, elements, planets, ancient ways of knowing the world. It was a way back to my intuition—my attunement to plants, animals, cycles, the ability to pick up on subtle data—an inner knowing I had to suppress while married. I would intuitively pick up plants on walks and hikes, only to later look them up and find that my instincts were always right, and specific to my situation. I just knew that this broad, velvety leaf had a purpose, which it did as ceremonial tobacco; one day I boiled rosemary to make a tea for my hair and reverse my stress-induced hair loss; I was drawn to a wild plant called *Artemisia californica* on hikes, and read later that it was used for fertility rites, labor pain, and sexual trauma. But my intuition didn't stop at plants. I worked with oils, flowers, and candles according to no guide, instead building offerings through intuition and the act of metaphor. And spirit talked back—animals would appear in the strangest contexts, and a deep sense of knowing, a connection to some other intelligence I had since I was a child, was unblocked, and stronger than ever.

There is a precedent for this kind of belief and behavior in my family. My tía Lupe was a vidente, a seer and medium who could communicate with the dead. The woman had a presence, tranquil but perceptive, like you could never lie to her; to do so would wound your very soul. And then there was my bisabuela Carmen, who performed barridas on me throughout my troubled adolescence, both of us moved to tears by her selfless but futile attempts to banish the shadow that had possessed me.

At thirteen I was caught between two healing modalities— therapy and curanderismo—each discipline distrustful of the other. I'd been expelled from school and was weeks away from psychiatric hospitalization. This created a kind of dichotomy between our familial customs and the institutions that sustained us—the more we abided by institutional assimilation to survive, the sicker and angrier we became, a dichotomy that played out in my mother's underpay and overwork, my father and the neglect of the music industry, my grandmother and the hospital's brutal experimental treatments, and me against the carceral logics of Texas schools. So when Abue and Tía Lupe would come to visit, they weren't just treating our ailments, they were treating the damage and institutional harms of white supremacy.

I'd never known my family's folk medicine practices as curanderismo, or folk healing. I'd only known them as everyday familial wisdom, an intimate generational knowledge practiced in relation to one another and to the land. It was only once I encountered writing on the subject in college that curanderismo even entered my lexicon, the word rearranging my core memories into an anthropological "ism" to be studied, divergent from established medicine and rooted in ancient, mystical Indigenous practices with shaman practitioners capable of some arcane healing magic. But that's not what I experienced. My bisabuela Carmen practiced these forms of healing as part of her faith, but never called herself a curandera outright. Such words had already been shamed out of our language by the colonial forces of science,

Catholicism, and borders, and internalized as the self-erasure of In-digenous knowledges.

I remember Carmen's serenity, the soft strength of her touch, how trustworthy her hands felt when she laid them on us. I learned about some of the herbs and their uses, from relieving something as simple as the common cold to the more intricate lifting of curses and treatment of disease. I knew these herbs by their Spanish healing names first, later overwritten by their English names, stripped of their medicinal contexts—ramas de albahaca became holy basil, yerba buena was now wild mint, romero now rosemary, laurel now bay leaf, manzanilla now chamomile. And those plants had Indigenous names before that, their ancient uses folded into names and rituals that would survive haciendas, borders, erasure. Back then, when my abue was still alive, I couldn't appreciate these knowledges as a gift. Forgetting, assimilation, and self-erasure were so automatic that they became how I defined "growing up," a leaving behind of the rituals and knowledges that made me and saved me. Over time we began to lose contact with our elders from Mexico and the Valley, and when they passed, they took their knowledge with them. And now, when all of my foremothers were gone, was when I needed them and their knowledge the most.

I am not a curandera, but I am descended from curanderismo and humble myself before it when I engage in its practices. At its core is the Latin word *cura*, circa 1300, meaning "care, concern, trouble" but also "study; administration; office of a parish priest; a mistress." But its primary use is a "means of healing, successful remedial treatment of a disease" (late fourteenth century). Women suspected to be witches were often just healers, midwives, "cunning women," women who didn't just dress wounds and treat disease but listened to others' pain and allowed them to externalize it, transmute it, and therefore heal from it.

Curanderismo, practiced as an attunement to ancestral presences, collective memory, a spiritual exchange with the energies of the land, is a syncretism—an Indigenous practice that survives hidden inside the language and symbols of Catholicism. Its practice is largely seen as superstition, a kind of magic, but its primary concern is medicinal, practiced by chamanes, spiritual medicine people, healers, abuelas—people who have retained the memories of their elders and continue to tell their stories through spiritual practice. In curanderismo, healing is a holistic practice, treating illness as a spirit that appears as a metaphor in the body, which is a symptom of the land, which is a site of collective pain that threatens collective survival.

In the year of disbelief, the year hurricanes dragged walls of water over the coasts and darkened an island, the year powerful men killed and lied, the year of alternative facts and mass gaslighting, the year relationships ended at the feet of power and youth turned to witch-craft and ancestral magic and protested en masse, that year we entered a new period of collective trauma, collective powerlessness in an alternate reality. Post-traumatic stress disorder, depression, and ADHD are scientific names for collective narratives, perfectly normal responses to unsurvivable conditions. Trauma is the name individualism gives to a suffering that must stay private, hidden, not part of a collective story. The closest thing to PTSD in curanderismo is susto, or shock that results in soul loss, which cannot be treated in a vacuum but must be addressed with others, with the land, shared and acknowledged as part of a bigger story. And what is healing but changing your story, and enabling it to go on?

Encyclopedia of All the Daughters I Couldn't Be

Mexicana

The day you come out of your mother, you are the first in your family to set foot on an American document, the proof your infant print in ink. Born in the north above the line, your first home is a one-bedroom trailer in McAllen, Texas, mere miles from Reynosa, Tamaulipas, the city where your father was born. In the Rio Grande Valley, you move along the river's seam—Edinburgh, Eagle Pass, Laredo, Alamo, Brownsville, Matamoros—a transborder community laced together by bridges, ties the idea of America will eventually unravel. To be the first citizen daughter of Mexican immigrants is to grow up between countries until a nation forms in you. You will not truly understand what *first-generation citizen* means until you learn how important it is to be good.

In Matamoros, your tía Lupe mops the floor to a Juan Gabriel disco. You are three, and your beautiful mother is at work in America, which means you've been driven across the bridge to Mexico to stay with your godparents for a while. You love their little white house with the red clay tile patio and tangled garden, tire marks carved into the tiny patch of grass. Behind the house, spindly wildflowers overwhelm a bare spigot in the ground where cold, crystalline water fills two large concrete basins for handwashing clothes and bathing the children. Sometimes your tía boils water and fills the basin to bathe you outside; other times you'd rather shower inside with your cousin Ivette, both of you shivering under the icy stream. The days are gauzy and long; after la comida, Tío Mario waters el pasto in the sun-streaked lavender evening until the last light sinks its blue into the streets, still bustling with bochitos. Ancient oak trees with painted white trunks extend their stately boughs over the vecindad, where music streams from mercados and courtyards with heavy wooden doors. If the night is cool, your tía will make a cafecito and open the windows to hear the music outside— she will put on Flans, Timbiriche, even *Thriller* for her daughters to dance to, *mama-say-mama-sa-mama-cu-sah*, as inside the smoke drapes heavier and heavier over the card game.

You love this side of the world, this

side of the line, so full of gentle people, everywhere a good and beautiful Mexican daughter: Iliana is smart and ambitious and wants to be a lawyer, to advocate for prisoners; Liz is helpful and kind, a nurturer who always asks her mother if she needs help; and Ivette is modern and chic, wants to be a fashion designer, and will be a newscaster in the future. Each an example of what a daughter should be, each a beam of pride in her humble parents' eyes. It is only then that you realize your loneliness—you are an only child in an expensive, lonely country, who has learned that to be good is to be silent and play alone. But in Matamoros you are never alone, and you love that every person is just in the next room, every *hola Vane* a bit warmer, every pastelito just a bit sweeter, every afternoon just a bit slower, different from the little brown apartment in Brownsville. This is what you remember: color and music and life on one side, work and silence on the other.

You will return to Puerto Vallarta with your mom at nine in 1991, but you'll stay in a beach resort meant for tourists. You are still Mexican then. But you will not return again until thirty, this time as an American on your honeymoon with a white man, who will already be looking for the way out, who will soon leave you.

EN ÚTERO

N THE SUMMER OF 1994, TWO FIGURES APPEAR AT OPPOSITE POLES of my identity: Selena Quintanilla and Kurt Cobain.

Nineteen ninety-four was a threshold year: I was twelve, in transition between childhood and adolescence, between my grandmother's death and my brother's birth. Back then family still came to visit, and that summer a van of tíos y tías sputtered up to Houston from the Rio Grande Valley to support us, though the tíos also came to catch a once-in-a-lifetime World Cup game in Dallas, the first time the Cup was ever held in the United States. One day I tagged along with my cousins to the pulga at the Astroarena, site of the Houston Livestock Show and Rodeo, and flea markets and trade shows in the off-season. There I bought my first two CDs from a vendor who also sold big brass belt buckles with words like CHILANGO on them. I needed something more from music, but I didn't know what. I flipped through the jewel cases one by one, half hoping to find *Amor Prohibido*, Selena's latest (and final) album, until I reached a strange image with a familiar name: Nirvana.

On the cover, an angel looked down with open arms, winged and serene until you noticed her brain, the frond of her ribs, her curling intestines, a clear plastic human anatomy model with angel wings, her body stuffed with organs. I opened the case. Printed on the disc was a photo of a masculine person in drag smoking a cigarette, black lingerie sagging on their crumpled body. I turned the case over. The back cover is a coral-tinted collage of discarded fetuses, lilies, bones—death and creation, the mess of the womb. I recognized every image on the album with my whole body, every symbol on the cover in my language: the anatomy figure, for a childhood spent in hospitals looking at anatomy diagrams and medical images; the lilies, for my mother, a florist who brought stargazers to my grandmother's hospital room every few days; the drag, for the clothes I borrowed from my dad and wore to school, trying to fit in and look more chola; the angel, for my grandmother, Angélica, her visible organs, her body experimented on, palms out, arms open, ascending, descending. And the title, In Utero, for my brother, who was already in my mother's belly the day I bought the album, and whom I would witness come into the world.

The Astroarena shares a parking lot with the Astrodome, where just six months earlier, on December 6, 1993, Nirvana played their final Houston show. Six months later, on February 26, 1995, Selena would play her final concert at the Astrodome. On the day I looked for Amor Prohibido and bought In Utero instead, I stood in the same place on earth Kurt Cobain and Selena Quintanilla would also perform, six months apart in either direction in time.

———————————

I have come to understand this period in my life, a preadolescence in crisis, as a series of thresholds—a liminal time I almost didn't survive. I've written and written about this period, trying to understand what happened—gender nonconformity, expulsion, rape, alternative school, suicide attempt, psychiatric hospitalization, all between the ages of twelve and fourteen—but only fragments surfaced. It wasn't until I started writing about Kurt Cobain and Selena, two formative figures previously compartmentalized into two languages, two separate aspects of my identity, that the memories from that time began to emerge and connect. I had to write this in the language of music because that was the language I spoke then, the only language I had to articulate my grief, my anger, my alienation. I begin at twelve because it's the age I knew myself least, the age I was trying the hardest to be someone else, the age I always skip. It's also the year *In Utero* came into my life to help me figure it out. Which is to say, we must begin with gender.

I got my first period at ten years old, just before I'd lose my grandmother to cervical cancer. *¿Ya se le bajó? Ay pero ¿cómo? Todavía está muy chiquita.* This was distressing information for my grandmother, who was hospitalized with a cancer that resulted from a lifetime of intimate violence. A childhood spent in hospitals and helping translate for elders already meant I had to grow up fast, but even then, my body was a mystery to me—I had no idea where to put the o.b. tampons I'd gotten with my fifth-grade puberty starter kit, and tried many places and orientations, none of them correct. This distressed her even more, knowing that as I entered this new phase, she would likely be gone and unable to protect me. For her, getting her period led to marriage and children, to a womanhood that began as a child bride and ended in a hospital bed, and a lifetime of crossing borders to escape violent men. My first period was not a rite of passage but another childhood cut short, running on a too-fast hourglass. With the final grain of sand, she believed, my life would run by an older, slower clock—the cycle of generational violence. *No quiero dejar a la niña,* she said to my mother, one of the last things she ever said.

The first image of a woman's anatomy I imprinted on was my grandmother's body, a terrain of scars. By the end of her life, all of her secondary sex characteristics were wounds. Cancer treatments had left her bald, cathetered, wombless, her torso an x-y axis, cut open from sternum to pubic bone, hip to hip, each cut a consequence of her sex. She'd known domestic and intimate partner violence her whole life, first from her father, and then from every man thereafter. She gave birth and fled her first husband as a teenager, then in her second marriage suffered multiple stillbirths, all delivered via vertical cesarean. She never had sex education or yearly pap smears—in the borderlands, gynecology was highly stigmatized, considered to be only for sex workers and loose women. Machismo is a culture not only of patriarchal power but also of shame that makes men vectors of disease—as Mexican men cheat, they also create barriers to reproductive care and screening through violence and shame. So when my grandmother began bleeding, she didn't understand the bomb a man had planted inside her, his repeating virus now shedding cells in her womb. She was undocumented when she was diagnosed with cervical cancer, a fact she wouldn't know until years later. When she finally went to the doctor, her test results were sent to a relative she was living with at the time, who withheld them, so the cancer spread like wildfire inside her, progressing until it became too late.

My grandmother had a full hysterectomy by forty, and upon moving to Houston she had to have her bladder removed. In its place, a stoma—a hole cut into her side where her small intestine, red and swollen, poked out of her body and connected to a tube that emptied her urine into a clear plastic pouch she wore under her skirt. She could never wear pants again. And when she emptied her urine bag in a public restroom—at the grocery store, at the movies, at the mall, at Astroworld—from outside the stall, her foot position made it look like she was peeing like a man, standing up. And still, in those final years of her life, she was happy, until her tumor returned to the memory of her cervix, now taking root in the ball of nerves at the base of her spine. Only experimental radiation and chemotherapy could possibly treat it. Then her blood became toxic, and she died.

What I know of womanhood begins with my grandmother's body—ungendered by the violence of men, the violence of sex, the violence of medicine, the violence of the state.

She passed just before my transition between elementary and middle school, which made my childhood fuse together with her life, remembered in Spanish, populated by family. She was the anchor in my Mexican identity, but when Spanish began its slow fade, a distance began to stretch between my two selves in language. Adolescence would become fused with death, loneliness, sanitized with English, a self bleached into an American one.

In the weeks following my grandmother's loss, I started acting out, seeking attention at all costs. Grief and alienation are unintelligible to the child body—all I knew was *need*. Alone in the house for the first time, I had no reason to be good when I felt this bad. I stole my mom's cigarettes, put on way too much makeup just to go play outside, and one night I went to listen to music in my uncle's truck and found condoms in his glove box, which I brought to school to show my friends. But all I succeeded in doing was getting in trouble, creating distance from others precisely when I most desperately needed connection.

I sometimes wonder who I would have become had my abuelita survived. While she was alive, I was good, and listened to her consejos. Home was a Spanish-speaking haven of safety and familiarity I could come back to after navigating a baffling language and culture. Although I did well in school, I couldn't figure out the English-speaking world's social expectations and enigmas—square dancing, the bogeyman, the

Alamo, language full of hidden prejudices I couldn't understand but always felt. I was an only child far from my primos y primas, in desperate need of friends, and her guidance had always helped me connect, kept me safe, out of trouble. But when she was gone the house rang dark with absence, no voices but the television echoing into the living room until someone got home from work. I didn't know who to be, how to be, now a latchkey kid raised by television, lawless and sensation-seeking, desperate to impress kids my age. And so I became a stranger, unrecognizing of myself.

During this time, two channels were always on in my living room, Univision and MTV—two worlds from which two figures would emerge, each the voice of their respective generation, each an embodiment of my becoming.

COMO LA FLOR

Sixth grade was when I began dressing in my dad's clothes to fit in with the cholas. They were the only friends who felt like the family I no longer saw, and they dressed in Dickies, white T-shirts, Starter jackets, and gold chains. In middle school, lunchrooms were no longer organized by classroom but had open seating, which began the slow process of students self-segregating according to race. This was confusing for me—I lived in a primarily Black neighborhood and had mostly Black friends, but was placed in gifted and talented classes with almost all white kids. I felt an unspoken understanding that I couldn't sit with either group—as a Mexican girl, I was expected to hang out with the other Latines, kids I barely knew, with whom I had a lot in common but little common ground. We didn't come from the same elementary schools, have the same friends, or live in the same neighborhoods. The only class I had with other Latine students was choir, so my only mode of connection was music. My dad being in a cumbia band was a plus, but I mostly listened to R&B and pop, so to fit in I had to fake my way through conversations and pretend I listened to Bronco and Los Bukis. As social homework, I began listening to the Spanish radio stations—music I'd heard at family gatherings but didn't care about one way or the other until I heard "La Carcacha," a danceable little rola by Selena y Los Dinos, a band I recognized from *Johnny Canales*. And I *loved* that song.

By that time, without my grandmother in the house, my parents were also exploring aspects of their American identities. Papi saw cumbia music as work, so although he knew "La Carcacha," he preferred to play along to jazz and study music theory in his free time. Mami was never much of a fan of Spanish music except mariachis, and since childhood she'd loved British and American rock, disco, and pop. After her mother died, Mami became drawn to Madonna in her high-fashion, sophisticated "Vogue" era, a symbol of sexually liberated American womanhood—the opposite of Mexican womanhood's chaste and self-sacrificing expectations.

Which is to say, no one in my family was all that interested in Selena except me, and in the short time I loved her, she made a deep impression. It was the first time I'd ever encountered a star who was so *familiar*—I could have sworn she grew up next door to us in Corpus. She wasn't just "relatable," she was your favorite uncle's mijita, the fun popular prima who spoke slangy English to the kids and perfect Spanish to the elders, knew all the latest Janet Jackson and Paula Abdul dance moves, had the good gel and pink tube of mascara with the green top, smelled like Big Red gum and hairspray, wore T-shirts tucked in with hoops and perfect red lipstick, the cousin everyone copied. Selena wasn't from distant American dreamscapes like the Midwest or LA, or an Italian street kid from Manhattan who made it big. Selena was *subaltern*, from Corpus Christi, a working-class

Mexican American girl singing in Spanish to audiences of immigrant workers, audiences invisible to the American imagination, and fully illegible to American culture. In other words, she was *ours*.

Selena was the first Chicana I ever saw become famous. It sounds absurd; surely other US-born Mexican American women had risen to fame? But none ever had, not even on Spanish channels, and certainly never on both sides of the border. And it was this rarity, this intimate recognition, this particular background, that made her so dear to us. Everything about her, from the way she did her makeup, her hair, and her fashion to the way she talked, refused assimilation. She was fully Chicana, Tejana, Mexican American, always displaying our particular fashion and beauty standards—permed hair with frosted highlights back to silky-straight black hair, bouncy sprayed bangs, updos with loose curling-iron spirals, slick buns with baby-hair waves, acrylic nails, dark penciled eyebrows, cow-print costumes. Her style was regional, specific to working-class Tejanos, seen at bailes, quinceañeras, high schools. But most importantly, she was the perfect Mexican daughter we should all strive to be—beautiful, feminine, gracious, respectful, and respectable—an embodiment of conservative values.

She was everything I was supposed to be. And I tried and failed, tried and failed, until I found *In Utero* at the pulga that summer.

At thirteen, while my dad was on tour with Los Super Villahnos, I had to be my mother's birth partner: wake up my uncle after a night of drinking and help him drive us to the hospital, coach her through contractions with a stopwatch, tell the doctors how many minutes apart. That must have impressed the nurses, because we were told that although children usually can't be in the birthing room, I was very mature for my age, and could stay in the room with my mom, watch my baby brother's head crown, then get pushed back in, I was mature enough to put on scrubs and a mask to watch my mother get cut, see her blood spill behind the surgical barrier, witness the stark fact of her insides, all so my brother could be lifted into being. And afterward, I was mature enough to sleep in the bathtub at the hospital, help mix formula, take all of his first feedings, all his first midnight diaper changes. Overnight, I went from only child to eldest daughter, a role I instinctively knew how to fulfill, having watched my mother be everything to her own mother my whole life.

This is what I remember: I needed to help, and I was bad. I'd lost a person, a language, an identity, a connection to family, a childhood, and while my dad was on tour, it was just my mom, a baby, and me.

———————

Although both Kurt and Selena were radical, groundbreaking artists and icons in their own right and technically contemporaries, they're rarely brought up in the same context. But for me, they were always in conversation. Would I look pretty and please, or present masc and disaffected? Would I conform or rebel? They were two suns in parallel universes, and in their light, the question was no longer how I would survive but what selves were possible.

Kurt Cobain was part of the white world, and radically different from any musician I'd ever known. Brilliant, defiant, intense, and rare, he was the anti–rock star who rejected wealth and fame and antagonized its most sacred stars and institutions. He was beautiful, but uninterested in his good looks, preferring instead to find obscure, avant-garde, experimental music that developed his craft. He'd show up to interviews and events with greasy uncombed hair, threadbare secondhand clothes, in dresses, even lingerie—in stark contrast to the materialism, masculinity, and artifice of the corporate arena rock of the time (and yet his look would be so meticulously imitated, it would become its own artifice after his death). Nirvana's music struck post-1980s, wealth-obsessed neoliberal American culture like a thunderbolt, channeling something so true, it made everyone else around them look vapid and fake. Cobain's music was challenging, raw, and strange, alive with dream-language that somehow still had mass appeal. But he was critical of that success, racked with guilt and conflicting feelings about selling out, and openly defiant of industry expectations. He refused to compromise his punk values to play nice with rich rock stars and music executives, people he considered frauds and charlatans—an integrity that only made him even more enigmatic and exclusive.

This might sound like typical teen rebellion stuff, but for a daughter of Mexican immigrants, Kurt changed everything I'd ever been taught about *how to be*. His working-class punk ethic was in full opposition to my obedient good-immigrant values. Although androgyny and drag was nothing new in my house—my parents liked Boy George, David Bowie, and Prince—Kurt's messy drag felt more like an affront than a fashion statement, and formed an early understanding of queer-as-in-fuck-you politics. Songs like "Polly" and "Rape Me" were my first exposure to explicitly feminist, anti-rape-culture songs and critiques of masculinity—and they were coming from a man. From interviews and television appearances, Kurt gave me the language to name and critique the homophobia and misogyny of my machista Mexican upbringing, exposed the patriarchal framework that structured my life, helped me understand the racialized oppressions specific to Mexican daughters by naming those specific to him in Aberdeen. And he was not afraid to name his whiteness, his masculinity, to name the whiteness of his fans, even going so far as to write, "If you're a sexist, racist, homophobe, or basically an asshole, don't buy this CD. I don't care if you like me, I hate you" in *In Utero*'s liner notes.

Principals, school counselors, and teachers tried to frame this change in me as a rebellious phase and gave my parents how-to-understand-your-troubled-teen literature. But the causes of teen rebellion in those books were stripped of race and class contexts, oversimplified as cries for attention, defiance, anger. The reasoning was hollow, and only made me feel less understood. What did make me feel understood was this: Kurt's father left him, and he was raised by his working-class single mother in a rural logging town. He survived homophobic bullying and violence from men, and the alienation he felt caused him to run away early, turn to drugs, become unhoused. I knew something about working-class machismo and running away, having grown up in a family of truck drivers and blue-collar workers and their runaway daughters. My anger came from a similar place: as the primary breadwinner, my mother had to work twice as hard and display impeccable respectability just to earn crumbs. She had to fight with my school not to put me in ESL, fight with the hospital to treat her dying mother, fight to be respected at work. My father was a brilliant, respected, legendary musician who no one ever gave a shot—not Americans, not his peers. My family was deferential and responsible and generous to a fault, and still struggled to survive in this country. We were outcasts, unable to get ahead, alienated by unbelonging, and it made me angry. I loved my parents, hurt for them, and watching them lose and lose a thousand times made me want to scream. I wanted nothing more than to say "Fuck you" to every white person in power, even if it meant hurting myself.

Be good. Be beautiful. Be respectful. Be pure. Be humble. Be generous and well-liked. Don't make waves. Don't invite gossip, the *qué dirán*. Be so good and beautiful, you get your fairy tale. This is what we teach our daughters—to please, to obey, to defer, to give. To value pleasing over pleasure, looks over intelligence, approval over integrity. But good behavior is never rewarded with love or safety, only the absence of harm. It is a hand always cocked in the air, threatening to come down. To be good is to never give the hand a reason to come down, a naive trust that if you're good, you'll never attract deception and danger. And if self-betrayal doesn't end you first, someone else's betrayal will.

When Selena began to blow up, I had the inside track. Although she was universally loved, my dad would provide the director's-cut commentary and let us in on how the sausage was made. He'd go on about how shrewd Abraham Quintanilla, her father, was in the business, how he squeezed the most money out of events, leaving peanuts for the other bands, how strict his Jehovah's Witness faith made him with Selena. She was never allowed to socialize with other acts after shows, or even to have friends. According to Papi, Abraham ran his family like a business, one whose star was kept in a tower in the shape of a tour bus.

And Papi would comment on Selena too—how beautiful and charismatic she was, so talented yet down-to-earth, but "bien pendeja para hablar." He didn't mean her pocha Spanish so much as how *ignorant* she was. It hurts to write that, but he wasn't criticizing her intellect or making fun of her; instead, he said it with a kind of concern or pity. He worried about how naive and small-minded she was, how limited her ideas and language were for a star with that kind of platform and reach with young Latinas. Her homeschooling was faith-based, done mostly on the road between gigs, and it showed.

In hindsight, it's no accident that the women in the *Selena* film and show have almost no lines. Selena's impeccable public character was sculpted by her father's hand. She pleased everyone. She wasn't just beautiful; she was radiantly charming, impossibly thin-waisted, with beautifully wide hips and big pompis for men. She wasn't just hard-working, family-oriented, and obedient; she was a Latina who didn't get pregnant, who waited until marriage (that is, until she eloped in an act of rebellion—more on this later), effectively serving as an anti-welfare billboard in a growing teen pregnancy crisis. She eased white Republican fears as an ambassador and role model for traditional family values, a counterbalance to the rise of gangs, dropouts, and hyperfertile Latino youth. She appealed to both Mexican Catholics and white Protestants by embodying their ultraconservative sexual mores in a language young people could understand. While her bold, form-fitting costumes and latest dance moves signaled pop sexiness, everything else about her was family-friendly.

In a 1994 interview, after recounting in her Texan accent how her dad "saw dollar signs" in her interest in music and performance and put the kids to work, interviewer J. R. Castilleja sees the opportunity to make her an example, not only of a good work ethic but of American values:

J. R. CASTILLEJA: You're a very, very good role model (*Selena thanks him silently*), and one of the problems with the Hispanic community (*Selena looks down, adjusts her outfit, and fidgets uncomfortably, takes a deep breath and tilts her head, seemingly annoyed and offended at where the interview is going*), especially with the teenagers, the girls, is teen pregnancy (*Selena mm-hmms, nods, on guard*). What do you have to say? I mean everybody gets into situations that it's hard to get out of, but I notice that the majority of them end up keeping their child—

SELENA: Which is good!

JRC: —which makes it rough, yeah! It makes it rough.

SELENA: Which is good, because I'm against abortions. I don't think that it's right. You know, everybody's entitled to their opinion but the way I was raised—it's kinda hard and it's very upsetting that you see people, especially politicians, and I don't want to get into politics, but they encourage kids to use . . . condoms, and I think parents should encourage kids not to have sex before marriage because you know, if you stop that right there, then you're not going to have teen pregnancy. You need to teach your children morals first before they get married, and then children afterwards. It should be marriage and children afterwards. But it does happen, it's very sad to say, but all we can do is educate the children, let them know what lies ahead if this happens, you know, and try to educate them afterwards.

The irony is that in this interview, she was *so close* to taking a pro-choice position. She starts out with typically pro-life answers, but as she follows her own logic, she arrives at sex education, not marriage, as the solution. "But it does happen, and *all we can do is educate the children, let them know what lies ahead, and educate them afterwards*"—that is a position *for* sex education, a contested topic in a time when a majority of pregnant teens didn't know sex led to pregnancy because it was a forbidden topic. The pro-life position was staunch: against sex education and contraceptives, pro-marriage and family values.

This is the kind of thinking that turned my parents off from her just before she died, having witnessed how little control or say young girls of color had over their sexuality or contraception. In Texas, factions of conservative Tejanos and Mexican immigrants transpose their machista values onto American politics. In voting pro-life, they also vote for anti-immigrant candidates; in seeking stable, high-paying jobs, they join the US Border Patrol; in search of community, they become evangelical Christians, all for the promise of inclusion into the American Dream. These are the kind of Tejanos the Quintanillas seemed to represent. This is what Papi meant when he criticized the Quintanillas—he saw them as symbolic of the lateral oppression Latines inflict on one another.

I have watched that interview angrily and uncharitably in the past, seeing Selena as all too happy to entertain racist questions and perform respectability while throwing young Latina girls under the bus. But now I also see how she was groomed to be a product—to be *good,* to please, to be liked, to be loved, even if it hurt her. She traveled the country in a bubble, never allowed to interact with anyone outside her family's circles. Once she was married, she went from being firmly under her father's thumb to a kind of freedom with Chris, where her celebrity combined with her down-to-earth approachable nature made her vulnerable to the darker intentions of others. Throughout her life, everyone around her who wasn't family was vetted, safe. Perhaps she never experienced playground betrayals and locker-room gossip, a first crush's rejection, frenemies and smear campaigns, obsession, intense female friendships that bordered on queer desire. Perhaps that antenna was never tuned. Perhaps being good, and liked, and pleasing is what puts others before ourselves, and that suppression, that self-denial, is what kills us.

There are glimmers of mischief and rebelliousness in Selena's life that I remember, and that I still love. She may have been sheltered and inexperienced in her everyday life, but onstage she was pure genius, able to channel the emotional truth of a song with raw intensity and drama. There's a performance of "Qué Creías," a ranchera sung by a woman scorned to her lover who has returned, where she acts out the scene of confrontation with a man from the audience. The footage is from July 1994, eight months before her death, on what appears to be a high school baseball field in Midland, Texas, a humble gig location for a megastar of her ilk, but typical for even the biggest acts from La Onda Grupera. Her magnetism is palpable, even through the poor video quality.

Selena Quintanilla dramatically leans back on one leg as she performs the song "Qué Creías" at a concert on a baseball field in Midland, Texas, July 1994. (Originally aired on Colores del Barrio, a Tejano music television show.)

Gorgeous in all-black form-fitting leather, she gets in the man's face, pointing at his chest with a perfectly manicured nail. The lyrics translate as, "What did you think? That you could come back and find me happy to receive you?" The lover has strayed, seeking the love of other women, and now that he's back, she gets the pleasure of deriding him before rejecting him. Theatrics are traditional in rancheras, but Selena's performance sparks with dramatic tension. She builds the world of the story in seconds, making you wonder if she's actually mad at the poor bastard in front of her.

She leans far back on one leg in an exaggerated flourish, holding a flawless note. A lean so dramatic as to be a provocation. The phrase she sings as she leans back, "contenta al recibirte" (happy to receive you), is a play on words that, on the surface, can be read simply as "take you back" or "take you in." But her body in performance is a text that implies another layer of meaning—Selena slightly bows, gets down on one knee, and leans until she is prone, illustrating "receiving" this lover lying down. While her gestures imply deference, begging, submission, the pose conveys nothing but pure feminine power, self-possession, passion, even rage.

Although sex is only ever implied in Selena's songs, she more than made up for it in the subtext of her performances. She was a firecracker, a daredevil, a provocateur, and an electrifying performer who could enthrall audiences like no other. This is what Mexican daughters do—we are taught to suppress our desires, taught to please and work and obey, until a wildness starts thrashing within, begging to be unleashed.

———

In my own family, running away is a rite of passage; perhaps it is the muscle memory of migration, when desire shares a border with survival and a father becomes a country. Grandmothers, great-grandmothers, tías y tíos, my own father, all runaways—in my generation alone, seven of us cousins ran away in our adolescence. I recognize Selena's elopement as a moment of agency, of freedom from a lifetime of strict control, the moment a daughter becomes a woman. Every once in a while a glimmer of rebellion would shine through: her incorporation of Black pop music into her cumbia sets, to the confusion of her audiences; her bustiers and tight costumes; her elopement with Chris Pérez; her growing awareness of her own racialization in American pop music. I find hope in the little moments—her somewhat defensive posture in that interview at "the problems in the Hispanic community," her skeptical *mmm-hmm* at the implication that "teen pregnancy" is a uniquely Latine problem and a sign of racial and moral decay. I see her bristle, and wonder what she could have been.

HEART-SHAPED BOX

The CD came to me a year after the loss of my grandmother to cervical cancer and the year before I would watch my mother give birth to my baby brother, see his black hair peek out of a rip in the universe before they cut her open on an operating table. The mess of death, the mess of creation. *In utero.* I'd find out shortly after buying the CD that Kurt had died by suicide mere months before I found his music. I'd never see Nirvana live, never experience their new music, our paths almost touching but never intersecting. My love for them would only ever be experienced in mourning, in memoriam, from recordings and footage and archives, with an ending I always knew was coming. To love Nirvana is to loop time, like trauma—once you get to *Unplugged*, you go back to *Bleach* again. This is how I love, I think—loops and loss.

In the opening shot of the "Heart-Shaped Box" video, Kurt, Dave, and Krist sit in a sterile hospital room, slumped in cheap hospital chairs across from an emaciated old man on his deathbed. As the guitar notes descend, the camera cuts to the band members, wilted but focused on the patient, concerned and exhausted, like family members who've been holding vigil and sitting with him for hours. It is a scene I recognize from my most intimate life—my family holding vigil for my dying grandmother, holding their bodies in the same posture, the same exhaustion, the same grief.

The first time I saw the video, I was thirteen or fourteen, watching late-night MTV. Upon hearing that opening A chord, I immediately hit record on the VCR. As the video played, I was transfixed: the images were like a dream memory, echoing from my unconscious. Red flowers, black blood, emaciated body, exposed organs, crosses, gnarled trees, a blond white child in what recalled a KKK robe. The video drew from an obscure but shared image system, connecting us across some collective unconscious beyond borders, beyond language, beyond life and death. I didn't have the words for it at the time; all I knew was that this song, this person, Kurt Cobain, spoke the same language as me.

My grandmother's hospital room was full of Valentine's Day arrangements that my mother, a florist at Kroger, brought to cheer her up. Red roses, red flowers in the video; white lilies, the same lilies on the back of the *In Utero* record, the same flowers covering the stage in Nirvana's *Unplugged* performance. In the 1990s lilies bloomed in every major event of my life—my grandmother's death, her funeral, birthdays, school dances, my own hospital room when I tried to take my own life. Lilies are a visceral flower, connecting the rooms of my memory. Kurt too loved white lilies, and in some other life, he might have interacted with my mother to buy them, his bored Pacific Northwest English made intelligible to my mother's playful Rio Grande Valley Spanish, exchanged in the common language of flowers.

I could not remember the countless hours I spent in her hospital room, watching her skin turn paper-thin and gray, her lips go blue, her cheeks sink in. The experimental radiation treating the tumor that had climbed the base of her spine and rooted into her vertebrae was slowly poisoning her blood. To remember her like this called on a different part of my brain—less of a memory and more of a dream, filled with stargazer lilies, bladders of morphine, red heart-shaped boxes of chocolate, holes in her body, bruised veins. Valentine's Day—two days before she died. She was going on her third month in the hospital, because by her bed was a Polaroid a nurse had taken when Santa visited the radiation floor in December. After the new year, the whole family came up from the Rio Grande Valley to stay with her in her final days, keeping vigil in shifts, tías in flowered skirts and sweaters sleeping upright in cheap hospital room chairs. She died the morning of February 16, 1993, a Tuesday. The morning sky was still pink when my mother called with the news, and a planet of unimaginable rage would burn in me for thirty years afterward, determined to wage war against every layer of violence, neglect, injustice that cut her life short. Memories I couldn't access until I watched the "Heart-Shaped Box" video.

Kurt's body position in particular still affects me to this day. He is canted over to one side, legs crossed, hand supporting his forehead, the position a body comes to after hours of worry, grief, witness. Family members slept in chairs, brought tortillas and meat to the hospital so she wouldn't have to suffer the hospital food, lit Sacred Heart of Jesus candles, burning like rubies by her bedside as my bisabuela prayed novenas. The long-haired elderly man from the video, upon dying, climbs a cross in a field and hangs, suffering like Jesus. *I wish I could eat your cancer when you turn black.* I'd never heard that word in a song before. I'd never seen that situation—the hospital room, the waiting, the grief, the colors and symbols—reflected back at me so clearly.

One night I was listening to *Unplugged* with the lights off alone in my room. Papi had just taken my door off its hinges, which meant that I had no privacy and the rest of the house could hear what I was listening to—a common disciplinary tactic with Mexican daughters. Anyone walking by could check up on what I was doing, and that night my father saw me crying.

"Mami, ¿qué pasó?" he asked.

I'm embarrassed now, but back then I trusted him with a sentiment I didn't fully understand—overwhelming grief that Kurt Cobain had died. This offended him, made him angry. ¿Cómo chingados Kurt Cobain? How could I mourn este pinche pelado, a stranger, an addict, este blanco who would never love someone like me, over my own family?

For my father, Kurt Cobain represented the worst kind of white entitlement, hypocrisy, and privilege. He couldn't understand Nirvana's popularity when their music was just basic power chords, no innovative scales, no technical proficiency. He thought their bratty anticorporate stunts the height of childishness and arrogance—career-ending behavior only English-speaking musicians could get away with. How could I not see the hypocrisy in saying "Fuck you" and seeming to bite the hand that feeds while absolutely taking the check? How could I support rejecting money and fame, knowing our house was in foreclosure and our cars were in danger of being repossessed?

While my father struggled for scraps, worked tirelessly at his craft, reading music theory books and listening to jazz guitarists, and scrimped and saved to buy used equipment at pawn shops, here were these entitled white men playing their biggest hits poorly as a joke, only to end their set

Still of Kurt Cobain destroying his guitar after antagonizing the audience, from Nirvana's performance of "Lithium" at the MTV Video Music Awards, September 9, 1992.

by breaking their guitars. It was inconceivable to him to waste such tremendous opportunities, to destroy such beautiful and expensive instruments, when all he had was a cheap black Fender Stratocaster, the most basic model, a well-worn starter guitar he had to weld, unscrew, replace, tune up, and adjust before every gig.

While his band coordinated matching villain-themed stage costumes, Nirvana rolled out of bed and played in the ratty clothes they slept in, didn't brush their hair, antagonized audiences and interviewers. My father was from a generation that idolized Studio 54, disco glamour, and high-fashion nightlife. He couldn't understand wanting to look and sound bad on purpose, couldn't see what it achieved. He'd only ever experienced the music industry as an immigrant, not as a white man. He would never be afforded the privilege of acting out onstage, insulting celebrities, or destroying his instruments. As a former rock-and-rolero playing rock in Mexico when rock was illegal there, a former runaway, an immigrant musician, everything about my father was already "punk," illegible, subaltern—the very fact of his existence was a rebellion. But my father was also a product of a machista upbringing,

115

beholden to strict gender performance and respectability—despite being sensitive, artistic, experimental, and chic in his dress and mannerisms, he could never get away with the rebellious antics Nirvana could get away with. That kind of behavior was inconceivable to him. And what Kurt was selling me—defiance, subversion, gender nonconformity—I too would never be able to get away with it. I would not only close doors on myself before they'd ever open, I was putting myself in danger by acting like him.

At that age, I didn't understand that I, his own daughter, had become just one more person in America who couldn't see him, couldn't hear him, didn't choose him or his music.

Nirvana, and all the artists I loved, created a tension between my father and me for a long time. But aside from their music, what resonated with me the most about the band was their distrust and disrespect of institutions, their critique of masculinity, their irreverence for authority, their refusal to "sell out." That was a mind-blowing concept—the refusal for ethical reasons to sell your soul for money, connections, and fame, and the choice to remain loyal to your communities. Kurt saw the music industry as a necessary evil, a medium through which to distribute music, and one that should only be worked with in malicious compliance. That reframing of power toppled the giants in my world, including Selena, and finally gave me a kind of courage my parents couldn't understand I needed to stand up for myself, opposite from their teachings, to refuse silencing or self-betrayal—a courage that, more often than not, incurred the wrath of authority figures. After watching my parents do everything right and still struggle, Nirvana helped me unlearn my "good immigrant" manners—to be nice, good, hardworking, and utterly invisible in deference to authority and whiteness—and not to be so grateful for scraps, never to give up my ethics for the crumbs of inclusion.

When I asked my dad if he would ever "sell out," he said he wouldn't think twice about it, and neither would anyone he knew. Cumbieros and norteños would give anything to partner with Pepsi, to sell their songs for a commercial, to be *valued*. (In fact Fito Olivares did just that—he sold "La Gallina" for a Burger King commercial. That saxophone riff stays with me to this day.) I started to hear the commercial in everything—the artifice in people's voices, the canned interview responses, the derivativeness of their music, who they pandered to, what they held back. But when Kurt Cobain spoke, his voice was a lightning bolt that pierced every layer of artifice, wild in its own power, defiant of polite norms. He couldn't pretend for a paycheck even if he tried. To me he was an oracle, unwavering in his bold antiauthoritarian courage but also forever an outcast, heckling Axl Rose on the red carpet while holding his baby next to RuPaul at the MTV Music Awards. He *loved* RuPaul.

And slowly I began to understand what else he was speaking to: my queerness. I began collecting every magazine Cobain appeared in, pinned up his pictures on my walls, stayed up all night to record Nirvana music videos from MTV onto VHS, wrote poems based on his lyrics. I bought *Come as You Are: The Story of Nirvana* by Michael Azerrad and read it in two days. And the more I read about him, the more I came to terms with my own sexuality and gender identity. He identified as gay in grade school because the only friend he had was a gay boy, and later, his friends were primarily women, feminists from the riot grrrl scene who dressed him in drag. He was an outspoken feminist whose fluid sexuality and gender nonconformity gave me a middle ground to question. I love that Gen Z has claimed Kurt and turned his gender performance into a site of queer and trans speculation—why he grew his hair long, why he wore makeup, how he slumped over in big sweatshirts like dysphoric kids do. It's a discourse and a provocation I'm sure he would have welcomed. And if I were young today—never married/divorced, with a child, and having already lived so much of my life as a woman, if I weren't so exhausted from my body being a gendered battleground—I know I'd be nonbinary, without question. Perhaps it's not too late; perhaps one day, I will.

I don't remember where or how, but shortly after I ordered every Nirvana, Hole, and Tori Amos album Columbia House had (twelve CDs for one penny!), I found the most important tape of my life— *Nirvana: Live! Tonight! Sold Out!*, a VHS tape compiling concerts, television appearances, home movies, interviews, and tour footage from the band's *Nevermind* days. I watched that tape almost every night through my most troubled years—when I was expelled in eighth grade and sent to alternative school, when I was sold acid at said school and did it at home for the first time, when I was admitted to a psychiatric hospital after alternative school, while coping with the guilt and shame of sexual assault, while brokenhearted, while grounded and lonely. Nirvana's performances—their messiness, their intensity— were raw, physical, agonizing, vulnerable, but also *fearless*. Two in particular stand out. The first is a performance of "Aneurysm" in a major stadium to a bunch of jocks at the Hollywood Rock festival in Rio de Janeiro, January 23, 1993. Kurt is in drag—a black lace nightie stuffed with balls for breasts, the fabric sagging under their weight on his rail-thin frame, topped with a diamond tiara. His hair is shorter, shaggy, and dyed brown, his beard is scruffy, and his voice is elevated and gravelly. The show is kind of a disaster. With any other band, that would be sexist rock-star bullshit, but Kurt was at a peak in his drug use then, and there was no malice or misogyny or derision in his drag. It felt earnest, experimental, challenging, and just as messy as him.

The second is a performance of "Love Buzz" at Trees, a small punk venue in Dallas, Texas, on October 19, 1991. The camcorder footage is blurry and poor quality, but the show is packed, the energy in the room thick and vibrant as the music thunders against a wall of bodies. A bouncer sits on the edge of the stage. Kurt is dynamic in a navy cardigan and torn jeans, his messy blond hair swaying over his eyes with every guitar note, and at the crest of the solo he jumps back-first off the stage into the crowd. He crowd-surfs briefly, his guitar throwing feedback while something tangles him up in the audience. Kurt starts bucking on a sea of hands, struggling to dismount and find the stage, but as the crowd tries to guide him back, the bouncer aggressively pushes him away, blocking him from the stage. Something happens—he's being jostled. Then Kurt slams the heel of his guitar into the bouncer's face, then raises it to hit him again. *Boom. BOOM.* He briefly sinks into a hole of bodies, then resurfaces on the stage. As Kurt regains his balance, that's when the bouncer punches him in the back of the head, then kicks him while he's down. Mid-beat, Dave Grohl instantly, effortlessly jumps over his drums and restrains the bouncer with Krist, the bassist. As the bouncer yells at the other two band members, blood runs down the side of his face. Kurt was always slight, at five-seven and no more than 120 pounds, and this ponytailed bouncer was at least double his weight. But despite their size difference, Kurt hit this giant dude anyway, no fear, no hesitation, knowing it was a fight he couldn't win.

For me, Nirvana is not just a band but the catalyst for a personal catharsis and self-realization during a painful adolescence. I was drowning between identities, languages, countries, realities, the anchor of my grandmother's loving voice fading from memory, and her Spanish along with it. I have spent a lifetime trying to find the right language to give to that little girl, to help her understand the magnitude of what was happening to her. *Fox bell. Long pine sun. The morning's back.* These are lines I wrote in my first Mead spiral notebook just for poetry, just like the one the cover of his collected journals would show Kurt also used, published ten years later.

I've been able to suture the wound of memory from that time to footage, ephemera, bodies in performance, the dates that anchor time to album covers, how I performed a version of each of them as myself. And through that somatic information, I now remember the tension they each represented. I saw in each of them how the obedience expected of me was self-betrayal. Being good would never save me. However backward this may sound, back then, Kurt Cobain represented feminism and freedom, while Selena represented oppression and patriarchy. And both of their deaths felt personal, like outcomes of my own disempowerment—Selena's misguided trust in people, her naivete, Kurt's depression and invisible disabilities. And somewhere between these two extremes—Selena, the beautiful virgin daughter I should be, and Kurt, the artist I wanted to be—I emerged.

I revisited that first spiral poetry notebook from 1996, where during free time in detention, I copied a passage from a book on Greek mythology about the twin gods Apollo and Artemis. Apollo, the god of music, poetry, (male) beauty, and oracles, could never lie, and Artemis, the virgin goddess of the moon, nature, and the hunt, was a protector of women and children. Only now do I make the connection—Kurt burns blond and bright and true in one half of me, while Selena, named after the moon, pulls me back and protects through the strength and virtue of femininity. They were not opposites but halves. That's just one reading, maybe a stretch. Poetry is the closest I've come to understanding ourselves. I meet them at the gate of our dream language, a memory of no-time. It is there I find the words to help that lost girl become themselves; give them the language in the middle of both of my heads.

Encyclopedia of All the Daughters I Couldn't Be

Virgen

Sin permiso.

The new moon hangs dark and heavy as a plum overhead as you sprint through the bayou-damp thick of a Houston summer night. You are thirteen, and the very air is electric with danger as you sneak out to meet the wrong boy. It is the summer of 1995, two years after your grandmother has passed, and a chthonic force has begun to lash so wildly in you that any risk is worth the promise of love. Maybe this boy will love you. Maybe this boy will make what the others did right.

Earlier that summer, Mami finally gave you permission to spend the night at Amber's, a white girl. This mattered because, culturally, you were vulnerable to white suggestion, and there was no common ground with white parents, who were more permissive with their daughters but all too ready to blame you. So you've never spent the night at anyone's house but your cousins', much less the house of a white girl, but because Amber lives just down the street, Mami has conceded. She had every right to be suspicious, though: this is the story of how you get raped.

When you arrive, you two have the house to yourselves. You are thrilled by the grown-up feeling of being alone, but Amber says everything is boring. She has an older cousin who drives her own car and lives just down the freeway, she says; her cousin can come pick you both up. Years later, you still don't remember that girl's name, but you're pretty sure it was something like Crystal.

You only have access to lower-middle-class Walmart whites, not the fancy ones. You don't know the difference yet, just that you have access to white people that your parents never had, and that feels like something you should want. You sit in the backseat blowing smoke out of the roll-down window, quiet as the white girls talk shit in the front. You don't say much around new people, but it doesn't matter. Amber has just had her fake nails done and is wearing a tank top and cut-off shorts to show off her tan. Ever the stranger to girlie things, you're in ripped jeans and a baby-doll T-shirt with black pen-covered Chucks.

When you arrive at Crystal's trailer, there are beer cans everywhere from the party the night before. Crystal, no more than seventeen, has been emancipated from her parents and often has parties at her trailer. She offers you a beer, and even though you're only thirteen and have never had a drink before, you accept, then move into the bedroom so Amber can get ready in the mirror. As she drags eyeliner back and forth under her eyes, they talk, and you find out there's going to be a party that night, and some boys are coming by later to chill. You recognize some of the names as boys from your neighborhood. "They're my hookup," she says. You don't fully understand what that means.

On the nightstand by the bed, there are about six white rectangular boxes of generic medicine just like the ones you've seen your family bring back from Mexico. Except they only ever brought back creams and insulin. These boxes all say ROHYPNOL on the front, with a half-used silver blister pack sticking out of one. Crystal offers you a pill, but you say no—you've barely touched your beer and things feel surreal and dangerous and overwhelming and you want to go home. Crystal starts bragging about how much she loves Rohypnol, how it makes her mad, makes her want to *fight*. She balls up her fist and mimics punching someone fast, and repeatedly. She

says she takes the pills all the time, and sometimes she kicks bitches' asses just for fun because the pills make her do it.

Evening darkens the pines, and you begin to feel anxious—you're too far from home, too remote, and your parents have no idea where you really are. You wonder if Amber planned this all along, and now you're stuck here with this girl, this stranger, who seems unstable, menacing.

A black pickup truck rolls up on the grass, and a guy gets out and knocks on the door before he lets himself in. Crystal seems to have an open-door policy with her friends, and this one is delivering the kegs. Crystal asks you if you know how to tap a keg and you say no, which makes her laugh because there's just something so *inexperienced* about you, so naive.

Once the boys get there, Crystal gets drunk pretty quickly, and by the time everyone has refilled their cups from the keg and smoked off the blunt, she's taken off her shirt to reveal a hot-pink string bikini top underneath, which she wears with tight denim Wranglers and boots. Someone puts on Jodeci, and she starts rolling with one of the older boys. You look for Amber, but she is nowhere to be found, but then you notice the door to one of the bedrooms is closed and locked.

You step outside to smoke in the deep wet night, alone. You drink the same beer from that afternoon between the pines in silence until the world starts to feel like it's tilting, and you're sliding down it into something softer than a dream. Did you swallow the moon? You're being led into the trees. And somehow you are on your knees in the dark and a boy is standing in front of you, pushing your head into him. It's Dante, the most beautiful boy in the neighborhood, staring down at you with his hazel eyes. There are other boys there, watching. He finishes, and then you black out.

You don't remember the rest of the night, or the next morning, or coming back home. All you know is the guilt dragging like an anchor in your center. The next memory you have is your neighbor Pierre ringing your doorbell when your parents aren't home. He says he heard you're good at sucking dick and asks if you would do it to him too. You try to close the door, he catches it, but you manage to push it closed and lock it.

You pretend it never happened. You try to fall in love to make it go away. Tonight the neighborhood is quiet and sleeping, but you've never felt more alive. You've agreed to meet Jordan at the playground at midnight, and your body is humming as you pump your legs forward. He will ride his BMX through the dark, soggy ditch between your houses and, sweat-soaked blond and sour, lay you down on a carpet of white clover, where you will give him your secret tongue. You will take each other's clothes off and touch each other too early in the rupture you make between childhood and consequences. You do not understand the animal grief has made of your body, or how far it will go for love. You will push your want into each other and he will fill your mouth with a river of stars and you will need it so much you sneak out again and again until one night, you go too far. You break into an empty house and try to go further, all the way, until a light shines in. Headlights. Your mother has found you after driving around all night looking for you, with your newborn baby brother in the back. And as the Chevy headlights flood your shame, the child in you slams back down to earth. Your mother will have to pay for the broken window and other damages, and you will not understand how much damage has really been done until he dumps you days before the first day of eighth grade because he's gotten what he wanted and he will tell everyone what a slut you are and how you did everything but have sex because you were too tight and it will hurt so much you want to die.

When they call the line for evening meds, you stand behind Naomi, a voluptuous blond thirteen-year-old girl with smeared black eyeliner. She's nice, suspiciously nice maybe, and seems like all the other normal nice white girls from your middle school—bubbly, preppy even. Until she's triggered. Then she throws chairs at the group leader and has to be carried out by two nurses and put in a room until she calms down. Naomi is your new roommate, and in a few days, after lights out, she will invite you into her bed, where you will have sex for the first time—at fourteen, with a girl, in a psychiatric hospital. And this time, you take the lead, in charge of your body, always in sync with Naomi—not like it was with Jordan, or Dante. But now that you've made those choices, sex with a girl is another, deeper kind of shame, another fault you have to bury.

Before you even have sex, you have already come out as bi to your mother, who after consulting *When Good Kids Do Bad Things*, the book recommended to her by your school counselor, decides that this is just a phase, another form of rebelling for attention. You'd learned the term from Rickie Vasquez on *My So-Called Life*, read it in books, heard friends try it on for size on themselves. But it had always been you, before you even knew the word. Coming out didn't soothe the shame, or make anything clearer. The next morning, you and Naomi ignore each other in a kind of mutual denial of what happened between you. You weren't her first, and you tell yourself she will be your last. *Aquí no quiero jotas.* You cannot be fucked up in one more way. Especially not this way.

It all happens again.

Tienes que pedir permiso, you have to ask permission, is how every good daughter moves through the world. Allowed. This is how choices are made for her. And when she begins to make her own choices, she doesn't know if it's allowed, learns to doubt herself without the validation, or permission, of others. You want to make everyone proud. You need to tell the truth. These desires are always in conflict. You write this without permission. You may get the details wrong.

You look up the hospital on the internet while writing your first book. Gulf Pines Psychiatric Hospital no longer exists, and your mother has misplaced the records, or so she says, except your intake photo. You put the photo in your book. Poems arise from the unspoken, link the gulf between the pines. Forgive her for trying to forget—it's why she came to this new country. To erase the past.

MEMORY, A LACUNA

MY MOTHER AND GRANDMOTHER WERE BORN IN "THE LAND of the lake," La Comarca de la Laguna, a cradle of fertile land in the northern Mexican desert between the Sierra Madre Occidental to the west and the Sierra Madre Oriental to the east, two mountain mothers, two guardians that keep the land between them a secret. It is where the Nazas and Aguanaval Rivers break their pact with the ocean and empty fresh water into the land, flooding the expanse with wide, glassy lakes—a miracle that enabled life in miles of landlocked desert and made impossible soil fertile for thousands of years.

The Comarca de la Laguna, its first word derived from *marca*, or border, is itself a borderland in El Norte that spans the states of Durango, my grandmother Angélica's birthplace, and Coahuila, where my mother was born, land that also borders the United States. It is also a site of colonial atrocity and Indigenous resistance, where New Spain established las haciendas laguneras, a robust cotton industry whose economy was built on the encomienda system, a legal system of forced unpaid labor by subjugated Indigenous people who had been dispossessed and detribalized through systematic extermination and unspeakable acts of genocide.

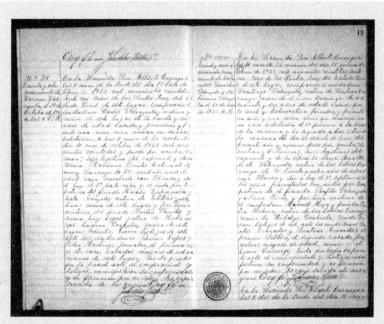

My great-grandmother Carmen Valenzuela's Catholic church birth record

No. 38 Treinta y ocho

Nacimiento de Carmen Valenzuela el 11 de Octubre de 1922 a las 9 p.m.

En la Hacienda San Alberto Durango a las 5 cinco de la tarde del día 13 trece de Febrero de 1923 mil novecientos veintitrés ante mi Jesús de los Santos Juez del Estado Civil de este lugar: compareció el ciudadano Carlos Valenzuela, nativo y vecino de este lugar de 36 treinta y seis años de edad, casado, y jornalero, y presentó una niña viva nacida en su casa habitación, a las 9 nueve de la noche del día 11 once de octubre de

1922 mil novecientos veintidós y puesolé por nombre: "Carmen," hija legitima del exponente y de la Señora Marciana Benites nativa de Jimenez Durango: de 28 veintiocho años de edad raza mezclado con Blanco y dio a luz el 6 sexto niña y es nieta por línea paterna del finado Marcelo Valenzuela y Justa González nativa de Huertillas Zacatecas vecina de este lugar y por línea materna del finado Martin Benites y Señora Luz Lopes nativa de Matamoros Laguna Coahuila, vecina de este lugar: viuda.

At the Hacienda San Alberto Durango at 5:50 p.m. on February 13, 1923, nineteen hundred and twenty-three, before my Jesús de los Santos, Civil State Judge of this place: the citizen Carlos Valenzuela, native and resident, appeared from this place, thirty-six years old, married, a day laborer, and presented a living girl born in his home, at 9:00 p.m. on October 11, 1922, nineteen hundred and twenty-two, and gave her the name: "Carmen," legitimate daughter of the exponent and of Mrs. Marciana Benites, a native of Jimenez, Durango: 28, twenty-eight years old, mixed race with white and gave birth to her sixth, a girl, and is the paternal granddaughter of the late Marcelo Valenzuela and Justa González, a native of Huertillas, Zacatecas, a resident of this place, and by maternal line, granddaughter of the late Martin Benites and Mrs. Luz Lopes, a native of Matamoros Laguna, Coahuila, a resident of this place: widow.

The "land of the lake," with rich soil replenished by the flooding rivers, was an ideal location for these haciendas, and for New Spanish colonists to begin their cotton enterprises for the crown. The frequent seasonal flooding was an ideal form of natural irrigation. In the middle of hostile, arid desert, this was a fertile oasis, virgin and unknown. Eventually the land of the lake was covered in cotton, a sea of whiteness. But cotton is a thirsty crop. It exhausts the soil of nutrients; the water it consumes leaves behind a kind of salt, stripping the land to such a degree it becomes a wasteland, requiring abandonment and expansion, usually into forests.

In fantasy, and poetry, we build the memory of the world through metaphor.

My maternal grandmother Angélica was born on one of these haciendas to farm laborers, and the only way I knew to trace my way back to my foremothers was through Catholic missions, known to keep excellent records.

My mother does not remember her birthplace, Torreón; she was a toddler when she and her mother fled. No one ever talks about Jesús, her father, or what happened while they lived with him before they fled to Tampico. All anyone in my family knows is that he, a thirty-six-year-old man, married my grandmother, a fourteen-year-old girl, and after she had a baby almost exactly nine months later, they lost all contact with her. The silence became so extreme that my tío Joel, my grandmother's brother, took it upon himself to find and rescue her. And when he finally found her, she was battered, pregnant with another baby. So he took them—my grandmother and my mother—and secreted them away in the middle of the night, but not before punching Jesús in the face.

Land is the only record that remains. And that land between them was once flooded by rivers that became lakes, lakes that due to construction, development, agribusiness, resource extraction, are disappearing, if not already gone. But the land remembers.

We all come from the land, eat from it, drink from it, touch its surfaces. The land is memory made material. It is the first object ever to come into existence; anything that exists after it is because of, and part of, the land. Therefore its formations and materials, when interpreted, are undeniable; they trump false narratives. Ice cores, tree rings, the amount of water left—these facts build a sequence, a story.

It is why in school my favorite kind of rock was the sedimentary rock, the layers of time visible in cross section, time itself made material, the story it told. My mothers' histories may be forgotten, but the Sierra Madres still exist.

Lacuna (disambiguation)

Lacuna (plural lacunas or lacunae) may refer to:

Related to the meaning "gap"

- Lacuna (manuscripts), a gap in a manuscript, inscription, text, painting, or musical work
- Great Lacuna, a lacuna of eight leaves in the Codex Regius where there was heroic Old Norse poetry
- Lacuna (music), an intentional extended passage in a musical work during which no notes are played
- Lacuna (scientific), an area of science that has not been studied but has potential to be studied
- Lacuna (linguistics), an accidental gap, a word that does not exist but which would be permitted by the rules of a language
- Lacuna (law), a non liquet ("it is not clear"), a gap or absence in the law

In medicine

- Lacuna (histology), a small space containing an osteocyte in bone, or a chondrocyte in cartilage

- Lacuna (muscular), a lateral compartment of the thigh
- Lacuna (vascular), a medial compartment beneath the inguinal ligament
- Lacuna magna, the largest of several recesses in the urethra
- Lacunar stroke, the most common type of stroke

Other uses

- Lacuna model, a tool for unlocking culture differences or missing "gaps" in text
- Lacunar amnesia, loss of memory about one specific event
- Lacuna Coil, an Italian hard rock/metal band
- Lacunary function, an analytic function in mathematics
- Lacunarity, a mathematical measure of the extent that a pattern contains gaps
- Lacunary polynomial, or sparse polynomial
- Petrovsky lacuna, in mathematics

Laguna (disambiguation)

RESEARCH IS A LOGICAL PROCESS, AND EVIDENCE MUST BE OBJECTIVE. Responsible research has little to no speculation. Here are the logical facts, arranged into a problem.

Logic problem:

The Rio Grande is the border between the United States and Mexico.

Land O' Lakes is a butter company that once used an illustration of an Indigenous woman with a feather in her hair, kneeling in front of a lake, as its label.

In 2020, in response to criticism, the depiction of the Indigenous woman was removed from the label. Now only the land, and the lake, remain.

Rivers empty into the ocean, and the end of the river is its mouth.

Rivers empty into the ocean, except the Nazas and Aguanaval, which empty into disappearing lakes.

A lake is a lacuna, and a lacuna is also a gap in memory, an absence, a silence.

If the river is a border, and the end is its mouth, where it empties, it speaks.

The Rio Grande empties into the Gulf of Mexico.

Synonyms for *gulf*

gulf, noun.

1. *Our ship sailed east into the gulf.* Inlet, creek, bight, fjord, estuary, sound, arm of the sea; bay, cove.

2. *The ice gave way and a gulf widened slowly.* Opening, gap, fissure, cleft, split, rift, crevasse, hole, pit, cavity, chasm, abyss, void; ravine, gorge, canyon, gully.

3. *There is a growing gulf between the rich and the poor.* Divergence, contrast, polarity, divide, division, separation, difference, wide area of difference; schism, breach, rift, split, severance, rupture, divorce; chasm, abyss, gap; rare scission.

The Rio Grande speaks into the abyss/void/rupture/divorce/ chasm/abyss.

Los ríos Nazas and Aguanaval empty into lakes, or lagunas.

The rivers Nazas and Aguanaval speak into the land of lakes.

A lacuna is a gap in memory.

"Laguna de Mayrán, Vega de San Pedro, Laguna de Viesca, Laguna del Caimán are long forgotten landscapes, long forgotten names." —Francisco Valdés-Perezgasga, *Orion Magazine*

The lakes have disappeared.

AT A TALK GIVEN AT THE NEW YORK PUBLIC LIBRARY IN 1986, TONI Morrison said, "You know, they straightened out the Mississippi River in places, to make room for houses and livable acreage. Occasionally the river floods these places. 'Floods' is the word they use, but in fact it is not flooding; it is remembering. Remembering where it used to be. All water has a perfect memory and is forever trying to get back to where it was. Writers are like that: remembering where we were, that valley we ran through, what the banks were like, the light that was there and the route back to our original place. It is emotional memory—what the nerves and the skin remember as well as how it appeared. And a rush of imagination is our 'flooding.'"

WHEN MY MOTHER IS SO OVERWHELMED, SHE BECOMES FORGETFUL, she says, "Ando bien lagunas."

WHILE LOOKING FOR PHOTOS OF TORREÓN, I SAW A HEADLINE: "Tras 6 años seco, corre agua por el lecho del Río Nazas." *After six years dry, water runs through the riverbed of the Nazas.* The photo showed a wide, gentle, lazy river, almost like a lake. Also called El Río de la Laguna, or the river of the lake, it is now contained by the Francisco Zarco dam, constructed in 1968, and has been dry ever since. Once naturally irrigated by seasonal floods, the damming of the rivers has had a devastating effect on the area, forcing the people to use groundwater that is laden with arsenic. The return of the river would replenish the aquifers and solve the arsenic problem, but the dairy industry needs the water to grow alfalfa, the thirstiest crop and single largest user of water, which feeds the cows, which produce the milk. On the US side, the problem is mirrored: alfalfa consumes 80 percent of the Colorado River's water supply, to feed the cows, to produce the milk and meat, and the river is disappearing.

The dry riverbed of the Nazas, the one the water returned to, linked the cities of Torreón, Coahuila, and Gómez Palacio, Durango—my mother's and grandmother's birthplaces. After the rains, the dams could not contain the excess, and the floodgates opened. And so the cities were linked again; the land remembered the river's path, and the river ran and spread, like always, into a lake—a river that defies its borders.

IN SEPTEMBER 2017, IN WHAT WOULD BE THE FINAL DAYS OF MY marriage, my grandmother's ghost called me to Mexico. I flew to Chetumal, Quintana Roo, in the Mexican Yucatán, to interview my grandmother's last living sister, my grandaunt Imelda, whom we lovingly call Tía Mela. I'd received a small grant from the gender studies department at USC for research, and I wanted to find out as much as I could about their lives before I lost another elder.

It's difficult to get my tía to talk candidly in front of the camera. Usually loquacious and always offering coffee, now she touches her neck every few minutes and lowers her voice to a whisper.

TÍA MELA: Everything was fine. Nice man, came from a good family. They did everything right, he kept her respectable, she gave him two babies, one right after the other. Your great-grandfather was grateful, he'd picked cotton his whole life.

ME: Cotton?

TÍA MELA: Yes, your great-grandfather worked for a Spaniard, a cotton plantation owner, and our house was on that land. Jesús, your grandfather, knew the Spaniard.

I hadn't known this. I ask my mother, and she didn't know either. I can only guess that housing was given in exchange for labor, and that price must have changed at some point in time. Later that evening, the laughter, cigarettes, and coffee lighten the mood, and she's ready to tell me more. The story is as extraordinary as always, but now I have details—I already knew about the intimate violence, physical abuse, and the part about my tío Joel stealing her and the children away one night, but not before punching Jesús repeatedly in the face with a warning to stay away forever, which I knew was true because it never changed. Then her new life in Tampico, a repetition with the second husband, escape, migration. I take the story in, and with the concretion of every detail, I feel more estranged than ever.

After five days I head home, uneasy, grateful to come back to the simple pleasures of domesticity. My husband informs me that he's done; he's filing for divorce. No reason, no answers in sight. Another dead end.

And when I go looking for my grandmother in the archives, the only proof she ever existed is her death certificate.

I PRODUCED ALMOST A DECADE'S WORTH OF DOCUMENTS FOR DIS-covery, only to receive a flimsy, redacted, incomplete discovery from my husband's lawyers. He was covering his tracks, seeking to discredit me. To prove my claims, I had to produce the records he was hiding, retrace every hidden credit card statement, parse every transaction, investigate every text and phone call, all while inundated with reading for exams. And it was during that desperate time, at my most unbelieved, that I began searching for my grandmother in the archive.

Divorce and the archive present opposite ends in the confounding problem of the Document. Experiencing both at the same time, I was suspended between two states of the document—excess and absence. To this day, I can't find any records of my grandmother's life in Mexico, can't access her hospital records or prove she existed at all beyond her death certificate. Meanwhile my Google Drive, email, and filing cabinet are redundant with doctored records from my ex-husband's deliberately incomplete discovery. I have no documents proving the existence of the woman who loved me the most, and an excess of documents proving that of the man who didn't.

But that's not the confounding part. It just stages the problem: the documents I needed, in both cases, both did and did not exist. They had been erased from memory by someone's hand. Like Schrödinger's cat, it was a problem of observation: if I searched for the document, it did not exist. If I didn't search for it, it existed.

For example, my grandmother's birth certificate does not exist. It must exist, however; she was born, went to school, got married, had children. But gendered violence and forced migration have buried her name somewhere in time.

Another: the things my ex-husband hid are what actually happened, and that's why he disappeared the documents. The statements exist, but there are just too many cases on the docket for anyone to care, and thus the documents disappear from institutional memory.

The problem of the document—identification, passport, birth certificate, green card, diploma, deed, title, receipt, statement, license, contract, census, tribal roll, paper trail, digital footprint—and the state of being undocumented—illegal, enslaved, unauthorized, unrecorded, dispossessed, uncredentialed, unhoused, unprovable—is a narrative one.

The presence or absence of the document as the very matter of memory determines who does and does not exist, who is and is not remembered, what narratives we privilege, what stories we live. The document is an *act*, with the power to make and unmake history, the power to literally change the reality of the present—from someone's gender, immigration, or marriage status to AI generating a painting Edward Hopper never painted. The document has the power to make or unmake the world.

I'VE BEEN OBSESSED WITH JACQUES DERRIDA'S CONCEPT OF hauntology for a few years now, broadly defined as the "nostalgia for lost futures." To me, a more accurate definition is much closer to that famous line from the penultimate episode of *WandaVision:* "But what is grief if not love persevering?" Hauntology is a state of grief in relationship to history, where what is lost and what could have been are temporally entangled, the past ever-present and refusing to be forgotten. It is the postcolonial condition of forgetting and being forgotten in the aftermath of violence, of longing for a homeland that no longer exists, and of the specter of the past, of what was and what could have been, haunting the present.

As colonized people, to begin the impossible project of tracing our ancestry through the empty fields of national amnesia is to acknowledge what haunts us; to grieve the futures we've lost; to grieve our dead; to imagine the fantasy of home; to imagine our collective futures; to look power in the face and examine its violence through language.

What draws me to Derrida's hauntology is that it's deeply engaged with the specter—the past, the ghost, the ancestor—as the persistence of cultural and collective memory that compels us to "set the record straight." The specter that haunts the archive asks to be found. For Derrida, every archive is unreadable because it is curated by someone in power, defined more by its exclusions and excisions rather than its records.

ACCORDING TO THE MEXICAN STATE, MY MOTHER DOES NOT EXIST, and neither does my grandmother. Or at least, according to the names I know them by: [María?] Angélica López [de Gutiérrez?], b. 1942; Silvia Angélica Gutiérrez, b. 1958. Where their names should be in time, instead there is a lacuna. The line tracing me back to them disappears for one hundred years, until a name I know resurfaces in the

My great-grandmother Carmen López with my grandmother Angélica López in a sailor outfit as a child (left). The other two children in the photo, the baby and the little boy, are unknown.

record: Carmen Valenzuela, my great-grandmother, born in 1922 on the Hacienda San Alberto, in Durango.

This is very strange. In genealogical research, usually parents are a given, and each ancestor becomes progressively harder to find the further back you go in time. My mother swears that I know their true names. Perhaps this is intentional—in case anyone ever thought to go looking for them, their names would become a dead end when every search came up empty-handed. Or perhaps I'm just a writer with a fanciful imagination and a flair for dramatics. But one day my mother sent me a newspaper clipping from Tampico where a childhood picture of her appears, calling her "la simpática niña Silvia Angélica López." Her birth father's surname—the name of the man she and her mother escaped when she was still an infant—is Gutiérrez. Her name *had* been changed. My mother first appears in the public records of

LA SIMPATICA niña Silvia Angélica López engalana nuestra sección de sociales, ella es candidata a Reina de la Primavera del Jardín de Niños "José María Morelos".

Paseo en Honor de una Simpática Candidata Infantil

UN PASEO en automóvil por las principales calles del centro de la ciudad tuvo la pequeñita Silvia Angélica López. Ella es princesa del Jardín de Niños "José Maria Morelos".

Top left: Newspaper clipping of my mother as a child with her surname changed to my grandmother's maiden name—Silvia Angélica López—erasing her father's name. In it, she is announced as a "charming candidate" for the Queen of Spring title for a parade in Tampico, Tamaulipas, around 1965.

Bottom left: Newspaper clipping showing my mother as the Princess of Spring in the same parade. Tampico, Tamaulipas, around 1965.

the United States on my birth certificate, and my grandmother's only existing record is of her death. There is more than one way of being undocumented.

FROM HERE, WIDE EXPANSES OF FORGETTING BEGIN. I CAN ONLY tell the rest in fragments.

IN ENGLISH, THE WORD *RECORD* IMPLIES A DOCUMENT, OR AN artifact—a hard, serious thing that corroborates an event, validates a story, documents a person. Records are the matter of history, kept in file folders, drawers, vast bookshelves, hard drives, the databases and libraries that make up an archive. Even its usage is a speech act. To record: to put down in writing, preserve history, commit to memory. On record: official speech. Set a new record: proof of the unbelievable. A testimony.

In Spanish, *recuerdo* is a memory—a fonder, fading thing, as recalled by a last living elder. *Recuerdos* are not records but a form of longing, a method of time travel, mementos from a bygone era. *Recordar* is not to record, but to remember. Memory itself is the record. But this also makes *recuerdos* vulnerable—the stories of our elders, names, mothers passing on recipes and cures, they can all be so easily lost when those elders start to pass on, taking both their stories and their silences with them.

Then there are those of us—descendants of survivors—for whom memory is a battleground. For those of us caught between memory and record, the reliability of our memory is questioned, discredited without proof. *That never happened. You have a terrible memory.*

TO BE A MESTIZA IS TO BE STRANDED IN TIME AND SPACE. MEMORY itself is a fantasy—who my ancestors were, where they lived, how they lived.

ANY TIME I BRING UP NOT BEING ABLE TO FIND HER OR HER MOTHER in Mexican public records, my mother gets defensive.

"Mami, is it possible that she changed your names in Tampico, or in the United States? So that her first husband couldn't find you guys?"

"Ay, Vanessa, no, siempre se ha llamado Angélica López."

"Well, you said that her first name is also María, and Dad is always joking about your real name being Alma. And you weren't allowed to call her 'Mamá' when you moved to Tampico—you had to call her 'Tita.'"

I can feel the tension between us tighten on the phone. I don't blame my mother—she may truly not know. As a child, she witnessed the two men my grandmother was married to commit unspeakable acts of sexual and domestic violence against her. And now here I am, asking her to recall memories from that time.

MY GRANDMOTHER'S LIFE IS SHROUDED IN SILENCE. THESE ARE THE things I know:

She was the eldest daughter of cotton laborers.

They lived on a hacienda; she was a child bride sold to a man twice her age, and had her first two children less than a year apart. She lived her entire life at the hands of extraordinarily violent, abusive men, trapped in the vise of an even stricter, more confining patriarchy than I've ever known.

Mexican civil records only improve after the Mexican Revolution— from handwritten testimony to typed data. But so far I haven't been able to find my mother and grandmother in any record. Until my great-grandmother Carmen appears. She was the daughter of a "nativo jornalero," or Indigenous laborer, Carlos Valenzuela, and Marciana Benítes, born at the Hacienda San Alberto, Durango, the Mexican near-equivalent of a cotton plantation, where she would also go on to work at the age of eleven. The Mexican civil records and Catholic church records corroborate each other perfectly. And from these three names, I can trace back my Indigenous family, all born at home to laborers. Then the names disappear. Until I check the bracero records from Tucson, Arizona.

My great-great-grandfather Carlos Valenzuela and the rest of my maternal line are listed in other documents as "originario," a word meant to denote a detribalized Indigenous person. Later I would find that this same great-great-grandfather, Carlos Valenzuela, was listed on the 1950 US Census as a bracero who worked as farm help in Arizona. Per the record, at the time of this employment period, he was sixty-three years old, working eighty-four hours per week.

———

IN SIXTH-GRADE GEOGRAPHY, EACH STUDENT WAS ASSIGNED A country and culture to report on for our major project. Most students were assigned European countries—Germany, France, Italy, the Netherlands, Sweden, England, Ireland (*Yes!* they would exclaim)—while the students of color were assigned stereotypes. Stephen, who identified as half white and spoke no Spanish, was assigned Spain. Heather, one of two Black students, was assigned Jamaica, although she was not Jamaican. Katherine, a Filipina student, would report on China. And my friend Edward, who was also Black, was assigned Ancient Egypt. Not Egypt, Ancient Egypt.

Following this logic, when the teacher got to me, I fully expected to be assigned Mexico.

"And Vanessa—you will report on the Aztecs."

"The Aztecs? Not Mexico?"

"Well, Mexico's a little too easy," she said. "It's right next door, and we already know a lot about Mexico from Texas history and the Alamo. Plus, Mexico doesn't really have the kind of history and

142

sophisticated culture of countries like France or England. What, are you going to bring tacos to class?" Laughter.

I've long forgotten that teacher's name, and what she said exactly before the taco comment is an approximation. But I've never forgotten how it ended: *What, are you going to bring tacos to class?* Of course. Americans already know everything they need to know about Mexico—margaritas, fajitas, tacos, and cheap anonymous labor. Mexico is Texas's footnote, and it has no place in *real* history.

In retrospect, I'm impressed she even thought to assign the Aztecs, although I know it wasn't out of care or thoughtfulness. I just had a Spanish surname that came late in the alphabet, I was darker-skinned and more stereotypically Mexican-looking than Stephen, I guess, and by the time she got to me, she was out of ideas.

On research day, I couldn't find a single book on the Aztecs (that is, Nahua and Mexica peoples) in the school library, and I didn't have the language to understand why. Colonial erasure in its most mundane, everyday form is simply encountered as absence, omission—the excisions and sutures of narrativized time. While librarians helped other students check out entire books on their countries and cultures, the only books I could find were on Native Americans of the United States. There were no entries for Aztecs, or any precolonial Mexican history, for that matter, in the card catalog. As far as Wunderlich Intermediate was concerned, Mesoamerican peoples were little more than a sidenote, absent from the memory of the world. The only book I could find that mentioned them was an encyclopedia of the ancient world, which dedicated less than a page to them as part of the entry on Christopher Columbus.

I began to get nervous, unsure about what I could do for my project with only one book and so little reference material. Compared to other students, I looked lazy, like I'd wasted my time in the library, checking out only one measly book, and a general one at that. And the more I worked on it, the more that anxiety grew into acute alienation and shame. As other students prepared their presentations on knights, castles, and pyramids, the stranger the culture I was assigned began to feel, like I was reporting on the savages from *Indiana Jones*. I began to desire the ease and familiarity of Europe, its ample, detailed history and fairy-tale beauty.

At home, I expressed this frustration to Mami. "Why do I have to report on the stupid Aztecs?" Big mistake. Even Tío Javier, five beers into his evening drinking and smoking session, joined in. *The Aztecs were an advanced Indigenous civilization! They had plumbing, and astronomy, and math, and agriculture! This is their calendar! We have chocolate because of the Aztecs! The eagle with a serpent in its talons! Tenochtitlan, the great city built on a lake! You should be proud! You're descended from them!*

A city built on a lake? I'd just read about the Lady of the Lake in T. H. White's *The Once and Future King*, the water spirit that gave Arthur the sword Excalibur. In my mind, *lake* the symbol fused with the *lake* Tenochtitlan was built on and the *lake* of Arthurian legend. All were stored in the deep collective unconscious of imagined history, and finally through the Aztecs and their city on a lake, I could picture myself in history, an alternate history forged between fantasy and erasure.

Later on, in the eighth grade, our long-term project was to create our family tree. We'd just learned about heraldry and the symbols on family crests as an early form of genealogy. We were given a sheet with a hand-drawn tree to fill out in class and then finish with our families at home, which we would look up and cross-check on the microfiche machines later that week. Once I began to fill out all the names I knew, I quickly hit a dead end. I could name twenty cousins off the top of my head, but in terms of direct genealogy, I only knew my grandmothers. No grandfathers.

The point of the project was to develop our research skills, and perhaps discover something interesting about our family story along the way—a distant relation to an immigrant who came through Ellis Island, or a soldier who fought in a war. As students found their family's names in military records, immigration rolls, and land documents, I remained in the blank space, unable to write a name. All of our histories were rendered neutral, little fun facts, as if they bore no weight or consequence in the present. One boy proudly announced that he was descended from a Confederate general and plantation owner.

When I asked Mami to help me fill out the tree when she returned from work, she only added her grandfather's name, Aurelio, and Papi's father, Amadeo, to the tree. But she left her own father's name blank.

I got an F on that project.

Since then I have tried to piece together what it must have been like to be my great-great-grandmother. She was purchased, according to matrilineal recounting, by a man who was extremely temperamental and quite wealthy. I try to imagine what it would have been like to have a discontented white man buy me, after a fight with his mother about prolonged bachelorhood. I wonder what it would have been like to have a thirty-five-year-old man own the secrets of my puberty, which he bought to prove himself sexually as well as to increase his livestock of slaves. I imagine trying to please, with the yearning of adolescence, a man who truly did not know I was human.

—PATRICIA J. WILLIAMS, "GILDED LILIES AND LIBERAL GUILT,"
FROM *THE ALCHEMY OF RACE AND RIGHTS*

IN MY FAMILY, THE DAUGHTER-MEMORY IS THE GHOST VESSEL, tasked with preserving the family record of the living and the dead: their names, narratives, recipes, rituals, ceremonies, their Catholic-Indigenous faith—the record that, as a young girl in the thick of assimilation and self-erasure, I had not realized, or cared, was slipping away.

THE LURE OF ANCESTRY.COM IS THE HOPE OF RECLAIMING THE LOST from the databases of state and institutional memory and the radical subversion of the state document, so often an artifact of violence, as a tool to name, affirm, and record the lives of those lost in the fallout of colonization via labor, migration, and borders. The comprehensive digitized records—birth, marriage, death, census, immigration—compress time into a searchable syntax, a kind of cosmic phone book second only to the scrolls of heaven. I notice that the names are mostly in English, and remember this quote from novelist and poet Morgan Parker: "Meanwhile, black Americans don't and will never know our real names; commercials for Ancestry.com feel like a personal attack."

I enter the names of my grandmothers into every catalog. They do not exist. Somehow this dead end is not a disappointment; it's just the way things are. The past has not changed, it's the same absence I've always known, but now, with age, I understand that their erasure from the past was also an erasure of their future.

MAGICAL/REALISM

NAVIGATING A SILENCE IS DIFFERENT FROM HAVING A SECRET KEPT from you. One is a ghost, the other is a locked door.

For example: as a child, my mother remembers seeing her mother in the hospital on life support, her face swollen and unrecognizable at the hands of her husband and his mistress. "He was a murderer," she says. This would be the last of many late-term miscarriages she lost to domestic violence. My mother remembers her being pregnant, but never having the baby; she remembers being told she'd have brothers and sisters; she remembers being sent away to Mexico City, to Guadalajara, to stay with relatives for no reason. She imagines it was because my grandmother needed time to heal, and didn't want her children to see her bruised and battered. She remembers my grandmother's beauty and elegance, her expensive dresses, her upswept hair.

IN HER CRAFT ESSAY "THE SITE OF MEMORY," TONI MORRISON REframes the writing of memoir in a specifically Black literary heritage— the slave narrative. Written in a time when there was a "hunger for 'slave stories,'" those firsthand accounts had to tread the delicate ground of documenting the horrors of slavery while also appealing to the white reader. Written ultimately to persuade white audiences to abolish slavery, their accounts were self-censored, full of silences and omissions, lacunae of archival forgetting. Instead, slaves had to compliment the "nobility" and "high-mindedness" of the white reader and tone down their emotions, drop a veil over "proceedings too terrible to relate." They had to keep their stories palatable to the people with the power to end slavery. But in dropping that veil, they also omitted any trace of their interior life.

Western history is a project of domination through narrative omission. Morrison points us to the thinkers of the Enlightenment and quotes philosopher Georg Wilhelm Friedrich Hegel saying in 1813 that Africans had no history because they could not write in modern languages. He moves to omit the entire African continent from human history: "At this point we leave Africa, not to mention it again. For it is no historical part of the World."

"First of all, I must trust my own recollections. I must also depend on the recollections of others," Morrison writes. For her, writing memoir is not a solitary act, but a contribution to, and collaboration with, collective memory, repairing a record where a silence once was.

I AM THE PRODUCT OF FORGETTING. I CANNOT TRACE MYSELF BACK. Silence is my ancestor, itself a record of survival. Silence marks a time when an unprecious life had no listener; when to speak was to be unheard, unacknowledged, unbelieved; when truth was not recorded because it had no power against the violence of men, the violence of the state. But the story will repeat itself inside every daughter, lead her to make the same choices, until she remembers.

Encyclopedia of All the Daughters I Couldn't Be

Doctora

At the hospital, when your mother is not in the room, you translate the nurses' questions for your grandmother. Basic things like *Do you have enough water, Are you in pain, Has the doctor come to see you.* She has always told you that you are smart enough to become a doctor, to be the one who discovers the cure for cancer. This becomes your purpose—to become the doctor who cures your grandmother. You want to possess this knowledge, have this job, more than anything in the world, but you doubt your abilities. And soon the world will too.

After she dies, in the fifth grade, your assignment is to write a poem. You write a book-length poem, illustrated with your own drawings, about your grandmother's death, about grief. Your Language Arts teacher is so moved by it, she shows the principal, who will then display

Fourth grade

the book in the library. A year later, in middle school, you will serve your first day in detention for being disruptive in class. The teachers seem to have a lower tolerance for the other forms grief takes in your language, and there you will stay.

ALTERNATIVE SCHOOL: A VERY SPECIAL EPISODE

Lean on Me
1991: The Year Punk Broke
The Voice of the Children, June Jordan and Terri Bush

WRITE THIS FROM THE UNLIKELIEST OF OUTCOMES—THE FINAL YEAR of my PhD program. Somehow I've ended up in Los Angeles, my dining room window facing the brush carving its way up the San Gabriel Mountains. I refuse to let it all become scenery. When I do remember to look at the mountains, really look at them in awe and gratitude, it's because I never thought I'd get anywhere beyond Houston.

In my early adolescence, they had many names for what I was. *Troubled teen. At-risk youth. Juvenile delinquent.* Now good white liberals in nonprofits use *historically underserved, disenfranchised,* and *economically disadvantaged* as their language. I am not exempt from this. Now a graduate student, I write in my CV, "Taught low-income, first-generation, immigrant youth in X Outreach Program." I have crossed over an invisible line, from *problem* to *solution*. But I'm still that scrappy punk in red eyeliner skipping school.

It's hard not to think, *They know who I really am. I'll be found out at any moment.*

Stand and Deliver

I do not consider my infiltration of academia a "success story,"[1] an inspiring tale of "Latina excellence,"[2] or achieving my "ancestors' wildest dreams."[3] It's tempting to read my story as an example of how a bootstraps mentality,[4] hard work, and resilience can overcome hardship. But that would be a lie.

This is a story about how easy it is to fall into the school-to-prison pipeline in the Texas public education system, where from top to bottom, Black and Latine kids with talent and merit lose their way. This is not a story about how academia is a path to liberation, or a site of equity. This is a story of discrimination, criminalization, and a mother's love.

That said, let's start with the odds.

---

1. Latines have consistently been the most underrepresented demographic in college enrollment since the 1970s. As of today, only 44 percent of all graduating Latine students will even be eligible to apply to college.

2. Latines have consistently had the highest dropout rate since the 1970s.

3. For many Latines, their parents' educational attainment does not surpass middle school.

4. Seventy-one percent of Latine students come from poverty and make up 73 percent of all homeless students.

1. First-generation student. I'm luckier than most, despite the immense struggle children of immigrants face in American schools. My parents spoke English—my mother better than my father—and bought a house when I was in first grade. I grew up in a working-class suburb. We almost lost the house a couple of times, and got a couple of cars repoed, but we made it through. I was the first to graduate high school, and the first to attend college in my family.

2. On the FAFSA, I answer truthfully. Father's highest education level: middle school. Mother's highest education level: high school, no diploma. These are technicalities. My father is a genius—a self-taught guitarist and sound engineer who only got up to about the eighth grade in Mexico. My mother is also a genius—a student with a near-perfect GPA, ineligible to graduate because of her undocumented status—who had to drop out of high school in the Rio Grande Valley to work and support her family. She taught herself floral design, and with no training became one of the most in-demand professional florists in Houston. In my eyes, they're the most accomplished people in the world.

3. Latinas continue to be the lowest-paid demographic in the United States, work the most hours, and face the largest wage gap among women. My mother has been the sole breadwinner in our family since 1996. I would start my first full-time job at sixteen in 1998, and worked two full-time jobs from 2002 to 2011. We made it through, but we shouldn't have had to.

4. Up until 2010, Latine students consistently had the highest dropout rate of any racial or ethnic group in the United States, and the poorest educational outcomes. After the death of my grandmother, I began exhibiting behavioral problems I now understand as grief, also due to undiagnosed ADHD, then misdiagnosed as depression. Once a gifted and talented student, by the time I reached middle school, I lived in detention and in-school suspension.

5. In high school, I worked full-time and barely attended the eleventh grade, nearly dropping out. By some miracle, I graduated.

Mad Love

Dazed and Confused

Come as You Are: The Story of Nirvana, Michael Azerrad

In the 1990s, girls of color were at a brutal intersection of unholy cultural forces: popular psychology and self-help culture crossed with the alarmist crises of teen pregnancy, adolescent depression, the war on drugs, zero-tolerance policies, and tough-love parenting, all resulting in the boot camps, psychiatric hospitals, rehabilitation camps, and halfway houses of the troubled teen industry. Troubled teens were a firmly entrenched trope in pop culture. The Partnership for a Drug-Free America ran the now infamous "This Is Your Brain on Drugs" commercials, where an egg is held up to demonstrate: "This is your brain," and then is cracked and fried: "This is your brain on drugs," followed by dramatic footage of a teen destroying their kitchen, or a star swimmer diving into an empty pool, only to end with, "Any questions?" Sitcoms would have "very special episodes" where the normative characters would encounter drugs, or pregnancy, or AIDS, and learn a powerful lesson to model good behavior. Before the ten o'clock news broadcast, the channel would run a "Do You Know Where Your Children Are?" spot to purposely terrify exhausted boomer parents. Talk show hosts like Phil Donahue, Ricki Lake, and Jerry Springer made their bread and butter interviewing "out-of-control teens," usually just poor, working-class, queer and trans, or subculture teenagers with no support systems or affinity networks, while movies like *Mad Love, Kids,* and *Dangerous Minds* capitalized on the cultural panic.

Parents were made to be afraid of their teenagers, while teenagers were framed as dangerous rebels on the verge of risky or criminal activity that required firm discipline and surveillance. The tough-love parenting that adolescents endured at home turned into zero-tolerance policies at school, with disciplinary procedures that operated by carceral logics. Adolescents, being considered minors, were rightless in the hands of authority figures, subject to illegal searches and self-incriminating questioning. And the most vulnerable in this severe climate were Black and Latine kids, economically disadvantaged kids, and mentally ill kids. I was all three.

Dos mujeres, un camino (1993–94)

I want to look like Bridget and Linda, the second-prettiest Mexican girls in sixth grade. They dressed so cool, like my cousins from South Houston on my dad's side: tight low bun, hairsprayed and laid. Baby hairs gelled down in waves. Extra-long lashes, liquid eyeliner, brown lipstick. Big white T-shirt or body suit, Dickies work pants, Timberland work boots or Jordans.

Everyone knows Natasha is the prettiest, and not just because she's mixed Mexican and Black. She just is. She's also the tallest and fastest and could easily be a model. Bridget is la morena, the coolest one that all the boys like and respect. Linda is funny, the ride-or-die, the lightest but also the poorest, with the heaviest accent. Claudia has green eyes and the most developed body. Everyone loves Soni because she's better at basketball than the boys and dresses like one—jerseys, Jordans, and shorts wangos (Spanish for "baggy"). Juan will fight for anyone and can get you weed. Everyone sags their starched pants just the perfect amount—not too low, except maybe Juan.

I dress like Claudia Kishi from *The Baby-Sitter's Club*, Lisa Turtle from *Saved by the Bell*, Denise from *The Cosby Show*. I have round flip-up nonprescription sunglasses like Dwayne Wayne from *A Different World*. When it gets cold, instead of a Starter jacket with my favorite sports team, I wear a shoulder-padded leather jacket, purple tights, and a green sweater. They tell me I look like Barney. I don't have Timberlands or Jordans or Dickies. I don't know Tejano bands or sports, just Selena, Los Tigres del Norte, and my dad's band, Los Super Villahnos. I am hanging on by a thread.

Linda asks me for two dollars at lunch so she can get a fiestada from the snack bar, a Mexican pizza with yellow cheese. She's the nicest to me but also asks me for money a lot. It doesn't bother me. My mom gives me three dollars a day, and Linda and I split it. We go to the bathroom together to do our makeup, and in the mirror she says, "Let me help you." She lines my eyes with dollar-store eyeliner, outlines my lips in black pencil, and fills them in with brown lipstick. I at least have knockoff Timbs by now and am starting to wear my uncle's work pants to school. He's a truck driver, but he wears a forty-two-inch waist, and they're way too big, hard to keep up on my hips. I'm an impostor, and I feel like they'll find me out at any minute. Linda asks me if I want to get jumped in. I don't know what that means. *Yeah, to our crew.* She tells me to think of a name. Bridget is Goofy, Juan is Sleepy, and she's Tweety. All the good WB and Disney characters are taken. I like Nintendo, so I choose Yoshi. She says that it'll happen when I least expect it, but they'll go easy.

My mom won't buy me liquid eyeliner or brown lipstick, so I shop-lift Revlon Toast of New York from Kroger and use a Sharpie to line my eyes. My dad's band is struggling, and we're having real money problems this time, so I can't get Jordans or a Starter jacket. I shoplift a pack of white men's T-shirts from the corner store and wear them with my dad's and uncle's work pants and knockoff Timbs.

One Friday afternoon I'm walking to the bus, and Juan says, "Hey, Bridget needs to tell you something." This might be true—we're both altos in choir and in the same sight-reading group. Bridget is the most popular, and today she wore wispy sprayed bangs with her hair half up, gold hoops, and green jeans. Since she started going with Eric, the only middle-class kid in our group, she's been untouchable. If she calls for you, it is an honor. Juan runs ahead toward the track, and as I try to catch up, six or seven girls jump out from behind the temporary buildings, run after me, and tackle me.

Getting jumped isn't like the fights in the movies—a slow narrative dance where one punch flies, then is returned by another. Instead you get blindsided and punched in the same spot really fast: boom boom boom boom boom boom boom. One girl takes the head and face, the other the back, the other the front. Juan and Armando and Eric are laughing on the sidelines. *Oh damn! Dale sus chingazos!* There is no time to think or react, just shield and crouch down. I fall onto my side and see Bridget's and Natasha's faces as they start kicking. They look mad, vindicated. Linda yells, "Teacher!" and they all run behind the baseball field and into the neighborhood. It has lasted less than four minutes, but the pain is agonizing. When the teacher runs up and asks me what happened, I say it was some kids from another school. I don't narc, but I miss my bus and have to walk home. That one cop always, always, turns on his lights when he sees me walking.

I can't tell if I've been initiated or betrayed. All I know is that I feel more alone than ever.

When I open the door, someone is home. This usually doesn't happen—I use my key and have the house to myself until a little after six. But today my dad is back from jira and watching TV. I try to run to my room and change, but he sees that I'm wearing his khaki Dockers and a plaid shirt, buttoned only at the top. *Ven para acá, pinche huerca. ¿Por qué estás vestida como hombre?* Why are you dressed like a man? I start to tell him that everyone dresses like this, but I'm shaken and nervous. I don't know what to say. He takes me by the throat and slams me down onto the couch. *Aquí no quiero jotas.* I don't want dykes here. It was only a matter of time before I got caught in men's clothes. I get the belt. This is how the fathers in our family make girls learn.

No one calls me over the weekend.

I start talking different, try to regain my accent, talk like I used to before I learned midwestern English from TV. I try to undo my anglicized pronunciations, stop swallowing my *l*'s and bring them to the front of my mouth again. Try it: say "Really." Your tongue is toward your soft palate, probably. Now move your tongue directly behind your front teeth for the *l*. *Reallee.* It's a tiny shibboleth that becomes automatic and breaks along racial and class lines. It signals: Have you assimilated? I try to sound "hard." That means being fearless, mean, streetwise, ready to throw down for your homegirls, taking no disrespect. But I'm not streetwise. I just want to read and draw and write. Instead of doing homework, I work at being accepted in the friend group. I listen to Spanish radio stations, watch Rockets games, make drawings of their names and characters in bubble letters.

That Monday, I give them all their drawings. They accept my offerings, even like them, but not enough to change the power dynamic. Instead, because I always had Sharpies, I become the group tagger. *Ey, can you make me one that says Bridget -n- Eric 4-evr in Old English script? Tag NORTHCLIFF LOCAS in the bathroom right quick.* Other kids catch on, ask me to draw their names with Crip signs in stylized lettering. I don't really know what a Crip is, just what I hear other kids talk about and hear in music, but I make a C with a cross and dots, like the ones I've seen on notebooks. I add sparkles in the corners of their names. *Damn that's tight, do you tag with spray paint?* Not yet. The teachers think I'm drawing gang insignia, so I get sent to the principal, then the school counselor. They ask me if I'm in a gang. I don't know what's happening to me.

It is not an exaggeration to say that I spent more than half of my time in middle school in detention. But this was a blessing in disguise, and did two important things for me: it put me in a silent room for eight hours, and it gave me free unstructured time to "do my assignments," which I always finished early so I could spend the rest of the day drawing, reading, writing. I read easily three books a week, mostly horror and fantasy novels, and *Dune*. I did better on my own with unstructured creative time. I felt better within the walls of my study carrel, isolated from others. I was relieved to not have to switch classes, negotiate social groups, or be in classrooms with other kids and authority figures pulling me in opposite directions.

Live Through This, Hole

In life, my grandmother wanted me to look up to Lucerito, the white Mexican singer-actress, but her good-girl ranchera shtick never appealed to me. After my grandmother died, though, I began to gravitate toward pop icons who showed their anger, who were insubordinate, who were not afraid to dissent.

There's nothing more boring than a jaded old middle-aged person going on about the music of their day, but before 2000, it was musicians who taught me my politics, never to back down. Back then the genre of music you listened to was an implicit identification not only with a certain racial, gender, and class identity (more than it is today) but also with a certain set of values.

Before tweens had Disney stars like Britney Spears, Miley Cyrus, and Olivia Rodrigo to facilitate the transition into adolescence and adulthood, preteens in the mid- to early 1990s had to navigate forming their identities through a music industry meant for and by adults, a model that would forever change after the late 1990s shift to the Disney-to-teen-pop-star/boy-band pipeline. Even the most commercial pop was made mostly by adults with adult themes, such as TLC's "Ain't 2 Proud 2 Beg" video, which featured them wearing condoms on their clothes to bring awareness to HIV/AIDS. Pop music was not apolitical, but a medium of expression and a gateway into the world's more weighty themes, from Salt-N-Pepa and TLC's pro-sex HIV/AIDS awareness to Prince writing *slave* on his face to protest the music industry. Underage pop stars even sought to appeal to adults, not tweens—LeAnn Rimes was considered a prodigy at thirteen for sounding just like Patsy Cline in her 1996 hit country song "Blue," while artists like Aaliyah released *Age Ain't Nothing but a Number* at fifteen years old, and the band Silverchair released their 1995 debut album, *Frogstomp*, at sixteen.

To choose what music to listen to was to engage a subculture's politics early. Before church-camp-friendly stars like Taylor Swift, the music that appealed to the preteens of my generation scandalized adults, was banned from radio and television, and was labeled with PARENTAL ADVISORY: EXPLICIT CONTENT stickers. Apolitical positive-role-model pop like Amy Grant's "Baby Baby," Mariah Carey's "Dream Lover," or Michael Jackson's "Black and White" had no real chance against artists like N.W.A., Nine Inch Nails, and Public Enemy—family-friendly pop was *corny*, for school dances and Christian lock-ins, until Disney stars and Kidz Bop would find a market there ten years later.

"What kind of music do you listen to?" was not only about what subcultures you identified with but also a litmus test for whether you were a *poser* who listened to *sellouts*.

To be a poser, or a person faking being indie, alt, or punk, was the worst possible thing you could be. You couldn't pretend to be a skater, or a punk, or a rebel. You had to *be* what you believed, risk everything for the ideas in the music, have the guts to back it up.

Under the Pink, Tori Amos
SubUrbia (1996)
Poetic Justice (1993)

Once I went to the mall with my friend Sonia, the daughter of a roadie for my dad's band. Her dad spoke no English and drove a 1986 copper-brown Chevy Astrovan with wooden beads on the front seats and an Eagles tape in the deck—very different from the sleek Lexuses and Audis in line ahead of us. A little over an hour after he dropped us off, two security guards flanked us outside a store and told us to come with them, escorting us through the back concrete hallways to a sterile white holding office, where we were told to sit in brown metal folding chairs while they reviewed video footage from Sam Goody, the CD and music merch store we'd excitedly gone to first. The employees found it strange that Sonia and I sat in a corner quietly for almost an hour reading *Sandman* graphic novels, band biographies, and guitar chord books—the same thing I'd done just weeks prior with a group of white girls from school. Determined, the rent-a-cops went through our things, patted us down, and questioned us as they went over the footage multiple times, threatening to call the police and "throw the book" at us for shoplifting, but of course they found nothing, so they had to let us go.

We couldn't let them disrespect us like that. We had to get our lick back, so we staked out Sam Goody and watched for the shift change. Once in, we shoplifted two T-shirts: for her, a black Metallica T-shirt, and for me, a white T-shirt with a photo of Kurt Cobain. I pretended to shop the Michael Bolton CDs to cover for Sonia while she ripped the plastic security tags out, leaving a small hole in each shoulder. Then she rolled the T-shirts up so that they fit in our pant legs (flared-leg 1990s jeans! a classic) and gave me a nod when it was done. *Vámonos.* On our way out, we flicked off the all-white staff behind the counter. *Fuck Sam Goody, and fuck your dumbass rent-a-cops!* We hadn't intended to steal. It hadn't even crossed our minds until it crossed theirs.

A few months later, my blond, blue-eyed friend Bree would get caught shoplifting a formal dress from 5-7-9, accessories from Contempo Casuals, and a bottle of GAP Dream body spray, all for the eighth-grade dance. That night, even though I was with four white upper-middle-class girls, I was still nervous that the security guards might recognize me from the Sam Goody incident. Maybe they'd even added my picture to the suspicious persons bulletin board in the office. My heart was pounding in my throat as they asked Bree to put her bag on the counter and open it, thinking they'd clock me any second. Instead, after finding the items, they said all she had to do was return the merchandise to the stores and apologize, promising to never do it again.

Although I was darker in my youth, I was still a relatively light mestiza by comparison. In my middle school years, I quickly learned that standing in a circle of white kids kept the cops at bay. Despite us all being between thirteen and sixteen, my friends could smoke openly outside the food court alone or in a group, while I still had to palm my cigarettes and blow the smoke down my shirt. Suddenly I could move freely around campus, walk along any road, go into any store in peace, so long as I was the quiet one in a throng of white kids. But if I went anywhere by myself, or with one of my Black or Mexican friends, it would be only minutes until we were followed, or asked to open our bags upon exit.

I've come to understand this part of my past as the invisible riptide of whiteness—an imperceptible, all-consuming force that drags the very earth under your feet even when you're standing still. It takes you unwillingly, until you find yourself so deep in its pull, it's impossible to swim against, dissolving the boundaries of you into its one big self. This is how I came to understand whiteness as a social project: when you're hypervisible as a potential source of trouble, safety means being able to go unseen. This is the eternal privilege of non-Black people of color—self-dilution, and the ability to cloak in ambiguity.

I remember swallowing the last remnants of my Rio Grande Valley accent by practicing dialogue from television, mimicking Kurt Cobain's bored, disaffected Pacific Northwest articulation in Nirvana interviews.

One day I went over to Pat and Kiki's house to kick it and watch TV like we usually did. In the last few weeks, the conversation hadn't been flowing like it used to; ideas for what to do weren't coming to the surface like usual. I wasn't up on the latest music on 97.9 the Box, couldn't talk about that week's episodes of *Showtime at the Apollo* or *Martin*. The cultural divide in shared social space between Blackness and Latinidad that we'd bridged so easily as kids had begun to be pulled apart by bigger, older social forces. Like with the kids who all sat together in elementary school and self-segregated by middle school, some silent field between us began to widen, no matter what I did.

Pat lifted weights outside and asked me, "You got ISS this week?"

"Yeah."

"You changed your style, huh. You a banger now?"

Nirvana: Live! Tonight! Sold Out! (1994)

I don't remember if it happened in autumn, but it must have. In Houston, the leaves don't change in a memorable way—one day summer just ends, and a clammy, wet cold strips the trees gray and bare. That's what I remember, abrupt change and bare trees, when maybe a month into eighth grade I was expelled from Wunderlich Intermediate School for bringing two joints to campus, despite never being found in possession of them, nor ever having done drugs in my life. I was put in handcuffs, illegally searched, and sent to an alternative school, an experience that would eventually drive me to a psychiatric hospital.

––––––––––

I was navigating the particular loneliness of a strange body that could not be grouped—racialized, gender-nonconforming, working-class, illegible, hostile—the kind of body that has to find other outsiders to survive. Think Nancy from *The Craft* crossed with Angel the cholo gangbanger from *Stand and Deliver*. Janis Ian from *Mean Girls* crossed with John Bender from *The Breakfast Club*. Anger as a defense mechanism, angst as the driver of bad decisions.

Enter Hunter and Dylan—two working-class white punks from rough neighborhoods and broken homes, each one strike away from some bigger consequence. For Hunter, it was Christian boot camp, for Dylan, it was something more serious.

Dostoyevsky said there are only two stories: a man goes on a journey, or a stranger comes to town. Dylan was that stranger. He was the new kid who dressed in all black and talked about drugs. He never mentioned his family or told us where he lived. He never took the bus, no one ever came to pick him up, and he'd find a way to disappear before goodbyes. He was always amped up on Mini Thins from the gas station, and already at fourteen he had endless stories about "tripping balls" and being high at shows, at parties, in the streets. He was fascinating to listen to and good at romanticizing the high. The following spring, Ewan McGregor would remind me of him in *Trainspotting*, but by then, he'd be long gone.

We all wanted Dylan's approval. He was real, experienced, of-the-world in ways no one else was. We were all sheltered posers, sweet summer children next to a real punk from the street. And he also saw something different in me—I was always surprised when he ran up to walk me to class, found me sitting alone at lunch, invited me behind buildings to smoke cigarettes. He would eventually ask me to "go out" with him, but I don't think he really liked me like that. (We kissed once; it was strange and open-mouthed and . . . tongueless?)

Looking back, I think I was a mark. He knew what he could get from me because of how alienated I was, and the kind of neighborhood I lived in. He'd say things like, *Man, if I only knew where to get a dime bag, I lost all my connects.* He and Hunter must've worked some kind of stoner inception, because eventually I *offered* to get them weed despite not knowing the first thing about where and how to get it. I did know one boy, Antoine from the house at the dead end, who talked a lot of shit and made it sound like he had the hookup.

That afternoon I took Dylan and Hunter's twenty dollars, got off the bus, and walked to Antoine's house. When I arrived, his brother Dante was in the garage. I got a head nod. I knocked on the door, and Antoine poked his head out and wordlessly gave me two joints in exchange—of course I didn't know how much $20 buys, and neither did he. The next day I brought them to school. The joints burned a hole in my pocket. I was holding a powerful piece of street cred, a shortcut to notoriety. Before first period, I showed the joints to two white girls in my class—good, wealthy white girls who would go on to be our valedictorian and salutatorian—mistaking them for friends. I never suspected that one of the girls, Calliope, a horse girl who took high school English classes in middle school, would snitch, and allege that I'd come to school high.

I found Dylan and Hunter after first period, gave them the joints, and went to my next class. Ten minutes in, a principal showed up at the classroom door. Something was different this time—both assistant principals had come to escort me downstairs, where two white campus policemen were waiting for me in the principal's office. I recognized one of them as the cop who always turned on his lights and chirped his siren at us when we walked near campus, rolling slowly behind us and asking, "Where are you supposed to be?" The policemen instructed me to place my backpack on the chair and turn around. I was put in handcuffs and restrained while Mr. S., one of the principals, searched my backpack. The back wall of his office was a panel of windows; a brown-gray finch fluttered onto a branch, flew away. I realized what had happened, and what they were looking for.

"I don't have anything," I said.

"Turn around and shut up."

My heart beat high and fast as a hummingbird in my throat as Mr. S. went through my things. I could see his reflection through a mirrored plaque on a shelf as he held my textbooks up by their covers and shook the pages, thumbed through my notebooks, opened a note from a classmate. They found no contraband except some old stray tobacco leaves in my pencil bag, no more than you'd find at the bottom of an empty cigarette box, which I confessed came from some cigarettes I'd stolen from my uncle. The principal nodded, and I was guided to a chair.

"Where are the joints, Vanessa?"

"What joints? I don't know what you're talking about."

"Don't you dare lie to me, young lady, there are multiple witnesses."

"I gave them away."

"To who?"

I would not rat out my friends. Were they my friends?

"This is a serious crime. Are you high right now? Do you want to go to jail?"

I didn't know what to do. They had not found me to be in possession of marijuana, which meant the police wouldn't get to make their arrest. But I was still technically in possession of tobacco, which qualified as contraband. They released the handcuffs, and I was expelled for the rest of the semester.

When my mother arrived at the school, she was still in her uniform—a white blouse and black skirt—furious and defensive, and a relief to see. When she asked me what happened, why I would do this, who the joints were for, I told her everything.

"You need to find those boys. They used her, and they're getting away with it," she told the principal, who said he couldn't search anyone without probable cause. My mother would not back down. "She will not take the fall for them."

The principals brought down Dylan and Hunter, who denied even knowing me, and said I was a bad influence, made up some story about me peer-pressuring them to buy weed. After talking to them, something clicked for Mr. S., as a story arranged itself behind his pale blue gaze. By washing their hands of me, Hunter and Dylan had made an accusation that escalated the charge—it was no longer possession, but possession with intent to sell, a felony. Soon after, Hunter's grandparents and Dylan's caregiver arrived and advocated fiercely for the boys on the basis of their whiteness, and my obvious deviance. My bad behavior was to be expected, given my family's likely *illegal* status.

"And how many languages do you speak?" my mother asked them. They wouldn't even look at her. But she held her ground and would not allow herself to be slandered. "If you searched her, then you better search them," she said. "Don't hold her to a different standard."

The principal asked Dylan and Hunter to open their bags and empty their pockets, found nothing, and let them go. As Hunter and his grandparents were on their way out, suddenly they were stopped, and a charge in the air changed. One of the assistant principals, a Black woman, had just gone through all three of our lockers. Mine was clear, theirs were not. But I was the only one put in handcuffs.

Hunter was pulled out of school and sent to Christian boot camp, while Dylan and I were expelled and sent to Klein Annex, a disciplinary alternative school next to the district police station, for the remainder of the semester. The school was a drab redbrick rectangle, with reinforced windows and school police guarding the exits. Pending good grades and good behavior, I could petition to re-enroll the following semester.

A few days into alternative school, I saw Dylan in the lunchroom. We were supposed to be silent, so he passed me a note as he walked by my table. In it, he asked why I had snitched, why I didn't just say I flushed the joints down the toilet. Said I was a stupid little girl. A few days later, he would get into a fight with a Black student. They would be violently separated and both slammed onto the floor, put in hand-cuffs, and escorted out of the building. And that would be the last time I ever saw Dylan.

Against all odds, I actually enjoyed alternative school. The school had no social hierarchy except the severity of what had gotten us there. It was a school populated by mostly Black and Latine students, queer students, blue-collar white kids, punks, and goths. We'd all been failed by the system, thrown into a building as rejects the state didn't know what to do with. I was finally among my people.

We had one teacher, a middle-aged white man who dressed in various shades of brown and beige and sat at his desk with the cross-word puzzle all day. Each student was assigned a curriculum packet, a legal envelope filled with reams of stapled worksheets to be completed via self-directed study. When I went up to get mine, the man said, "Uhh, Villarreal. Oh, that's the one we're still waiting on. No one knows what curriculum to give a Gifted and Talented student, too fancy. You're our first." I was eventually assigned a ninth-grade curriculum, which I completed in two weeks. (Take that, Calliope. I took high-school-level classes in eighth grade, too.) That left the rest of the semester for inde-pendent reading. This self-direction and lack of structure turned out to be exactly what I needed to concentrate, to apply myself, to excel.

But alternative school was also a place where kids who struggled with addiction, substance abuse, and violent oppositional behavior were sent to be disciplined rather than supported or helped. And any-time a fight broke out or a student talked back, the police were always there to enforce order by using excessive measures. It was where I learned to hide cigarettes better, how to smoke while we walked around the track during PE. It was also where I would buy my first two hits of acid—Black Fly, two tiny pieces of paper with a fly printed on them, each wrapped in a tiny square of foil.

Although I would survive the semester, the thought of going back to my assigned school filled me with dread. So over Christmas break, I attempted to take my own life. In response, I was hospitalized at Gulf Pines Psychiatric Hospital, a popular destination in the troubled teen industry, advertised as an alternative to juvenile detention. Both facilities—the Klein Annex alternative school and Gulf Pines—were stops in the school-to-prison pipeline, operated by carceral logics.

Both experiences were an outsize response to an all-too-common problem: discrimination, loneliness, the need to belong.

When Good Kids Do Bad Things, Katherine Gordy Levine
Girl, Interrupted, Susanna Kaysen
Prozac Nation, Elizabeth Wurtzel

White womanhood has its tragic mentally ill figures: Marilyn Monroe, Sylvia Plath, Amy Winehouse. Their mental illness is enshrined in fragility and victimhood, making it okay to not be okay.

The only movie about institutionalization I can find with a woman of color lead is *Gothika*, with Halle Berry, which was universally panned. We don't get to be Winona Ryder or Angelina Jolie in *Girl, Interrupted* or Drew Barrymore in *Mad Love* or Kirsten Dunst in *Crazy Beautiful*, manic pixie dream girls who change a man's life. We don't get to be fragile, fucked up, or "crazy" when our labor is the thing that's valuable.

When you grow up having trouble with authority, trouble with authority itself becomes the cop in your head. Discipline becomes your demon, your nemesis sabotaging every move you make. You can't be bad again, you can't fail. So it's you or the demon, and only one of you can win. "Getting better" means mirroring, acting the way authorities want you to act, which means you must question yourself at every turn, learn how to mask. The future was never a blank slate again, but rather an extension of grace, a life spent making up for your failures before you're found out to be the piece of shit you truly are. That's discipline. No one polices me more than I police myself.

Figure 8, Elliott Smith

Senior year, I became friends with Calliope, the same girl who snitched on me in the eighth grade. You might wonder why I would let somebody like that into my life again, the person who made racist comments and set off the chain of events at the center of a major personal trauma. I couldn't really tell you, other than the fact that we worked for the literary magazine together, and the only way forward was to forget. That was a version of me that no longer existed, and just as I was not defined by the worst thing I've ever done, she wasn't either, and I extended that same grace to her.

We were also both on the newspaper staff, and would go out to lunch in her Suzuki Sidekick, listen to music, laugh, and smoke cigarettes. We were both writers, book people, music nerds. We had so much more in common than whiteness would let us believe, were so much more alike than class and invented politics and her parents would allow. Except she had a second house, a horse ranch in Huntsville, along the same highway as the Texas State Penitentiary.

Somehow, in the final year of high school, she finally saw me for who I really was. I think she carried the guilt of what happened to me, and over time, instead of resenting me for what I got away with, was surprised to learn who I really was, what racial stereotypes and ingrained fears didn't let her see before.

She would eventually get accepted to Harvard and drop our friendship—class and race would become real again, and our friendship could not withstand the realities and pressures of Harvard networks, especially when opening doors is all about who you know. After our respective first years in college, Calliope met up at IHOP to debrief on our first years, our classes, what it was like going to school with *Natalie Portman*. I told her about how much I loved the Honors College, and asked her if Harvard had anything like that. "It's Harvard. The whole thing is an 'Honors College,'" she said. She wrapped up her visit and made a quick exit after that. A few years ago she followed me on Instagram, but we don't interact, and I don't think about her much at all anymore. But recently, on a Christmas visit home, I found my senior yearbook, and the note she wrote to me in the back. I was moved by what she saw—I'd recently been diagnosed with severe ADHD, and was putting my past back together from that knowledge, regretting a life that could have been with medication and support. Part of me doubted the diagnosis, dismissed it as a trend among grad students and LA creatives. But there it was, in her note, all along. It reads:

> *When I tell people about you, I say, "Vanessa, my best friend, is the most gifted artist and poet I will ever know." It's not like a "probably" or a "maybe I might meet someone who can match her at Harvard," it's a "she is." I think part of the reason for all the tension is pure jealousy . . . And of course another reason for the tension is your unfocused-ness—it drives me NUTS to see you not fulfilling your awesome promise [. . .] I will miss you [. . .]*
>
> *Calliope*

MY BOYFRIEND'S MAID: A REVERSE CINDERELLA STORY

TODAY I NEED YOU TO WASH AND DETAIL THE LEXUS, AND THEN when you're done, wash the Dually and Isaac's car." His mom hoisted a shop vac out of the detached garage into the driveway, where some old towels, various cleaners, polish, and a pair of cheap tooth-brushes lay inside two stacked plastic buckets. "One toothbrush is for detailing the inside. Make sure to get deep inside all the cracks, handles, knobs, seams, and scrub really well. The other toothbrush is for the outer details. Use newspaper on the glass and towels on the body. Let me know when you're done with the Lexus—do that one first." At 7:45 in the morning, the day was still steely and cool between the tall Texas pines, but by 9:00 the sun was high and white and searing the suburban con-crete in the boggy Houston heat. The high temperature that day would be 102; inside the Lexus it would be at least twenty degrees hotter.

By 11:00 my body was damp and dripping with sweat. I should have started with the inside of the car. As I vacuumed the Cheerios under the seats and dragged a blue plastic toothbrush across the seams of the dashboard, I saw Isaac and his two sisters come out in their bathing suits. He looked over and gave me a sad little wave. He needed to spend more time with his sisters because his mom said he was spending too much time with me. He was going off to college soon, and then he'd only see them on holidays.

I waved back, smiled, maybe too approvingly. *Yes, go, spend time with them, I'm great over here!* As they played in the sun, splashed in the water, and jumped on the trampoline, I scrubbed the handles, the plastic liner, the individual tire bolts, hosed down the mats, polished and shined the headlights into diamonds. When I was done and asked for her approval, after fixing a few minor details, it was nearly three in the afternoon. But I was only done with the Lexus. I still had to wash his stepdad's truck and Isaac's Saturn.

"Those two'll be easy, you just have to wash, wipe down, and vacuum. Piece of cake."

She was my boss, so I did. Because the summer after I graduated high school, I worked for my boyfriend's family as their maid.

IF DESIRE IS SHAPED BY THE FIRST FACE YOU IMPRINT ON, FOR ME, that face was my father's. Curly black hair, olive skin, a long bony nose, and deep-set almond eyes. Although he's Mexican, he's always been ethnically ambiguous, commonly mistaken for Arab and, by my white friends, mixed-race Black. (His band nickname was "The Arabian Knight," and one night, when the band members were introduced onto the stage, a DJ mistranslated it "La Noche Árabe.") The first men I loved all resembled my dad: my first celebrity crush was Prince in

Purple Rain, shredding a solo on guitar in ascots and floral jackets on a small club stage; then Michael Jackson, spinning in glittery socks to "Billie Jean," whom I only loved more when *Bad* came out, his hair now styled with long black curls in the back, like my dad.

Then my desire began to branch outward to the boys in my neighborhood. My first kiss was a boy named Chauncey; my first neighborhood crush, a boy named Pat; the first boy who called me his girlfriend, a tall, thin Desi boy named Danish; my first close, hot dance was with a Salvi boy named Ariel at one of my dad's bailes; my first obsession was Mayín, the son of one of my dad's bandmates, a Mexican boy who loved Nirvana as much as I did and had a real Fender Jagstang, Kurt Cobain's signature guitar. My first official boyfriend was Tyrone Moye in sixth grade, who gave me his Rockets jersey to make it official, took me to see *The Mask* at the dollar theater, and still holds the title for the most beautiful smile I've ever seen. In terms of desire, whiteness was never on my radar. In fact, I was a bit scared of white boys after one hit me on the nose with a bat when I was in kindergarten. I never really looked at white boys, much less believed one could ever love me. They just weren't part of my world.

Not until a boy named Brandon—wealthy, blue-eyed, with chin-length blond hair—started paying attention to me. He sat in front of me in Honors Texas History, and toward the end of the period he'd turn around and we'd sit on top of our desks facing each other, our legs intertwined in the dip of his chair, and he'd hold my hands in his and stare deep into my eyes through his wire-framed glasses in silence for what seemed like hours. I'd never even noticed him; suddenly, he became the most beautiful boy in the world.

It never went further than that. But its impact was lifelong—as a girl who was constantly surveilled and getting in trouble, I noticed that being near him granted me a new, if temporary, buff. For those few brief weeks in the sunshine of Brandon's company, for the first time, I was treated like a person, not a problem. I'd never experienced that kind of calm, that acceptance, that *protection*. That brief experience of freedom opened up the world.

Brandon was the first time I'd experienced proximity to whiteness, and the privileges that come with that status. I was the first in my family to gain that proximity, but I never learned how to earn my way in through respectability politics like good grades, good test scores, good behavior, neutrality, and silence. All white proximity passes are conditional, but mine was earned for being off-limits.

Before I understood what respectability politics were, I'd already rejected the terms. I was never going to convince white people I wasn't bad, angry, or dangerous, so I didn't try. And *that's* what made me attractive to whiteness—they chose me *because* of my provocations, *because* I wasn't afraid to talk back to authority figures, *because* I smoked in the bathroom, *because* I lived in *that* neighborhood, the farthest one south just before the tollway. Respectability explained why most of my peers of color distanced themselves from me once I began showing signs of trouble—their status was already predicated by their assimilation and docile behavior. That sounds unkind, but the more trouble I got into, the more they distanced themselves from me, and the better-behaved they became. They weren't trouble like me, and maybe if they got the best grades, did the best work, and made the least amount of trouble, they'd get chosen by white kids as their tokens.

Here's a secret. Proximity to whiteness earned by the *opposite* of respectability—by being someone's danger and rebellion—has different terms and conditions. White feelings for me were intense and obsessive, only to disappear overnight. I was always losing white friends without explanation, only to learn later that their parents saw me as not just a bad influence but a legitimate threat to their future—a Jeze-bel stereotype that would drag them down into my underworld of poverty, crime, and dead ends. They forbade their kids from interact-ing with me because they tacitly couldn't bear the thought of their child living a life like mine.

But that doesn't mean I didn't benefit. Despite their parents' rejec-tion, my new proximity gave me access to a world I'd never known was possible. Two-story houses with curved staircases and "wings," families with second houses and horse ranches, tutors and college legacies and ideal lives, bored moms in Diane Keaton kitchens in spar-kling houses who drove cream Mercedes and had coke problems. Once white boys acknowledged me as an object of desire, I met white parents for the first time, and in their mothers I witnessed a version of womanhood I'd never known, beyond my teachers—comfort, luxury, Martha Stewart hospitality, security.

Before I go any further with this story, I must address its two prob-lems, complicated by feminized, racialized labor: the future, and the desire for whiteness. These are the dual drives of mestizaje, a desire shaped by the promise of safety, where the onus is on the woman to find a white partner and "improve the race" to survive. In exchange for the protection of whiteness, the woman provides domestic and inti-mate labor, and self-erases until she disappears.

DIDN'T YOU HAVE ANY SELF-RESPECT? WHY DID YOU AGREE TO BE their maid? It's not what I was originally hired to do. His mom and step-dad ran a successful plumbing business, and although they were from blue-collar backgrounds with only high school diplomas, they became millionaires almost overnight. I was supposed to help his mom in their home office with administrative duties, but after the first few days, my tasks began to move out of the office, and by the end of my first week I had a mop in my hand instead of a pen.

For a long time I thought I ended up as their maid by accident. Maybe she had to find tasks for me because I was hopelessly bad at math and messed up their accounting; maybe it was because I didn't know what an invoice was, or a lien (still don't); maybe she just really did need more help around the house, and with her new baby, than in the office. Either way, I had a car note to pay, and deep in the gauzy bliss of first love, I trusted her. Besides, I was *great* at cleaning and infant care; having spent the majority of my adolescence grounded, in trouble, and helping raise my baby brother, domestic labor was how I atoned, how I earned back trust, forgiveness, permission to go out and be a teenager.

I thought if I did the best possible job I could—if I was the best house cleaner, the best car washer, the best laundress, the best nanny, the quietest, hardworkingest, most deferential girl—I might someday even be asked to join their family. But that wouldn't ever be my future. Instead, being their maid did exactly what his mother meant it to do— divide our futures.

It doesn't matter now.

I MUST STOP AGAIN HERE AND ACKNOWLEDGE A FEW THINGS. I AM a light mestiza; some might even say I'm a white mestiza or white Latina. While I accept that label in relation, I will never self-identify as white because of my formative experiences as a Mexican American in

Texas. Believe me, I tried everything I could to pass as white in my youth, but every time I claimed it, it was denied. In middle school my friend Olivia gave me her disposable blue contacts when she was done with them, and I wore them until I couldn't stand the pain. I used light makeup, like my mom told me to. I stopped speaking Spanish. I disidentified with all Mexican and Latine culture. I even thought about changing my legal name to Kate Bennett, the plainest, most unassuming name I could think of. But as much as I performed and desired whiteness, no one ever let me claim it as my identity.

When I would say I had French or Italian ancestry, white people would respond, "Hmm, I don't see it." A MySpace date once said he was surprised to see my body in person because I was so *wide*, and that my face was rounder than my pictures, "almost like a Mayan sun." I still don't know what that means. When I would tell people my birth certificate said my race was white, I'd promptly get a history lesson on how Texas needed to manufacture a white majority for XYZ reasons, and that's why Mexicans were white "on paper." When I acted white in front of Mexicans, they would say, "Te crees bien gringa pero tienes el nopalote en la frente." *You think you're so white but you can't hide the big old cactus on your forehead.* The more I desired the safety of whiteness, to just be the default, the more everyone denied it to me. Still, I have to own this.

This is the deep programming of mestizaje. I'd interpreted all the signals from my environment correctly: to be racialized is to exist in a perpetual state of fugitivity, and to be feminized is to tie survival to men, both of which are futureless conditions. The desire for safety, which is the desire of a future, becomes a desire for whiteness.

Now whiteness consumes me without my consent. After a lifetime of being denied entry to whiteness, I am now denied the identity it took a lifetime to claim.

I'M NOT ASHAMED OF HAVING BEEN A MAID, ALTHOUGH IN HIND-sight, the position was *meant* to shame. Nothing quite puts you in your place like cleaning your first love's toilet, or filing away his perfect SAT scores (1590), or detailing the family Lexus with a toothbrush while they play in the pool. Labor shifts contexts between people, under-lines their origins and determines their futures, divides a story once headed in the same direction into different endings.

Anyway, his mother was right about me. My grandmother was a maid and an elder caretaker. My mother has held the same grocery-store job since she was eighteen; my father did roofing between bands; my uncles drive eighteen-wheelers; and the rest of my family come from, or are, farm laborers. I could not conceal my background in an office setting by dazzling her with my knowledge of e. e. cummings. I would never be more than a maid in her eyes, and she needed her son to see that before he ruined his future. As a Mexican girl (that's how she referred to me, *My son is dating a Mexican girl*), now Mexican woman, my primary value in America has always been, and will always be, my cheap labor. And I'm always so grateful for the chance to do that labor, for being chosen. No matter how many degrees I get or books I pub-lish, I will always be the help.

IT OCCURS TO ME NOW THAT THE CINDERELLA STORY NOT ONLY MIR-rors the immigrant dream of a "better life," it is also the core narrative that shaped my ideas of love and romance. In high school, the only rom-com I remember between a white and Latine lead is *Fools Rush In* with Salma Hayek and Matthew Perry, where Matthew Perry literally rides a mule through Mexico looking for his bride. At its core, the Cinderella story is a bootstraps narrative where love is inextricable from labor—it is not beauty, but the humility of labor that makes Cinderella exceptional, and therefore worthy of love and a fairy-tale ending.

That is also the narrative that drives the "good immigrant"—exceptional labor will make you worthy to the state, and with enough hard work, you'll get that house, that truck, that middle-class life. To be a good immigrant, a good worker, a good student, a good wife, is to begin every relationship from a disempowered position, where love is conditional. And when love is conditional to your value, safety is conditional, and even documents of permanence make no guarantees.

DOMESTIC LABOR IS A KIND OF TIME—THE HARDER, SLOWER LABOR invisibly turning the largest cog in the mechanism of the universe. It is the least valuable form of time, but the most necessary, which means those who do it become invisible people; they're literally in a different time. Migrant farmworkers, truck drivers, construction workers, janitors, maids—all specters of slavery and colonialism, all bodies outside of time. Wealthy white women hire help because their time is valuable and meant for more important things, like blowouts; motherhood sabotages even the most progressive careers because they lose valuable after-hours social time to their children. More time equals more future, and borders are sites of time extraction—the United States extracts labor, and therefore time, from the border, which results in more leisure time and longer life spans; and when you extract time from domestic workers, you extract entire futures.

My relationship with cleaning is fraught. Today I am an overworked single mother who, after a lifetime of cleaning up after men and boys and trying to earn love with labor, finds it hard to clean unless absolutely necessary. I'm disorganized and procrastinate on chores. Even washing my own dishes feels like standing in an anthill. My therapist says that it is a form of rebellion after a lifetime of being exploited, similar to "revenge bedtime procrastination," where mothers stay up late and sacrifice sleep to get some precious alone time for themselves, independent of children, family, or work demands (something I also do). And that's what it comes down to—time. I'm not messy because I'm undisciplined, I'm messy because I want the future I have constantly been denied.

So if the corners of my house fur at the edges with dust and hair, if every surface is covered with clutter in exchange for a future, so be it. I will never hire help—not that I can afford it. I can't stand doing my little computer job while someone else scrubs down my counters, makes my bed, mops my floor. I've been extracted from my whole life, and even though I desperately need the help, a kind of survivor's guilt holds me back. I refuse to take a little bit of someone's future for myself.

I also never want my son to be able to say, "We had a maid." He will never witness an immigrant woman, or her daughter, cleaning up after him as her job, as her place in the world. That has to break something in a child—some basic pillar of compassion. But when he won't clean his room or pick up after himself and I have to do it, it takes me back to myself at different points in time: at thirteen trying to earn an outing to the mall by cleaning the bathrooms; at eighteen detailing that three-story house in Spring, Texas, for eight hours; at twenty-six trying to show the man who would become my husband how good I was at domestic labor; at thirty-three cleaning the house between pumping sessions at two in the morning, ignoring the pain from my C-section scar. Domestic labor is how I have earned love from everyone, and I wonder if it's already too late to change that with my son. If he already sees me as the maid.

BY SENIOR YEAR, I'D BEEN THROUGH SOME SHIT—EXPULSION, ALTER-native school, mental hospital, sleazy jobs with sleazier bosses, multiple sexual assaults. So I skipped school constantly, which made adults suspect me of drinking or doing drugs. But substances were never my thing, except coffee and cigarettes. No, the only high I've ever chased is love.

I promised my mother I would at least graduate, so when I did come back for senior year, my college-bound white peers were surprised to see me. They thought I'd dropped out, fulfilling every stereotype they'd come to know about Mexican girls. So I found friends outside school at this all-night diner called Jojo's where the goths, geeks, stoners, and art punks gathered to drink coffee and smoke cigarettes among middle-aged blue-collar workers. The decor was wood paneling and macramé straight out of the 1970s, but the place was cheap, delicious, and unpretentious, and served as a commons for outsiders to find one another, play chess, and argue about music or politics or Star Wars.

One night two boys walked in—a slim, sandy-haired boy in Beat-poet cosplay and a theater queen in ripped jeans and eyeliner. They sat with us, liked my drawings, asked to go through my sketchbook, and sat for a portrait. And that was it. Isaac, the sandy-haired boy, be-came my favorite subject—I drew and painted him, wrote aching love poems, took dramatic black-and-white photographs of him with my Canon AE-1, documenting our once-in-a-lifetime romance. We were the stars of our own love story: that was Isaac's particular magic, the way his deep attention and spontaneity could make every moment feel as bright and thrilling as a living film, cameras rolling somewhere in the periphery.

Isaac was a *thespian*, a word I learned when I met him, and he indeed had more than a flair for the dramatic. To spend time with him was to seize every electric moment of life, where even the most mundane strip mall parking lot could become the site of some ridiculous obstacle course, any diner a stage for an ever-more-absurd improv game, any secluded circle of pines the most private, tender bed beneath the stars. The poet in me thrived on the intensity, on the shimmer of a white middle-class freedom I'd never known. Part of the romance of Isaac was that he lived a kind of Kerouacian dream life I could never pretend to claim, or fully surrender to. He could make every friendship feel like a romance, fashion his friends into the Dean Moriartys of East Texas (I'm still not a Kerouac fan), rewrite suburban kids as timeless, forever-young gods. The way he saw people made them see the eternal youth and beauty in themselves; by being tender, he could pull out your tenderness, by being silly, pull out your silliness, and for me, his love peeled back my armor, exposed my vulnerability, made the world feel brand-new.

This was the boy who, while driving through heavy traffic, spontaneously rolled down our windows, stuck his head out, and yelled, "I love Vanessa Angélica Villarreal!" over and over to anyone who would listen. I could never act like this in public without being followed or harassed by security. But to him, it didn't matter—love was not shameful, or dangerous, or embarrassing; caring was not yet creepy, nor simping yet a word. To him, love was vital, proof of life worth demonstrating to the world. Something softened in me with that kind of unashamed love, and I gave myself over to it completely. I'd never known a love like that, and haven't since.

But no one was more important to Isaac than Ren, a Black gender-nonconforming bisexual boy and self-proclaimed theater queen, and Isaac's best friend. Ren's Blackness and queerness would not be such a remarkable detail except for the oppressive whiteness of their rural Texas high school, and the rarity of such interracial, cross-class, queer platonic friendships between teenage boys. Their friendship was special, intense, loving, and wrought with erotic tension. With Isaac, Ren was safe—he could indulge in his queerness, wear makeup and costumes, sing, dance, act out. It would only be a matter of time before the forces of destiny ripped them apart—Isaac had a pending future, and Ren was bound for the military after graduation and already engaged to his long-term girlfriend (platonic or romantic, their relationship was unclear). And in the end, all of our classes would matter. The military would "fix" Ren's nonnormative behavior, lest he be disowned—all he had to do was give a few years of his life in exchange for a full-ride college degree. The military gave kids in hopeless situations a shot at a future, but only if you played Russian roulette with your life.

The last time I saw Renny was in the spring of 2000. He had glitter on his eyes and fuchsia lipstick. I taped the dragged heel of his jeans to a page in my sketchbook. He was leaving for the army soon, so Isaac drove us through a corridor of pines at midnight to an empty field to say goodbye. When he popped up on Facebook as someone I might know twenty years later—"Renaud" now—he was handsome and clean in his military uniform; married, subdued. I wanted something different for his life, but was so glad to see he'd survived, seemed happy. When the three of us first met, I loved Renny first—there was an instant recognition between us. We were both queer kids of color from the same side of the tracks, who both loved an impossible boy—a boy who, incredibly, loved us back.

ISAAC BROKE UP WITH ME IN 2001. THAT YEAR, AND IN THE YEARS that followed, it seemed like every depiction of white-Latine romance was a Cinderella story, some even explicitly about a maid: *Maid in Manhattan, Crazy/Beautiful, Spanglish.* Bennifer.

Perhaps the white-Latine love story with a Cinderella subnarrative is an echo of colonial conquest. Love between the Native woman and the invader legitimizes the conquest by depicting Indigenous acquiescence. From Rahab to Pocahontas to La Malinche to Neytiri from *Avatar,* the Indigenous woman is a metaphor for the land, and the love story between the white man and the Indigenous woman is the narrative that justifies the settlement of her land and people. Now, as an academic, I always want to historicize, look at the underlying social forces that trigger fantasy—why were Latinas being paired with wealthy businessmen in movies? There are many ongoing issues, like immigration fearmongering, gangs, but in the 1990s, there was a myth of a US-Mexico romance that would become exploitative, and that myth was NAFTA.

I hated *Maid in Manhattan.* Or I should say, I couldn't bring myself to watch *Maid in Manhattan,* despite my dad's love for Jennifer Lopez, and rom-coms being our thing to watch together. It was released in December 2002, the first of many years I spent lost in the dive bars and indie venues of the Heights in Houston, searching for Isaac in other people. I'd get a stomachache every time I saw the *Maid in Manhattan* poster, but I never put together why until writing this twenty years later. I finally watched it in 2021.

Maybe I couldn't watch it because I couldn't handle the irony of Jennifer Lopez going from playing Selena, a Mexican American icon— Grammy winner, record-breaker, entrepreneur, cultural titan—to playing a white man's maid. It felt personal, like being mocked. Even as a fantasy there's just no way a man of that class and status would ever fall in love with an immigrant brown hotel maid. You can't even get white men to tip housekeeping, much less see maids as human enough to date. The only way he even notices her is because of a case of mistaken identity when she tries on, and low-key steals, an important white woman's coat for a few hours. That's not a bibbidi-bobbidi-boo transformation—that's fraud.

I also hated Jennifer Lopez during this time for reasons I couldn't place, despite loving her long before anyone knew who she was. She first caught my attention in the early 1990s on *In Living Color,* where she was one of the Fly Girls. She was one of the first Latinas I saw on mainstream American television in a non-Latine context. Then I recognized her again in Janet Jackson's "That's the Way Love Goes" video. As Selena, she was incandescent—not just because of the way she played the singer but because she was the only person who *could* play her. One of Selena's main influences was Janet Jackson, a singer Jennifer Lopez was a dancer for. She understood the music that shaped Selena's body, structured her moves, how she moved the way she moved. It was destined, somehow. I have never been able to suspend disbelief in a biopic, but with *Selena,* I didn't even have to try.

Which is why JLo's 2000s career felt like such a betrayal. It seemed like she'd used the success of *Selena* to launch her career so sky-high, she transcended the stratosphere and entered the orbit of whiteness. After *Selena,* she embarked on her spicy-white era, playing ethnically ambiguous white women, most notably the Italian American Mary Fiore in *The Wedding Planner* (2001). Accounts vary as to why she played Italian—some say that film executives "felt the moviegoing public [had] no interest in the love life of an actual young Puerto Rican woman" and whitewashed her to remove any implication of WASPs engaging in racial or ethnic mixing. Others say Lopez was invited to change her ethnicity in the script, but she insisted they keep her as Italian. I get it—even if it was her choice, the rom-com is a genre about white upper-middle-class people falling in love, and the pressure to whitewash yourself, either to fit the genre or just to be taken seriously as an actress, is well documented in Hollywood history. Either way, no one bought it, and it hurt her in the film's reviews.

But perhaps the biggest symbol of her A-list status change was in her shift from dating men of color—rapper Sean "Puffy" Combs and Filipino dancer Cris Judd—to getting publicly engaged, with a million-carat Harry Winston pink diamond, not just to any white man but to Oscar winner, leading man, and Hollywood golden boy Ben Affleck in 2002.

It's hard to overstate how controversial their relationship was at the time. In the late 1990s to early 2000s, Ben Affleck was part of an impenetrably elite circle of Hollywood royalty. Before JLo, his last serious relationship was with his *Shakespeare in Love* costar Gwyneth Paltrow, who won an Oscar for Best Actress while they were together. So when he went from the elegant blond Gwyneth Paltrow to Jennifer Lopez, a Puerto Rican singer-actress from the Bronx best known for her roles as a Mexican and a maid, the white backlash was brutal.

Isaac was only half-wealthy, with an eccentric, long-haired father who sold fireworks and worked odd jobs, which is what made him attracted to odd characters, eccentrics, queers, and misunderstood loners, able to see people's true essence beyond their circumstances. He wasn't the typical rich suburban kid who goes slumming to rebel against their parents or prove something to the world; he was a true old soul, with a wisdom beyond his years and a way of looking at the

Drawing of Isaac in my sketchbook, dated September 22, 1999. Jojos, Houston, Texas.

Drawing I gave Isaac as a gift in 2000. I asked for it back after we broke up in 2001, which he was reluctant to do.

world with an expansive generosity, like he was born in the wrong time. He devoured old books even faster than me, beyond the Beats, in any genre— *Stranger in a Strange Land, One Hundred Years of Solitude, Zen and the Art of Motorcycle Maintenance, The Lord of the Rings, Native Son,* Sylvia Plath's collected poems. I remember lying down on our linoleum kitchen floor one night, my parents stepping over me, because it was as far as the phone cord could reach, so we could talk about *A Farewell to Arms* for three hours because we were obsessed with the love story.

Although I never had to wonder about how Isaac felt about me, I was sometimes curious how he saw me. He knew all about my troubled past, the hardships I survived, my hospitalization, my money issues, what my house looked like, why I had to go to college in Houston and stay near my parents. When I graduated, my bisabuela Carmen and tía Lupe made the trip from the Rio Grande Valley and Matamoros, respectively, at great personal cost, to watch me graduate. They were both non-English-speaking, and most of the day Isaac was amid Spanish-only conversations, with the occasional kind smile at him and random hug from my family.

Every other time Isaac called my house, my dad would answer the phone—*¿Bueno?*—a detail Isaac loved so much that he started answering the phone with it anytime I called and GILBERTO VILLARRE popped up on his caller ID. "¿Bueno?" Isaac would answer, a smile in his voice. It was something endearing my dad did that Isaac echoed back to me, an intimate recognition of our difference that no one else thought to do.

To be truly known by someone, a peer I admired, and someone I loved for the first time, to be believed in, broke me open, exposed a deep hunger for meaning I didn't realize I'd been deprived of. And that's what excessive discipline, punishment, and racism does to a person—it deprived my imagination of meaning, purpose, possibility, belief in the things that drive someone toward a future. Maybe I wasn't bad after all; maybe I had been good all along. School became easy. My anger and cynicism were channeled into focus and belief. All it took was someone loving me. And what is the future if not wild imagining, purpose, belief?

———

THE IRONY IS THAT, WITHOUT EXAGGERATION, JENNIFER LOPEZ could have won an Oscar for her performance in *Selena* the same year Ben Affleck won for *Good Will Hunting*—the heads of Warner Bros. just refused to fund her campaign because the Academy "would never nominate a Latina," they said. By 1998, no woman of color had *ever* won an Oscar for Best Actress. That wouldn't happen until 2001, when Halle Berry would become the first Black woman to win the honor for *Monster's Ball*. It's an award that usually boosts careers, but for Berry it all but secured a string of heavily panned failures, including *Gothika* and *Catwoman*, an all-time "worst film."

A less-discussed statistic: by 1998 no Latina had *ever even been nominated* by the Academy for Best Actress. The first Latina nominee was white Brazilian actress Fernanda Montenegro in 1999 (who incidentally was beat out by Gwyneth Paltrow).

Gregory Nava, *Selena's* writer and director, strongly believed that Lopez's rare Golden Globe nomination—often a sign of a real shot at an Oscar for a white actor—should have been proof enough for Warner Bros. But *Selena* was a low-budget film for a culturally niche audience, produced on a mere $20 million ($50 to $100 million is the average). An Academy Award nomination requires studios to invest millions of dollars in a six-month campaign—there was no way they were going to spend half of the entire film's budget on an unknown Latina, not in the same year they were up against a film like *Titanic*.

I recognize that these are impossibly rich, successful celebrities who are hard to sympathize with, especially since Lopez is notorious for being rude to fans and service workers. But a celebrity's public life is a relevant cultural subtext that everyone shares, and its analysis is perhaps one of the only ways of making invisible cultural forces visible. Britney Spears's life and career, for example, is a global living text that has been extensively dissected not just to reveal misogyny but to make visible *how* misogyny works systemically—*how* misogyny enables exploitation, shapes public opinion, how it plays into mental health stigma and limits autonomy. The public analysis of her conservatorship is an accessible discourse that not only had a real impact on her life but has value as an articulation of mental health, labor, and disability rights.

The public breakdown of Bennifer has rarely been articulated. The fall from grace of Affleck, once known as half of the "genius" behind *Good Will Hunting*, was a sight to behold. It's almost as if the culture wanted to punish him for being with Lopez, for breaking some kind of invisible pact. When he costarred with Lopez in *Gigli*, both of their names became associated with one of the worst films of all time. It was considered good taste to hate her (Matt Damon reportedly *hated* her), and frame that hate as concern for Affleck's once-promising career. In screen tests for *Jersey Girl*, another film where they played a couple, Lopez was so reviled by audiences that they cut the majority of her scenes.

I started working at a used bookstore in 2003, at the height of Bennifer, when Lopez and Affleck appeared on the front page of every tabloid and were impossible to ignore. Back then, I was a hipster snob who was way too cultured to care about celebrities, so I ignored them when maybe I shouldn't have. One purple summer evening I took a copy of *Rolling Stone* out to the loading dock on my smoke break. I remember I wanted to read a profile on Franz Ferdinand but was embarrassed to be seen with the magazine because there was a terribly loud picture of Ben Affleck on the cover. The profile was short, so I skimmed the Affleck interview just to kill time as I finished my cigarette. Then this quote stuck out (italics mine):

> But it was his union with Lopez that really rankled, particularly when her glittering lifestyle drew him in, and *he traded his scruffy jeans and Red Sox caps* for *slicked-back hair and velour tracksuits*

(although who among you has not had a wardrobe tweaked by a new love?).

Affleck says he doesn't know why their union caused such a hostile reaction. "Hopefully I can get far enough away from it in time to be able to get a better sense of it," he says, although he suspects the hostility *"had something to do with race and class. That* pushed a button. This is a country that flew into a gigantic up-roar about Janet Jackson's breast. *There's still a heavy-duty puritan influence going on, and we still hold ourselves to a pretty chaste ideal, which includes, buried within it, the tradition of people being with people like them. We were thought of as two different kinds of people, not just racially but culturally." Perhaps that's why the tabloids have gone easier on Lopez dating singer Marc Anthony.* Affleck lights another of his menthol Marlboro Lights. "Basically, it just came down to, *Wow, I never thought those two would get together.'"*

The interview goes on to describe instances where Affleck played into his ex-fiancée's fetishization, namely when Howard Stern asked about JLo's ass. But this stuck out: *He traded his scruffy jeans and Red Sox caps for slicked-back hair and velour tracksuits.* Code for "He traded his wholesome all-American whiteness for urban streetwear associated with Black and Latino culture." And that's when it all clicked.

Affleck grew up in Cambridgeport, Massachusetts, a working-class ethnic enclave in Boston, formerly segregated and zoned for immigrants. He was raised by a single mother—his father was a semi-employed blue-collar jack-of-all-trades and a bookie with a drinking problem who left early in Ben's life. His working-class, inner-city upbringing was much closer to Lopez's Bronx than to Paltrow's South of France, but in America the invention of race is meant to make poor whites self-segregate from the rest of the working class and, through the status of whiteness, identify with the rich, so much that they will actively vote against their own interests. In the eyes of the American public, and encoded in American media, Affleck "fit" more with Gwyneth Paltrow, because he should be with someone white like him.

Later on in the article, the writer, Jancee Dunn, misspells the name of the Mexican restaurant they went to as Paquito Más instead of Poquito Más, probably conflating the word *poquito* with *taquito* and never bothering to get it right or correct the mistake. When I found the article online while writing this, the restaurant name remains misspelled twenty years later, no correction.

I could never bring myself to watch *West Side Story* either, not until I had to for research at thirty-nine years old. I don't like musicals generally—the music and mannerisms are so corny they give me secondhand embarrassment—but the way the Jets and the Sharks snap and jive at each other to externalize racialized conflict is over-the-top offensive to me. The entire play is an act of brownface. Everything about it is hollow and rings false. The story was originally supposed to be a New York take on *Romeo and Juliet,* but set in the conflict of anti-Semitism between Jewish and Irish Catholic neighborhoods; then later it evolved into the gangs of the Chicano turf wars in East Los Angeles, to be called *East Side Story,* but was moved back to New York's Upper West Side and changed to Puerto Ricans (interchangeable cultures, I guess) because no one involved in the production knew anything about Mexican Americans. And you can feel it—the writers of *The King and I* and *Peter Pan* never spent any substantial amount of time in Spanish Harlem, never listened to the rhythm and hybridity of Puerto Rican speech, never felt the island form between people. They just imagined what Puerto Ricans were like, what they sound like. Probably like the Lost Boys from *Peter Pan?* Making a little song and dance with jive talk is how whiteness sanitizes the heavy structural violence of segregation, aestheticizes its own gaze. But the worst part is the message: What is the consequence of a love that dares to cross borders? The death of the white man in the end, which fills Maria with hate.

I DIDN'T UNDERSTAND WHAT HAPPENED BETWEEN ISAAC AND ME, not fully in those first few years after we broke up. He seemed so regretful, so resigned. I remember finding his MySpace one night and reading two posts in his blog section, one that said something like "Hey ex-girlfriend, where are you? How are you? Are you happy?" and another, "I'll never forget this poem, it's almost absurd in its simplicity, it took you thirty seconds to blow my mind." The post was one of my short poems he'd memorized.

A few weeks after we broke up, I did my best to appear exceptionally happy and busy with bands from the Houston indie scene. One night I openly and loudly talked about seeing other people while he was within earshot, forcing him to put cash on his table and leave.

I don't remember how I received this card, I was so overwhelmingly crushed and grieving. Did he give it to me the day he broke up with me? Had he driven to my work to give it to me afterward? Did he drop it off at a table one night? I don't remember. All I remember is the pain. His final letter:

Dear Vanessa,

My world is literally filled with fragments of you. . . . There's still poetry on my wall that you penned. Pictures of you dot my wallet

*and my wall. . . . Part of me breaks whenever one of your fragments . . .
meanders its way back into my life. . . . It's most important that you
realize that we did not break up because of any shortcomings that
you . . . had as a girlfriend. We broke up because of a thousand
things that were eating our relationship and making it hard to
continue. . . . I will love you for the rest of my life.*

Isaac

When I opened the card, a photo of us was enclosed. We're at a
diner; he is dressed in a thrifted button-up shirt, I'm in my work
clothes after a shift, still wearing my Guitar Center lanyard. I have a
big smile on my face, but his mien is overcast, tender, somewhat sad.

I WISH MY FIRST LOVE WERE AS SIMPLE AS A RICH-POOR KIND OF
love story, like *Pretty in Pink* or *Dirty Dancing* or *The Notebook* or Selena's
"Amor Prohibido," where two kids from opposite classes but similar
hearts find love against all odds. Maybe there's a disapproving family
member, or a judgmental friend or community, but their disapproval
only intensifies the youthful rush of infatuation, the drama of not being allowed to see each other only heightening the electric tenderness
of nervous first times. When both parties are of the same race or ethnicity, class may separate them, but the future is still equally available
to both. But when one partner is racialized, especially the one with the
least power, the future *is* the complication—whiteness, once secure of
its future, must now contend with the condition of racialized futurelessness as its own fate.

Will the brown girl drag the white boy down? Where will they live? Will they have the same opportunities? What will the babies look like? I've seen how these questions play out with my own eyes. With my father, the darkest of his family, and how Dolores, his mother, always loved him the least for being the darkest, with a stranger's features and pelo chino, how she hated my most beautiful cousin for being prieta, and hated my mother for being morena, corriente. How on the night she met my baby brother for the first time, asleep and cooing in his car seat, she told my father the baby was too dark-skinned to be his, that my mother had stepped out on him and gotten knocked up by some chuntaro. Dolores already hated me for being my mother's daughter, but she wouldn't even acknowledge my brother—a doe-eyed, pecan-brown baby wrapped in a white blanket—the darkest, and most beautiful, of us all.

I've always bristled when people say, "You never forget your first love," because for me it's synonymous with "You never forget your place." I don't remember my first love in all its earnest innocence. Instead I remember myself through the eyes of his mother, how I must have looked to her—a poor, hypersexual, hyperfertile brown Jezebel who would trap him with a baby and ruin his life. And this is how our story ends; not the natural growing apart of first loves, its forking paths en route to separate futures, but because his bright future was threatened by my no-future, and that is the deepest betrayal of whiteness—the denial, and theft, of the future.

I am always complimented on my hair—its full, thick black waves. Once, when I was cleaning our house, my ex-husband said wearing my hair up in a bun did me no favors. It just looked really *stereotypical* when I cleaned the house. I had never seen myself through his eyes like that before. I wonder how I must have looked to Isaac's mother back then. Hair up, mop in hand. Maybe that's how she finally made him see the maid, the dead-end girl she saw. The memory of that house is still so sharp after all these years: carrying a mop and a bucket up the carpeted stairs, his room the first door on the left, me on my knees, scrubbing my first love's toilet for $7 an hour.

Too bad she never counted on me becoming a writer for real.

Encyclopedia of All the Daughters I Couldn't Be

Bien Educada

I will need the hospital records from Gulf Pines Psychiatric Hospital to apply to college, since it was technically my "school" during my expulsion, says my high school counselor. She asks me what colleges I want to apply to. I tell her the schools that sent me pamphlets: Reed College, Sarah Lawrence, Oberlin, Vassar. The University of Texas, I add. She's a soft, gray-haired, flush-pink white lady, with small, mean blue eyes, hard and shiny as marbles, and a heavy Texan accent, so that even the "tuh!" sound she makes has boots on. *Maybe Stanford*, I add, goading her. She tells me to brace for disappointment, to think about community college.

After high school, almost all my friends went off to college in New York, San Francisco, RISD, or their "safety school" (a mindblowing term—you should apply to multiple schools?), where they would be accepted by default to the University of Texas at Austin, thanks to the Top Ten Percent rule—a rule I never knew existed, but once I did, would never qualify for.

My parents wouldn't have known how to prepare me for college applications—a factor I'd never considered until senior year, when I fill out my first FAFSA: *Mother's highest level of education: Some high school. Father's highest level of education: Middle school.* They didn't know sophomore year was for résumé-packing, or that junior year was the "bear-down" year, your last shot at boosting your GPA, the year I almost dropped out. By senior year, I'd fallen out with nearly all my friends from advanced classes except the artists, the goths, the punks, the runaways, and the second-chance kids from PDAP, the Palmer Drug Abuse Program, a free group therapy program I occasionally attended with a friend. (I didn't do drugs at all—after sophomore year of high school, my vices were strictly coffee and cigarettes.) After being expelled, I was just trying to survive school, assuming I'd go to college one day but with no idea how, and as a result, my GPA was absolutely dismal. 2.7 something.

I didn't know if I could even apply to college with my troubled background. I was an anomaly—too fucked-up and angry for regular school, too soft and naive for disciplinary programs, too hopeful and optimistic for the psych hospital. "If you would only apply yourself," said every teacher, principal, coach, therapist, friend, and lunch lady. And I could, but only in art and humanities classes.

I had a decent list of achievements, most of them unofficial. I was the only student in Texas to win *two* Scholastic Gold Keys in both painting and photography one year. My test scores were nearly perfect in reading and writing, but so remedial in math, I had to retest, probably on suspicions of cheating. I was never nominated for an editorship on the literary magazine, but I did so much work for it, I was credited as "Wonder Girl" on the masthead—not as impressive as "Editor in Chief," which is the title Calliope had. I was in the National *Art* Honor Society, not the National Honor Society. And I played absolutely no sports, but due to the homophobic harassment I got in the locker room, I was allowed to run the five-kilometer route with the cross-country track team sophomore and junior year. I was invited to try out, but it wasn't something I could ever afford and, thus, couldn't put on my résumé.

My college application must have looked bizarre—a could-have-been-valedictorian in the arts and humanities but a troubled youth everywhere

else, like a scale with rare books and gold bars on the right side, and one shoelace, some gum, and a cigarette butt on the other. I could only afford to apply to two schools: the University of Texas at Austin ("the best state school in the country! Austin is such a great town") and the University of Houston ("commuter school, glorified community college, in 'the ghetto'").

By some act of god, I managed to get my GPA up to the top 25 percent of my class by graduation, like 3.75 or something. How? I really don't know, I'm not good at math.

I got into both schools. Sort of. The envelope from the University of Houston was large and heavy, and in the acceptance letter, a cream-colored invitation on card stock informing me I'd also been accepted to the Honors College. By contrast, the envelope from the University of Texas was a slim, standard letter-size envelope with one piece of paper in it, informing me I'd been accepted on "provisional admission," which meant I would have to enroll on academic probation for a year, and if after the trial period I made good enough grades, the school wouldn't publicly sacrifice me to a longhorn. Would I choose Houston, the school that actually wanted me, or would I choose Texas, the school that only conditionally accepted me?

Needless to say, for once in my life, I made the right choice and accepted Houston, and after a great freshman year (a C in College Algebra!), I . . . decided to transfer to the University of Texas. Someone I loved had chosen a future in Austin over me, and I was desperate to prove I could get there. And that's when I no longer qualified for provisional admission, and they rejected me outright. Twice.

Anyway, UT was right about me—I failed out of UH my second year. My Saturn was too shitty to handle the fifty-mile round-trip commute, and slowly broke down driving between school and two full-time jobs on opposite ends of the city. After my first year, I just couldn't hang on, and lost my grip. I failed precalculus. Twice. And failing one class meant that I didn't get credit for twelve hours, I got credit for nine, which meant I was no longer, by definition, a full-time student. I lost my Pell Grant, and because I couldn't pay my tuition, finally had no choice but to drop out. I just didn't know how to do this.

That disastrous second year, a woman started calling the house asking for my father. That's how I found out about his other daughter, a secret child he had with this woman

the year after I was born. She was calling because the girl was in juvenile detention and needed help. He denied it, of course, but when he finally owned up to it, he showed me pictures of a girl who looked kind of like me, and almost exactly like him—long mercurial face, black hair, bony features, deep olive skin. She wanted to meet me, he said, and gave me the address to send a letter to juvi—a fate that I had also been headed toward, and narrowly avoided. I'd just completed my freshman year of college and sent her what I'd read—*Leaves of Grass*, *Duino Elegies*, the novel *Caucasia*, band stickers. I wish I hadn't been so pretentious in what I sent. We never communicated again.

When MySpace came on the scene, I'd check up on classmates at UT, Harvard, NYU—they'd gotten Vespas, taken a gap year in Paris, interned at Google in vintage T-shirts and Goodwill loafers, had their first art opening in New York. Me? I worked two jobs, failed out of UH, and was taking one class per semester at Lone Star Community College. And I hated that feeling—not of jealousy, but of my own futurelessness, of living on another kind of time.

I had to get to Austin. But the harder I tried, the harder the city bounced me. Every few months I'd make the road trip there, hoping to run into Isaac, or anyone I knew, unsure of why I was really there.

On my final visit to Austin in 2003, one night I turned the wrong way on Guadalupe, a two-way street that became a one-way by the state capitol. As soon as I realized I was going the wrong way, two state trooper cars flashed their lights and wailed their sirens, indicating that I pull into a nearby 7-Eleven parking lot. I hadn't seen them behind me— my rearview mirror had melted off the windshield, and my side mirror had been broken off in a parking lot months ago and now dangled on the side of the car. But it was the only mirror I had, and I made the mistake of reaching for it to see behind us.

"KEEP YOUR HANDS INSIDE THE VEHICLE," one of them said through the PA speaker.

Upon running my driver's license, the one with the ruddy face asked me why I was in Austin.

"No reason, just visiting." (*A boy left a gaping wound in my chest.*)

His flashlight sliced into the car, onto the gearshift, into the backseat, where I had my guitar case and a bunch of books and CDs.

"Do you know you have warrants for your arrest?"

"No, I didn't know." I did.

He proceeded to list off my outstanding tickets—three in total, including one I'd just gotten in Giddings, Texas.

Here, the details blur. The second one asks me to step out of the vehicle, pushes me up against the side of the car, puts me in handcuffs, and begins to ask me questions, search me. They say nothing to the thin, blond, blue-eyed girl in the front seat named Lindsay, a coworker from Half Price Books, who had more than a quarter bag of weed in her floral hippie bag— weed that again, I didn't partake in. But they left her alone—she wasn't driving, and I was the one with unpaid tickets, warrants, an illegal vehicle with an expired inspection, no rearview, and a hanging side mirror. The one people have always wanted to teach a lesson.

Of course, they find nothing. "All right, miss, you have one of two options," one of them said. His uniform is tan beige, with a gold star on black leather on the breast. "You can either pay off these tickets now, or we can take you to jail. Your choice."

I couldn't go to jail. I'd lose my jobs. "I can't go to jail, I have to work tomorrow. I'll pay them, how much do I owe? Will it be enough to keep me out of jail?"

"Let me check." The trooper walks back to his car, speaks codes into the radio. After some time, he comes back. I must have been looking down, because all I remember are cowboy boots. "Including fees and penalties, $950."

I just didn't have it. My paychecks were $500 every two weeks at Starbucks, and $700 at the bookstore. But freshman year of college, I had signed up for a Capital One credit card, to help out with textbooks. That card had about a $900 balance remaining, I explain to the troopers.

"That'll work. There's an ATM in there." He nods at the 7-Eleven as he unlocks my handcuffs.

In the store, they don't know I'm a criminal, they don't know I'm paying the cops, do they? I walk to the back of the store to a small gray ATM. The screen is dim, white. The withdrawal limit is $300 per transaction, with outrageous transaction fees. By the third one, I don't have enough and can only come up with $780 cash. I come back to the officers. I explain the situation, the cash advance, ATM fees.

They take the cash and drive away. On the drive home, the transmission on my car will break down on Highway 290 and I will have to be towed back to Houston. I paid dearly for that trip, not just with every cent I had plus a payday loan but with a dream. I would never be good enough for Austin, or have access to the future it promised. I eventually fell behind on car payments. Months later, a tow truck came in the middle of the night to repossess the car, and as I watched it get dragged away, I finally got the message: I wasn't going anywhere. Now carless, futureless, dreamless, I get an envelope in the mail from Giddings, Texas.

The warrants are still outstanding, tickets unpaid.

Good Immigrant

My mother does not want me to write that she was undocumented, she wants me to write that President Reagan gave all undocumented immigrants amnesty in 1986. She does not want me to write who remains undocumented because they could not take advantage of Reagan's amnesty offer. She does not want me to write that she had to drop out of high school to support her family. People at her work might get the wrong idea about her. Some might find out she was "illegal," and therefore criminal.

What she wants everyone to know is that she is a good immigrant, and smart, and American. She wants you to know she supported her brother, her mother, and her family on her own dime without any help from the government, bought her own house *and* everyone's car.

And I want you to know that she has worked at the same grocery chain for over forty years hardly missing a day, and is not only outstanding at her job but exceptional; not just head and shoulders above her peers but a visionary who has completely revolutionized her field. All of that is also true.

Neither narrative does her justice. Her life is one lived in amnesty, under

My mom and me, with a Michael Jackson Pepsi cutout promo she brought home from work, in front of the chimney in our new house, 1988.

pardon for her "political offenses"— arriving as a child. To live under pardon is to live a life in constant gratitude, where your very existence is an apology, proving that you deserve that grace. That is a conditional life, lived by the value of her labor. She can't just be good, she must exceed the quality expected of others just to earn her place; she can't just be good, she must be exemplary in her behavior and performance; she can't just be good, she must maintain an impeccable record, or risk losing her value to the state. And as a mother, provider, caretaker, and eldest daughter, everyone depends on her value. Everyone she loves becomes the state.

VOLVER, VOLVER

If I, for instance, want to tell you that a man I loved, who died, said he loved me on a curbstone in the snow, but this occurred in time after he died, and before he died, and will occur again in the future, I can't say it grammatically. You would think I was talking about a ghost, or a hallucination, or a dream, when in fact, I was trying to convey the experience of a certain event as scattered, and non-sequential.

—FANNY HOWE, "BEWILDERMENT"

IN ANOTHER LIFE, I AM BOILING CUT POTATOES IN A LARGE, SILVER drum, awaiting the arrival of friends. It is the fall of 2014 and I scarcely recognize myself—I am thirty-two, married, and somehow, four months pregnant the minute after graduating. In this timeline, I like cooking for others, which I hope will translate into some maternal instinct I still do not have.

Tonight I am starting to show, so I will joke about how maybe I don't want children after all. It is a good joke because it's something I'm not allowed to feel about motherhood. Instead of joy, I feel dysmorphia, fear, grief for all the things I still wanted to do, disgust at how white and heteronormative my life has become, resentment at how despite all of my contraceptive efforts, I am the 0.10 percent that gets pregnant with an IUD. It was as if this baby willed himself into existence, my life now aligned to some cosmic clock beyond my control.

I wash my knife, rinse the cutting board. I spring the sausage from its casing, laugh a little. I'm being immature. In this moment, I've jumped years ahead to be silly with my little boy. No one ever tells you that pregnancy is a time dilation; I am no longer living my one life but am now a point on a timeline, a nexus of timelines, expanding into many pasts and many futures. I collapse into my own birth, my mother's birth, her mother's birth, the first

My grandmother Angélica López on her wedding day. She is fourteen or fifteen here, and the groom, my grandfather Jesús Gutiérrez, has been blacked out, ca. 1957.

birth, all stored as an ancient memory in my cells, the baby growing from an ancient blueprint. History imagining itself as the future. In my body are two brains, two hearts. It's a mysterious thing.

I think of my abuelita, remember how she'd look down at me while cooking to make me laugh. I have a very old portrait of her taken on her wedding day, in a past before my mother or I were born. She was fourteen when she got married to the first man she would escape from three years later. The original portrait had the groom, my abuelo, standing behind her, but in the version I own, he is redacted from the photo, his body replaced by a vertical bar of black. Somehow the photo is more true this way, with her standing alone on the border between black and blue, her face serene as the moon. The blue is what remains of the past, while the black is the hand that

206

overwrites it from the future. Looking at the photo, you'd have no idea anyone once stood behind her unless I told you. **He has ceased to be a part of her story, our history.**

'Cause you could never know that
In a time trap
—BUILT TO SPILL, "TIME TRAP"

I wrote the first draft of this essay while four months pregnant, on September 27, 2014, before I would read it to a live audience that same night. It was an expansive, hopeful time, forward-looking, full of possibility and uncertainty, hope and doubt. I was fresh out of graduate school and two years into a marriage that would end three years later.

When I found this essay later in the future, there was an uncanny feeling of recognition, as if no time had passed, but also embarrassment at my naiveté, moments that needed more precision, new insight and depth. But in those moments I could feel my younger self reaching toward some difficulty I could not name, some premonition of collapse. To reread this essay at forty, divorced, and mostly always alone, I can hardly recognize the optimism of my thirty-two-year-old self. It's a portrait of a self who dared to hope, but whose conclusions would not be true, and I needed to redact.

The version you are reading now is the product of the eight years that followed—a birth, a move to Los Angeles for my PhD program, the abrupt end of my marriage, the shift into single motherhood, extreme austerity, and hard work—but also the triumph of personal achievement, the space to live a writing life for a little while, to build a life finally on my terms. So like my grandmother's wedding portrait, in this essay,

I'm redacting and overwriting the past with my future hand. I've left the original **bolded and in gray**, with my 2022 additions set in regular text.

Yo sé perder, yo sé perder,
quiero volver, volver, volver.
—VICENTE FERNÁNDEZ, "VOLVER, VOLVER"

Yo sé perder
Pero, ah-ah-ay, ¡cómo me duele!
—SELENA, "COMO LA FLOR"

The art of losing isn't hard to master.
—ELIZABETH BISHOP, "ONE ART"

I'm afraid of raising a man who will hurt someone, and that's why I am ashamed to admit I wanted a girl.

When the nurse said, "Well, it looks like you're having a little . . ." her pause stopped time, flooded with scenes of **my parents, their** failures, my failures, **invented scenes of the past, an image of a little girl laughing with her** papi. **Was it me?** Or was **it the life I imagined I'd give my daughter?** I remind myself: *Gender is not essential, nor yours to assign. A daughter is not a second chance to redo your life. A son is not a reincarnation of the men who hurt you.*

My father never cared for **Vicente Fernández, or "Chente" as the people affectionately called him** before he passed away in December 2021. Instead, my father called him **"viejo sangrón,"** recognizing something toxic about his masculinity. *Sangrón* **means heavy-blooded, arrogant, and as a ranchero singer, he was famous for it,**

upholding an old-world machismo channeled through his powerful, mourning voice and classic heritage trajes. He was a kind of relic, a callback to a romanticized Mexico, when mustachioed men heroically ranged the land on horses and abducted their wives from the fields. (It happened to my great-grandmother, true story. My great-grandfather Aurelio abducted her on horseback from the rancho she worked on as a teenager. She always claimed she went willingly.) But Vicente Fernández was also emblematic of the conservatism common to Mexican machismo, often expressing regressive misogynist views and virulent homophobia throughout his career—familiar attitudes in my family that even my father struggles to evolve out of himself.

I have only ever known gender as a modality of violence. As an eldest daughter, I bore the corporal discipline of 1950s Mexico until I was nineteen years old. When I was thirteen, my father removed my bedroom door so that I could not sneak out or have any privacy. My brother and I often compare our starkly different childhoods—I was the only one raised this way. Mexican parents coddle their sons and punish their daughters, so my brother was never disciplined with a belt, a shoe, a slap across the face, or a hair pull. Machismo and marianismo are two sides of the same coin, and each gender role begins at home. I was expected to perform a respectable femininity by being obedient, hardworking, sexually pure, and self-sacrificing—a family's respectability is reflected in the obedience of their daughters. But no matter how far from Mexico my grandmother had to flee, somehow my parents still ended up reproducing the same compulsory gender roles, the same misogyny that manifests as violence and femicide in Mexico. Marianismo is a deeply encoded set of behaviors I carry in my cells—a role I still struggle to evolve out of myself.

Perhaps I did not want a girl but a daughter—to experience the mystery of daughterhood as an expression of time. I am the eldest daughter of an eldest daughter of an eldest daughter, a nested coil of matrilineal time. I was already in my grandmother's body when she was pregnant with my mother, present on this earth as a molecule of tissue in 1958. To be a mother to a daughter is to experience a lineage as simultaneous—by loving her in ways none of us have ever been loved, I could untangle my ancestors from some primeval, cosmic pain in the past while liberating the future.

A son can be a daughter.

My grandmother, and all the elder matriarchs of my family, loved Chente, just as they have always loved their men and sons best, no matter how toxic or violent. Perhaps his masculinity was less threatening from afar, instead reflecting strength, protection, safety, romance. For them, to watch him sing was like entering a portal into the past, or the past that could have been, calling from a sentimental version of home. For them, Vicente's voice had the ability to bridge impossible distances across time and space—Houston to Tamaulipas, McAllen to Mexico City, Edinburgh to Puerto Vallarta. There are no borders in the geographies of feeling and memory.

Arguably, his most famous song is "Volver, Volver," a ranchera slow jam sung by a man in a state of desperate, passionate longing and deep regret. He laments a lost love, dying to return to the woman he left—now, in a state of clarity, he admits she was right about everything. In my mind, the relationship he sings about was an abusive one. She once told him to listen to his heart, but his obstinacy ended everything messily, abruptly, decidedly. But although he longs for his lost love, still, his pride will not let him return. He talks to himself mid-song: "Y no vuelves porque no quieres, papacito!" *And you do not return because you don't want to, little man!*

It's not that he doesn't want to return, but that to return is to cede power. He will not let her win by coming back—to do so is to disempower **himself,** despite his feelings. It is better to hold on to power and endure a needless separation rather than apologize or plead to a woman. This is the kind of machismo taught in **Mexican** culture as a form of respectability. And this is also how I was raised: to accept the terms of **male** power and call it self-respect; to let men go; to never chase; to show nothing but strength and silent dignity through painful losses. And a man would be raised to be proud, prioritize his needs, believing that the world is for him, there is always something better, to never come back. *He does not return because he does not have to.* **We have been** leaving **one another for generations.**

The use of "**volver**" in this song is not just about the desire to return to **his** love, however, but about the endless loop of grief and regret—**he returns and returns to his thoughts, his lamentation, to scenarios** of what could have been. **His mind springs into a state of temporal simultaneity—a lamentation of the past, the forgone future, a fanning out of different scenarios if he were only a different kind of man.** The bliss of her love and the grief of losing her held in the same hand. In the loop of grief, **the present is infinite. Time freezes** when one is unable to move on. **The song itself stops time—** all the instruments go silent so that Vicente's voice is isolated, a cappella: "**Y volver,** volver, volver!" *Oh, to return, return, return!* But he does not; it is a wish sung into a bottle.

I have witnessed this state of drunken regret more times than I can count. While I'm lucky to have parents who rarely drink, as a child I saw my uncle and grandmother drink themselves into oblivion a few times. And much as in the song, when my uncle drank, he was full of regret. But when my grandmother drank, the past would return in a tidal wave of rage and despair.

Stars in her eyes
She fights for the power, keeping time
She grinds day and night
—BEYONCÉ, "6 INCH"

The first time I caught my spouse cheating was in February 2016, two months before the premiere of Beyoncé's *Lemonade* on HBO, and one year after our son was born.

Pregnancy sets off a chain of hormonal events in the bodies of both parents to facilitate intense bonding and safeguard against abandonment and betrayal. It's a kind of evolutionary safety mechanism, oxytocin, hardwiring the body's chemistry to create instinctual attachments. But even before our son's first day on earth, something had already begun to pull my husband out of orbit. My pregnancy was not a happy one, beginning with his suggestion that I abort, only to become a long, slow abandonment—a reality I was fighting to ignore.

One night, while I was feeding the baby, the heaviness in my marriage became too much to bear. The energetic signature of neglect, resentment, and conflict in the air took on a monstrous form, a dark presence in the room beckoning me to pay attention to my animal body, to the siren blaring deep in my amygdala. To survive my marriage, I'd had to disconnect from my body and suppress my intuition for years. But in the deep silence of feeding my child in the middle of the night, my inner voice could finally surface.

I didn't know what I was looking for until I found it.

As a rejoinder to "Volver, Volver," I think of the end of Beyoncé's song "6 Inch," the fifth track on *Lemonade*, the album I consider to be her magnum opus. The song comes after the prideful "Sorry," where she tells her cheating husband to "suck on [her] balls," and ends by assuring him that she and her baby will be all right without him. More than a visual album, *Lemonade* is a work of speculative nonfiction—a film about the pain of infidelity in a marriage, performed through personae, selves that, without divulging specific details, collage poetry, documentary footage, and music to stage a personal narrative of grief. In the film, the poet Warsan Shire writes the poetic connective tissue between the songs called "chapters" in the film, whose names reference Elisabeth Kübler-Ross and David Kessler's traditional stages of grief but in terms specific to Black women—"Intuition," "Denial," "Anger," "Apathy," "Emptiness," "Accountability," "Reformation," "Forgiveness," "Resurrection," "Hope," and "Redemption."

The song "6 Inch" is in chapter 5, "Emptiness." After the separation from her husband, Beyoncé's album persona must go on. The video is shot at night, and red is the predominant color of the lighting and set design. As Beyoncé is chauffeured alone in a car, presumably to or from work, the seedy corners of the city reflect against her privacy window, shining red light into the car. Gone is the spontaneous back-seat car sex of the song "Partition" an album earlier, where she pleads, "Take all of me / I just wanna be the girl you like / the kind of girl you like." But despite her efforts to be the kind of girl he liked, she has ended up alone in the car anyway. He has presumably found sex outside the marriage. The second setting of the video is a white Southern house with a long hallway and a door on fire, echoing the "Door of No Return" on Goree Island, Senegal, a primary site of the transatlantic slave trade. From here, the video takes on the visual elements of horror—as Beyoncé spins a bare red light bulb above her head in one of the rooms, she narrates "every fear, every nightmare anyone has ever had," revealing silent Black women seated in the room with her. The women are all trapped in the same nightmare—a man's secrets, a legacy of intimate colonial violence.

The red light in the "6 Inch" video has the connotation of rage, but also of empty eroticism and sex work. It is the color of lust, and the secret places in the city one can find it. But instead of being about sex, the song itself is about a woman who works around the clock, rendered through the metaphor of sex work. The themes of sex and labor are juxtaposed, fused together as a site of generational trauma going all the way back to slavery, and although the song is not about sex work in earnest, it is about the more abstract sex work of feminized labors: of being a wife, being desirable, the performance of sexuality, domestic duty, motherhood, care work—and of maintaining and balancing that labor while making the space to do one's own work. If being "enough" in a marriage is sex work, for Black women (and as a point of identification, women of color), all of it is racialized labor.

In order for a woman to survive alone, work fills the void of love, and constant work around the clock fills the void of grief. Although "6 Inch" frames work as a way of taking back power to distract from the pain of heartbreak and loss, there is a deeper, underlying despair that resonates: the erotic fury that arises from betrayal.

We marvel at how strong and powerful she is, how much she can work, how much she can earn, how good she is at her job, until the end of the song, when she finally breaks and reveals her vulnerability, singing in a whispered high falsetto the secret feeling that work hides: "Come back, come back, come back, come back, come back, come back."

I imagine there is a kind of seafloor in all of us—unmapped territory deep within the darkest, most unexplored parts of us, shaped by the subconscious information of feeling, fear, memory—information that, like the ocean floor, is composed of the oldest rock and the newest, a container for our oldest feelings and memory, spreading out every generation from its seam. The images of horror and fantasy are the affective mappings of that seafloor. Although they lack the documentary evidence and detail of nonfiction, they are tied to older ways of knowing—intuition. I don't know Beyoncé, and I would not presume to know the experience of being a Black woman, but I do recognize how the legacies of colonial violence repeat in intimate contexts—womanhood, marriage, and labor as sites of colonial domination and power—and how the patterns of colonial violence our mothers survived take shape in the men we love. *Lemonade* reflected back a woman's interior world shaped by a history I recognized intimately.

One of the questions that has haunted you: Would knowing have made you dumber or smarter? If, one day, a milky portal had opened up in your bedroom and an older version of yourself had stepped out and told you what you know now, would you have listened? You like to think so, but you'd probably be lying; you didn't listen to any of your smarter, wiser friends when they confessed they were worried about you, so why on earth would you listen to a version of yourself who wrecked her way out of a time orifice like a newborn?

—CARMEN MARIA MACHADO, "DREAM HOUSE AS TIME TRAVEL," *IN THE DREAM HOUSE*

I never understood the Schrödinger's cat thought experiment until I became pregnant. In quantum mechanics, the paradox holds that a cat trapped in a box (with radioactive material in it) is simultaneously alive and dead in different planes of existence, yet once the box is opened and its contents are observed, one will see the cat *either* alive or dead. This is where I would always get confused—*wait, so is it alive or dead?* The whole point is: it's both until it isn't. While the box is closed, one reality is *superimposed* upon the other, each one real at the same time. It's the observer who splits those states into two separate realities upon observation, posing the question: When does one reality stop being possible and become **another**? The experiment is meant to question the nature of reality, and prove that multiple timelines and universes can exist. It is also a metaphor for the state of possibility anything is in before we acknowledge it, the weight every single tiny decision truly carries. Reality is just a state of potential until we make it real.

It sounds morbid to compare a pregnancy to the Schrödinger's cat thought experiment. A baby in a belly is itself a state of superimposed realities, each one vibrating with potential before they become a person. Perhaps it is the inverse of the thought experiment: the baby is simultaneously itself and its future self.

In the history of Western science and philosophy, the vast majority of ontological discourse has been shaped by cis white European men, none of whom have ever been pregnant, and who can only conceive of pregnancy and birth in the abstract. Would Descartes have thought himself into existence and split human consciousness into unnecessary binaries—mind/body, reason/feeling, human/animal—if he'd ever carried another person? I can only abide by that fact if I assume that maybe some of the greatest scientific discoveries of our time have stemmed from times of irresolvable grief. Maybe regret gave us the theory of relativity in its contemplation of time as relative to its observer, and therefore simultaneous, ever-present, elastic, reversible; perhaps grief gave us the Heisenberg principle as the reason to finally stop looking, lest we continue to change what we observe by observing it. Perhaps terminal illness is the root of eternalism, or the idea that all points in time are real and happening all at once. Perhaps to hope is to create a parallel universe—longing as its own reality. To long for the kind of you that would never leave or mistreat the woman you love. The possibility that those who leave us come back. The state of reality that imagines a person into being.

It's possible I still don't understand science.

I suspect my grandmother, my mother, and the tías loved Vicente

Fernández because his music gave them the illusion of access to a man's vulnerability, that moment a hardened man softens. The masculinity I've known on my mother's side: men who hit their children with thick leather belts well into adolescence; men who rescue women in abusive marriages; men who hit their wives; men who take in their elders; men with secret children and second families; men who take full custody of children who are not their own. My uncles have been all of these at different times in their lives. And although my father has always been more progressive about gender for a Mexican man, my mother was always the steady breadwinner while he toured with his band. And he has also been guilty of things listed above. I suppose that this history is what has also shaped my continued misunderstanding of men, of masculinity, the ways I have misassociated gender with goodness or badness.

"Well, it looks like you're having a little . . . boy."

I learned to make love to a man / by touching my father. . . . He would
lift me each morning / onto the bathroom counter, / dot my small
palms / with dollops of shaving cream / so I could lather his face.
—EDUARDO C. CORRAL, "DITAT DEUS," SLOW LIGHTNING

Our sex chromosomes, X and Y, are divergent axes on a graph. X lies horizontal, flat in one dimension, while Y springs up, vertical in another. Perhaps our chromosomes are aptly named to show that gender is a field, as though each of us were points on a graph moving through space. We'd all fall somewhere between X and Y, rather than all women rigidly on the x-axis and all men confined to the y. It allows us the space to visualize the dynamic movement of gender expression, lets us spatialize the gray areas.

I am more masculine than feminine in most ways, including the ways I hold my body at rest. I identify with male characters more often than female ones, although I advocate for female characters and notice if they don't have an arc. Although I love makeup, beauty as a practice doesn't appeal to me. I don't do my nails or cut my hair into any style but *long* or *shaved*. Many of my femme friends consciously try to dress like "bimbos" as a politics, wearing miniskirts and heels in the house and sleeping in lingerie, and I fucking love them for it. I wear T-shirts, Chucks, cotton briefs, and practical bras with no lace. **Confession: I am a little bit proud that I have, in some way,** as a pregnant person, **grown a penis.** Not because I want one, but just because I can.

Before graduate school, I'd always rejected feminism, not because I didn't believe in gender equality but because I associated feminism with white upper-middle-class women. I'd never known a white feminist who applied their politics to migrant workers, Black or Indigenous women, or the poor. No feminist ever advocated for the reproductive rights that would've spared my grandmother's life, or protected my mother from wage exploitation. White feminists were not speaking to anyone but white men. In my eyes, men of color had fewer rights than white women, and as a criminalized, unprotected Latina growing up in Texas, even as a survivor of rape, I had more in common and felt more kinship with hypersexualized men of color than any white woman harmed. During my formative years in the 1990s, riot grrrl and alternative white women musicians, like Kathleen Hanna, Kim Gordon, Courtney Love, Tori Amos, and PJ Harvey—whom I loved—were speaking to white men, not about women of color. I could only ever look up to them, but I could never relate. "Girls to the front" was not my fight.

Once I knew the baby's sex, **I began researching circumcision.** Since that day, I have never returned to parenting forums. **Like all forms** of baby research, the question was fraught with fierce political agitation and ignorance. On baby forums, acronyms like FTM, which I had always known to mean "female to male," were used to mean "first-time mom"—an innocuous community abbreviation I took huge offense to. On these posts, gender was not only essential, it was biological. But any time I tried to communicate how heteronormative and transphobic these parenting forums were to my husband, doctor, or doula, *my* sensitivity and politics were the problem. I wanted to raise our baby gender-neutral, use "they" pronouns until they chose their gender. But that was a bridge too far for everyone involved. So he became he.

The entire experience put me on the offensive. Not only would I not circumcise, I would defend his agency to his body from birth, and the right to choose his own gender in the future. The same rhetoric that had empowered me to protect my body was the rhetoric I would apply to my son.

———

Between her beauty and his hands were the three of us, the children.
He didn't regret hurting her; he regretted that she hurt enough to leave.
—MARCELO HERNANDEZ CASTILLO, CHILDREN OF THE LAND

We often think of ghosts as light. The dead appear before us as specters, dots, glowing forms. But new souls are sound, formed from inaudible waves. A heartbeat from a machine, fast and distorted on the air. A first cry.

The waves churn on the beach. It is Labor Day weekend in Galveston; the sky is deep gray and heaving. The wind tosses the seagulls around, disrupting their graceful dives. In the summer of 2012, mere months before my wedding, I'm visiting family in Houston.

Over fried seafood, my mother tells me that my grandmother was always suspicious of my dad because she was suspicious of all men. She suffered greatly because of them, my mother explains, as she tells me these near fairy tales set in 1960s Mexico, with men as the monsters. Today, my mother and I are not speaking—because I've chosen to write about this family history, about gender violence, about our Indigenous origins. She says of my writing: nos ves como si fuéramos muy poca cosa. *You write us as if we were pathetic.* I am constantly being corrected: your great-grandfather was the *manager* of the cotton rancho; your **grandmother** married rich; we were middle-class; your great-great-grandfather was six feet tall with blue eyes and red hair.

In Marcelo Hernandez Castillo's memoir, *Children of the Land,* he writes about applying to get his mother, a victim of domestic violence, a U visa to migrate safely to the United States. But instead of writing directly about the violence, he writes about patterns, the structure of intimate violence itself reproduced in the immigration system, the indirect consequences of violence. "I was always falling in love, even as a child. As Apá tossed Amá against the wall, I wrote letters to my fourth grade crushes," he writes. This too is how violence made me love—early, intensely, as an escape. The way violence warps gender, makes us desperate for love, makes us withhold it. Every sentence is a seam, stitching together love, family, gender, childhood, and queerness threaded with the violence of the state. As his friend, I remember this process, this period in his life, and the poem he wrote about braiding his mother's hair. Perhaps witnessing, and surviving, domestic violence is what has made me so desperate for, and unable to hold on to, love.

When I first revealed that I was pregnant, **my father told me that he identifies as a feminist. That he never questioned his own masculinity, seeing my mother be the provider while he stayed home. He disowns machismo, he says, gossiping a bit about our beloved Tío George, who** just this year welcomed his twenty-ninth child into the world, this time with his home-care nurse. My dad doesn't drink, or smoke, or own guns. He is a slight man, thin and long-boned, with kind brown eyes and a wholesome sense of humor. He lives for his art, playing jazz on a semi-hollow-body guitar. I don't have the heart to critique him, to tell him that feminism is not allowing your wife to take on the roles of both provider and nurturer, breadwinner and domestic laborer.

On the way to our first ultrasound, my husband suggested I abort. Upon seeing the baby's heartbeat, he changed his mind. But he was cold throughout my pregnancy, and my body knew something before I did.

The day my water broke, I was in labor for nearly forty-eight hours but never developed any contractions. This is highly irregular. I was given three times the usual dose of Pitocin, a hormone that even in tiny amounts reliably induces a strong labor. But my body would not respond. When the nurses realized how much Pitocin had been pumped into my bloodstream, they said, "How is this possible? You should be screaming your head off right now." They said they'd never seen anything like it. I apologized for not being able to start contractions, but birthing processes are involuntary—my body had shut down labor in my husband's presence, overridden by some deeper sense of danger. Later I read that women whose water broke in war zones would enter a state of shock that prevented contractions until they'd reached safety. Elsewhere I read that failed labor was caused by low oxytocin—the love and bonding hormone. Although there was no physical violence in my marriage, my body was terrified of him, and had been so starved for affection, sweetness, support, and care that it physically could not bring our baby into the world.

Hours after I'd given birth via C-section, womb cut and bleeding through tubes, he screamed at me in front of my mother, who had flown in from Texas the minute she heard I was in labor. The baby and

I were finally in the same room after our first meeting on the operating table, and I asked my mother to lay the baby on my bare chest.

"You're still groggy from the surgery," he said. "You're going to fall asleep and drop him, or roll over him."

"I won't, I promise," I said. "Skin-to-skin contact is vital in the first hours, especially for C-section babies." Even in the twilight state after surgery, I was always quoting things I'd read back to him so that he would believe what I said, respect my wishes. "I'll know where he is at all times—just watch him and take him if I drift off."

"You're an idiot if you think you won't drop him," he said. "You're not some 'magic mother' with mystical powers."

When I wouldn't give up the baby, he exploded in rage, left the room, and complained to the nurses about me.

"Can you please explain to my wife why she can't sleep with the baby on her?" I heard him say. "She's breaking the rules." Muffled voices.

A nurse came in a few minutes later.

"You okay?" she asked me. I nodded, smiled. "Sir, this looks okay to me. As much skin-to-skin as possible is encouraged in the first forty-eight hours. Can you help your wife by keeping an eye on her if she falls asleep?"

He took the baby out of my arms anyway. Later, when he left the hospital to sleep and take a shower, another nurse approached me with pamphlets on postpartum intimate partner violence. I assured her he was just tired, and I refused the pamphlets. She wouldn't be the first.

I should have read them while he was at home showering. But all I wanted was for him to come back.

A few weeks later: *What if you just did a hundred squats every day?* A question he started asking midway through my master's program before we were married, and now postpartum, started asking again. *Thanks for going running this morning, keep pushing it.* Touching the cross-cut, nerve-numb, purple-scarred, and stretch-marked pouch below my belly in the shower: *Is this ever going to go away?*

After my husband left me, my father often said it was because I'd cut off my long hair, never dressed up, never lost the baby weight. That I should take a weight-loss medication he saw on television, or get bariatric surgery, to be beautiful again. I think about how growing up, my parents would both say "Andas de güila," that I was a wayward slut for simply going out and talking to boys, while at the same time, my father would joke about getting a sex worker to service my then-teenage brother so that he could get his first sexual experience out of the way early. These are the things I don't want to return to, or remember, but that inevitably leave their traces.

I can feel the invisible structure of gender shape my reality as a single mother. Joaquín, my son, often says he wishes I weren't so sad, or so lonely. He asks if Daddy left me because I got fat. He witnesses my constant labor, my sleepless nights, still there at the computer when he wakes up in the morning, my self-neglect, my loneliness. I'm often miles away mentally, cooking and cleaning on autopilot until I pass out on the couch. He often wakes up in the middle of the night and joins me there, his little body between the couch cushion and me. I am another model of gender and misogyny he will internalize and have to unlearn, one that, despite all my efforts, I have no choice but to live as my reality. I try to undo the damage by making conscious choices: I hug my son often, try to give him the most magical childhood, talk him through his feelings, try to be present and listen to him as he tells me the most minute details about his toys, or a Roblox game, or a Spider-Man suit variation. **Every decision I make is love, and I hope that will be enough to make a man who will not hurt**, will not lie, will not leave. Will always come back.

MAGICAL REALISM

Or the Objective Correlative as the Symbol of Madness:
A Domestic Realism Vignette

September 23, 2017. San Fernando Valley, Los Angeles

On the first real weekend in our first real house, as I pull milky stalks of wild lettuce up by the root from an overgrown flower bed, my husband is arcing a sledgehammer high into the air. Silent, he slams it down into the concrete behind me without warning. *Thud.*

It was a steely blue morning, cool enough for our toddler to play barefoot on the patio less than three feet away. But as the sledgehammer's blow came down and cracked the surface, the baby startled and began to cry. I rushed to him, picked him up, and comforted him. My husband hadn't considered that sharp white shards of concrete might fly out from the blast, or that the baby was within the projectiles' radius. He didn't consider most things before he did them.

We'd just closed the month before, in August, on the house—a dated beige four-bedroom tract home in the Valley in need of repairs, but our first real home, miraculously ours. We were only able to afford it because of his good tech job. I was in the second year of my PhD program, making a tiny yearly stipend, below poverty wages. We'd have to HGTV the repairs, but even that was exciting.

There was something wrong with the slab, I can't quite remember what. It wasn't level, maybe, or it wobbled, a problem only he could see. I was annoyed but not angry, careful not to show either emotion, and I explained why using a sledgehammer with the baby so close was unsafe. The morning was still pink along its edges as gold flooded the sky; his cheeks reddened. He left me talking mid-sentence and headed inside to work on the kitchen sink instead. Our oldest tension—me opening my mouth.

I followed him inside. "I'm talking to you," I said. Silence. "Are you going to respond?" Silence. I would learn later that I was being stonewalled—just one tactic he used to frustrate me, elevate my emotions so that he could be the rational one and take control of the conversation, punish me for having a point.

Moments later, after I'd come back to the weeds and begun turning the soil, he appeared at the threshold of the back door. "I can't do this anymore." I thought he meant working on the house, or the sink. "I'm done." I don't remember if he said the word *divorce*, but he must have; all I remember is falling off the world into a giant bell that had already been rung but was still radiating sound, the aftermath of the ring suspended in an echo that would not fade. I must have told him to leave, because after that, he went to stay at a hotel the next three nights.

You might see the metaphor I'm building here: my husband, bent on destruction while my back is turned. An unexpected, decisive blow. A crack winding its way through the foundation. The baby made witness, vulnerable and frightened by the fallout. In writing, this narrative technique is called the *objective correlative*: the use of the environment and its objects to reveal or externalize the emotions of a character whose feelings are not shown. The term was coined by T. S. Eliot to describe the madness of Hamlet, whose emotions and acts of destruction "exceeded the facts of the play." Later, a friend will console me by saying, "Sometimes, out of nowhere, men just blow up their lives. They freak the fuck out at midlife after having a baby, getting a mortgage. And then boom, they destroy their lives, and the lives of everyone around them."

Two years later, while I was parsing his discovery, I found phone records and credit card statements from that day that shattered the present and every point in the past, shattered reality as I knew it.

At that moment, a ribbon of time ripped in two. It's one thing to have someone take the future away, but it's another to have your past taken away—the past you thought you knew, the shared history you'd built your relationship, your life, your decisions, your family on. I had just been writing about how the erasure of colonization leaves the mestize stranded in time—no known ancestors or tribes to claim or trace back, and without generational identity, consigned to a foreclosed future. And that same force was at work on an intimate scale as my husband's deception erased what I knew to be the past. I was double-stranded in two timelines, unsure who I was in the story of the land, unsure who I'd been all this time, if I didn't know the man I'd married.

THE FANTASY
OF HEALING

GERALT OF RIVIA, THE HERO OF *THE WITCHER 3: WILD HUNT*, IS introduced to us naked, soaking in a wooden tub in a steamy postcoital bath. We are in the bedroom suite of Kaer Morhen, the witcher castle of the Wolf School, where Yennefer, the love of Geralt's life, is also nude except for the towel wrapping her hair, on a chaise, reading, her shapely figure posed to show off her perfect ass. Despite her objectification, Yennefer is all business: she sends a magical lobster into the tub to nip Geralt in his sensitive bits, reminding him of his promise to their adopted daughter Ciri that he'll train with her. The erotic tone of the scene is tempered by domesticity, family, the mundane threaded through with love and deep longing as its main emotional chord. For a fantasy role-playing game, the music is warm and folkloric—a slow, yearning melody played on classical guitar to evoke an almost painterly intimacy, unlike the grand epic symphonies of more traditional fantasy games. We are anchored in the vulnerable space between lovers the morning after—the home to come back to at the end of the hero's journey.

The scene is a training ground meant to teach the player the controls and introduce the world's mechanics, how Geralt moves, how to activate his "witcher senses." Gamers play as Geralt throughout, but here we watch him as himself, moving and talking on his own. It's a richly rendered, cinematic introduction to the characters, with a focus on the tension of Geralt and Yennefer's relationship. His desire for Yennefer goes unsatiated as he's rebuffed by her toying condescension, their spiky dialogue hinting at old conflicts. She is still wary of his womanizing past, guarded after a betrayal.

> GERALT: Of all the women I've known, you're the only one who [does her makeup] before.
>
> YENNEFER: Oh? You've known many?
>
> GERALT: [*beat*] What's it matter? Only ever thought of you.

Already, these weren't just characters, they were two people with a history. I found myself restarting the game a few times to play through this opening scene again and again. Something about it hurt, felt familiar in its undertones—the fragile intimacy the morning after a painful fight; the realization that you can never truly know your partner; the unspoken, knowing sense that he's been inside someone else.

———

The last place I expected to confront the pain of the end of my marriage was in video games. I'm not *The Witcher*'s target demographic. My time is measured in labor, responsibilities, obligations, and guilt, which is to say, I have none.

And yet here I was in the summer of 2020, on the couch slaying wights in a filthy apartment, ordering Postmates at 2:00 a.m. after not eating or sleeping for four days in a loop of avoidance and hypervigilance. In September 2017, one month after buying our first home, two years after our son was born, and on my first book's publication day, my partner of ten years abruptly ended our marriage. In the months and years that followed, a flood of long-hidden behaviors came to a bright surface, crumbling every structure of reality I knew to be true. In the interest of privacy, I cannot divulge what I endured in the aftermath, only that the consequences have obliterated every aspect of my health.

I was never hungry or tired on the ever-changing cocktail of antidepressants and amphetamines I was prescribed. But no matter how much they increased or decreased my dosage, I could not bring myself to pay my bills, do my taxes, text back, attach the file someone needed to an email, shower, or do anything other than keep my son abundantly alive. For the four years that followed the end of my marriage, I was unable to leave my apartment without risk of a panic attack. Running into a neighbor at the mailbox could set off a grid of emergency lights in my brain; unanswered emails would trigger my smartwatch to alert me of an escalating heart rate; meeting friends for dinner would leave me in shambles, sobbing in my car. This is complex PTSD, a condition that can emerge after a big traumatic event, but can also emerge after years of living with a constant low level of fear, paranoia, abuse, and a lack of security and safety. Trauma is commonly defined as "too much too fast," but in my case, it was also "never enough for too long."

To heal, I repeated the story of what happened every week in therapy. I saw it in everything I watched, read, listened to. I didn't mean to repeat it to eye doctors, at birthday dinners, to the TurboTax specialist at the 800 number. With every vulnerable post online came the polite distance of a mute, with every moment of honesty an act of professional sabotage; every attempt to seem better and connect was laid bare in its desperate grasping. The more I spoke, the more I disappeared—grieve too long, too loud, and you become the unspoken spam of your social circles, muted out by polite apathy. And yet the story repeated itself against my will, forced me to cast the same characters, enacted itself in who I desired. No matter how much I told it or didn't want to tell it, language only confirmed my powerlessness. This was a story I could not change or move on from, no matter how hard I tried. So I learned to silence this pain by isolating it. I locked every door. Something big was happening to me, but in the end, who would truly listen?

No matter the circumstances, divorce, frankly, is boring, and of all the things you lose, you don't realize you've lost yourself until you exit your body mid-sentence and watch yourself become terrifying and inappropriate, someone to avoid at parties, just another scorned woman who has let herself go. This too becomes a loop: how you embarrass yourself.

In the beginning I was unmoored, disconnected from reality and the passage of time. On the days my son was with his dad, the only thing that soothed me through the shock and sleepless nights was playing fantasy movies and television shows over and over—*Game of Thrones, Harry Potter, Lord of the Rings*. When they ended, I'd go back to the beginning and replay them until I had memorized every word, breath, beat. Ironically, the rich worlds of fantasy are what allowed me to regain my footing in reality. If I memorized the story, the lore, the maps, the family lines and sigils, I could always know what was coming, rely on my memory, double-check the details and reconcile them with what I was seeing. But after a while, even *Game of Thrones* couldn't numb the agony anymore. Immersing myself in the earthy realms of fantasy could not help me reimagine a more just world or liberate me from this one, a world in a constant state of emergency run by monstrous men, all happening alongside my own personal disaster. Nothing felt real. As the Amazon rainforest burned and the pandemic raged and my exam deadlines passed, I could not look at my life, much less confront the monster within: a grief that was trying to kill me.

Since childhood, the periods of deepest grief have also produced my most magical thinking. Amid personal devastation, as Bruno Bettelheim writes in *The Uses of Enchantment,* fairy tales are for children portals to places of recovery, escape, and consolation from the anxieties of abandonment—a coping mechanism I brought with me into adulthood. Fantasy is a space safer than memory to process trauma and escape abuse into a world where the helpless are empowered by magic, friends are found among outcasts and survivors, and a hero will defend you with his sword until you find the hero was you all along.

Perhaps I am so drawn to fantasy because it is also the space of immigrant dreaming, the projection of the self into an impossible imaginary to bear the reality of the present one. Its central question: Forces larger than myself have estranged me from my home; what can displacement into new lands make capable in me?

For survivors, fantasy can make the realm of the erotic feel safe again. If one has only ever known lovers as abusers, elaborate scenarios with beloved characters can make desire after violence seem possible again, reassociate deep wounds with magic and pleasure. In Western speculative fiction, the presence of magic requires that it be grounded in its own system of limitations and moral boundaries. This is something like consent—world-building as a contract for an agreed-upon set of rules. In role-playing games, to create an avatar or become the hero is to move through a world with a renewed sense of trust, where triggering situations become a kind of exposure therapy and trauma can be encountered and reenacted in a controlled setting, but this time with a sense of agency in the decisions, and outcomes, of the story.

Two years into this mourning period, in the autumn of 2019, my younger brother Gilbert came to live with me so he could help out with my son and try his luck in LA's music scene. He was often concerned about how far I pushed my body to work. I do not indulge in luxuries, and I could not waste a single minute—even leisure had to have a utility. I'd work at the computer until he went to bed and still be there when he woke up, having worked all night for the fifth night in a row. I'd grade for sixteen hours straight, forget to eat, write twenty pages overnight until my son woke up. I'd long lived this way, even while married, ever striving toward the fantasy of financial security.

"Bro, do you ever have fun though? Please chill," he begged. He suggested I try playing *Skyrim*, one of the most popular massive open-world fantasy role-playing games, to fill the void *Game of Thrones* had left behind. By March 2020, to distract me from doomscrolling the news between writing and chores as pandemic lockdown orders became mandatory and everything was canceled, my brother finally convinced me to at least create my custom character. Within hours, I was hooked.

I thought back to the hours my ex spent playing games on his computer, relieving stress, while I took on all of the domestic labor, put myself through college, held down two jobs. I thought about the toll two full-time retail and food service jobs take on the body, how my mother works more than eighty hours per week at a grocery chain and comes home only to take on all of the domestic labor after her shift. How she modeled these constant overloaded stressors as my baseline.

Killing draugrs with my enchanted ebony bow was not a productive use of my precious time, so *wasting* it, *wasting my time*, made it even more engrossing, despite the nagging guilt I felt. As I played, I felt a very old tension deep within me finally release, and over the next few days came complete surrender. I would sometimes cry after a long game session, realizing I'd finally spent hours not thinking. Every muscle in my body had been imperceptibly clenched with years of tension and urgency. By complete accident, I'd become grounded in the present moment, killing vampire elves in a snowy forest. When intrusive thoughts did surface, it was during dialogue exchanges, where my options for interactions were morally categorized as persuade, intimidate, and lie. But over time those thoughts lessened. I was letting go of something heavy, but I didn't fully understand what it was.

And then, amid a new set of quests in a little Skyrim town, a completely unexpected option was presented to me: my character could get married.

My husband, Rune—an NPC, or nonplayable character, who interacts as part of the game's storytelling—had only three lines: "It's good to see you," "I made you a home-cooked meal," and "We have a cozy little profit, love." He was kind, supportive, and mostly silent. We adopted two daughters, whom he raised while I went out and killed dragons. We built our house in the mountains by a lake, with a library, an alchemy lab, and a fish hatchery. He did not cheat, he did not lie, he did not neglect, he did not yell or make messes he expected me to clean, and when I returned, he was still there. He would never leave.

It's good to see you.

Gently, the game walked me directly to a wound: to live out a vision of marriage I never got a chance to live.

———————————

Recent case studies have shown that video gaming can be a more effective behavioral intervention for PTSD than talk therapy for lessening intrusive thoughts, fearful avoidant behaviors, and desensitizing triggers, from combat veterans' experiences with first-person shooter games to car crash survivors and the prevention of traumatic memory formation through Tetris. PTSD is characterized by the activation of deep psychological scars, which drastically alters behavior into learned patterns of avoidance and suppression, which reinforce themselves every time they keep the sufferer "safe." This is why it's so difficult to treat PTSD—patients may not benefit from talk therapy, especially as protective avoidant behaviors become more entrenched; narrating traumatic events doesn't work if there's no available memory to recall, or if to engage the memory is dangerous or so ingrained by repetition that it cannot be analyzed in such a way that it changes behavior.

EMDR, or eye movement desensitization and reprocessing, is an alternative therapeutic modality in which the patient recalls traumatic events while moving their eyes from side to side or engaging in an activity that requires their full attention. Researchers such as Harvard psychologist Richard J. McNally and Dutch psychologist Marcel van den Hout explain how eye movements, as well as other tasks that require short-term memory, "tax memory in such a way that trauma-related images become degraded and less emotionally evocative," alleviating trauma symptoms.

Video games do both, mimicking EMDR's physiological component by requiring that the patient engage both rapid side-to-side eye movements *and* short-term memory to complete tasks and quests.

Intrusive thoughts will inevitably surface during play for PTSD sufferers, and for veterans, first-person shooter games stage a site of recall by re-creating the environment of combat, allowing exposure to triggering situations and images in a controlled, safe environment.

———————

After my brother Gilbert and his PlayStation moved back home to Houston in September 2020, I did the unthinkable: I bought my own PS4. By then I'd finished playing through his copies of *Skyrim* and *Assassin's Creed*, gateways into the world of fantasy role-playing video games. In search of a new game, I finally came around to *Witcher 3* on fellow writer-gamer Carmen Maria Machado's recommendation. And it is here that the real confrontation with my demons began.

The Witcher 3: Wild Hunt, CD Projekt Red's massively popular, award-winning 2015 video game, is considered the gold standard across the board in terms of writing, character development, romance, and story in massive open-world role-playing games. Six years later it continues to rank first on best-of lists, with even a recent Netflix adaptation of the games and book series.

It's worth noting here that video games—even fantasy video games—have often been a hostile, even unsafe territory for women of color, beginning in 1982 with *Custer's Revenge,* a game in which General Custer, a pink man with a huge erection, must avoid arrows and make it to the other side of the screen to rape a bound Native woman. Previously, I'd associated gaming and its characters with shitty preteen boys at the mall arcade who called me a "button-mashing bitch" when I won as Kitana in *Mortal Kombat;* with bongs and bad boyfriends in dragon button-up shirts and JNCOs beating women in *Grand Theft Auto;* with my ex-husband, an avid, lifelong gamer with *Warcraft* posters up on his bedroom walls well into his thirties. I associated gaming with everything sexist, lazy, and impotent about white middle-class toxic masculinity. I thought gamers to be my total opposite in terms of politics, positionality, and priorities.

I remained skeptical of Geralt in the early stages of *Witcher 3* until I sensed that he was different from the misogynist archetypes in *Grand Theft Auto* or first-person shooter games. Geralt's character, and his particular expression of masculinity, began a slow process of building the trust necessary to expose me to a wilder pain just below the surface. But while I doubt the developers of *The Witcher 3: Wild Hunt* had someone like me in mind, playing as a male character known for his voracious appetite and sexual conquests, it turned out, still led me to encounter scenarios that would set off a near-deadly trigger.

You might be thinking, *It's a video game, it's really not that serious.* And maybe that's true, but as with any story, it's what we bring with us that's serious. I read the game through the screen of my pain as it reflected back my own monstrosity: Mexican womanhood is a state of powerlessness, where suffering and forgiveness are idealized in the form of Mary, and grief and rage are made monstrous in La Llorona—two myths forged in relationship to men. Mexican daughters are raised in a culture of shame, expected to obey and punished when we don't. We are shaped by guilt and disciplined through labor, groomed to emulate our mothers' sacrifice and endure a life in which family is an obligation and infidelity is assured. When everything is your fault, you learn to doubt your memory and the integrity of your actions, distrust your own testimony.

Today I cannot remember much of my relationship—when you are denied your memory, even your reflection in the mirror is not enough to prove your body exists in space. It's like waking up unable to describe the blank echo of a dream you just had, a dream that lasted ten years.

At the beginning of *The Witcher*, the first game in the trilogy, Geralt wakes up with amnesia, a narrative device that allows the player to discover the world alongside its hero. Geralt does not remember Yennefer or Ciri. Instead he enters into a sexual relationship with Triss, who takes advantage of his amnesia and seduces him with magic, withholding key information so that he will be unfaithful to Yen without his knowledge. But echoes of Yennefer throughout the games stir a strange longing in him, deeper than memory.

The first two *Witcher* games are not romances but complex political intrigues known for their strong characters and branching storylines with significant, far-reaching consequences. But perhaps the *Witcher* games are especially notorious for their explicit sex scenes, nudity, and adult themes. Amid brothels and princesses and sorceresses who practice "lesbomancy," in *Witcher 1* and *2*, Geralt's amnesiac promiscuity is part of the fun until the end of *Witcher 2*, when Geralt finally regains his memory.

By *Witcher 3*, Geralt has visibly matured and, having completely recovered his memory, has urgent priorities—to find Yennefer and Ciri and put his family back together. In the game's first quest, Geralt desperately tracks Yennefer, whom he now remembers as the love of his life—a reunion we have to wait half the game for, with many pitfalls along the way. Would I indulge every opportunity to be with someone else behind her back, or play it faithful, as if doing so would, in some universe, make someone remain faithful to me?

Geralt at middle age—handsome, grumpy, and gruff with his signature gravelly voice—still comes off as all hypermasculine, virile aggression. This was a turnoff for me in the early stages of the game. But as I played on, I took note of his devotion to Ciri, his love for Yennefer, how soft and silly he could be, his spiky sarcasm, the result of a lifetime reviled and alienated as a "freak."

But Geralt isn't a white knight or a romance hero; he also struggles with his own complicated humanity. As he unravels the truth behind a monster, he also unravels something in himself: the pain that animates a haunting, the betrayal that binds a curse. To be a witcher is not just about killing monsters or lifting curses, but about a solitary life dedicated to the reparation of harm. And while Geralt might use two swords and offensive magic to fight, he uses feminized folk practices to heal victims, homes, and communities. In *Witcher*, monsters are never just monsters but manifestations of human trauma, and of the monstrosities we inflict on one another that make demons, werewolves, and wraiths of us.

In *Witcher 3*'s central love triangle, Geralt has two options—mercurial Yennefer or sweet Triss—to choose as his life partner. True to canon, the game heavily encourages you to repair things with Yennefer and shows its bias by planting multiple in-game books, poems, ballads, and plays about their love story, and nothing about Geralt and Triss other than embarrassing rumors. (Not to mention that their queer daughter Ciri is firmly on the Geralt-Yennefer ship, as am I.) Geralt is affable, even playful, when he reunites with old friends throughout the game, many of whom are sorceresses, but upon reuniting with Yennefer at a funeral, he completely loses his cool:

GERALT: You look beautiful.

YENNEFER: Thank you. It's nice to see you. The eulogy.

GERALT: You smell wonderful.

YENNEFER: Geralt—we're at a funeral.

GERALT: You smell wonderful at this funeral.

[EULOGY CONTINUES]

GERALT: Haven't seen each other in two years. I want a solitary cottage by the sea. I want to lock myself inside with you, stay there for a week.

YENNEFER: What would we do there?

GERALT: Got so many ideas.

YENNEFER: The one with the rope you use for trophies, that one seems interesting.

GERALT: Stop reading my mind.

YENNEFER: Got something to hide?

GERALT: Don't like secrets?

YENNEFER: No.

Witcher 3 somehow manages to build so much tension in its romantic relationships that the sex feels emotional, yearning, and romantic (albeit also heteronormative and white). But reconciliation with Yennefer after Geralt's infidelity with Triss is not so easily won, requiring careful choices and multiple lengthy quests to finally earn her back for good this time, fulfilling the promise of the opening scene. (Failure to reconcile has its own consequences.)

Which is why it's disappointing that, once you reconcile with Yennefer, having spent half the game pursuing her, you immediately have the chance to cheat on her. Following their reunion, Geralt ends up at the Passiflora brothel, where one of the first dialogue options, unrelated to the quest, is to ask the madam about the girls on offer. Out of curiosity, I chose that dialogue option as my stomach sank with dread. Geralt, who had earned my trust in his role as father, devoted partner, and defender of survivors, at the end of the day was a character written for cis-hetero men, gamers, and fans who would read these scenes as a harmless indulgence of justifiable urges. After pursuing Yennefer for so long, Geralt deserved a reward, because in the end, she would stick around anyway. And that's the way it goes—the thrill of the chase is always more appealing than the daily grind of fidelity and commitment. Not even in the realms of fantasy could I be free from the terms of male desire.

The propositions at least were pleasant, not creepy or disrespectful. I could have skipped the encounters with the sex workers—they're there simply as a novelty—but I wanted to see for myself what it felt like to deceive, how to disconnect sex and desire from those who depend on your fidelity, how to not consider consequences, to just think of myself and my own pleasure first and "relax with a beautiful woman." I have never centered or prioritized my desire, but have always been at the mercy of men, of being or not being desired, of what they do or do not do with that desire.

Visiting the brothels as Geralt was not erotic or satisfying—more embarrassing and awkward, even heartbreaking. Still, I visited the brothels a lot, not for pleasure but with a strange compulsion to confront a painful scenario in the effort to *understand*, watching the same bouncing breast animations over and over—a kind of exposure therapy, sometimes numb, sometimes aroused, full of shame, mostly always in tears.

I felt empty, or perhaps emptied, of something when the scenes ended. But every time I went, it hurt a little less. In a flood of shame, I'd reload my last save to the moment before I entered the brothel, over-writing my infidelity to Yennefer like it never happened. Through role-playing Geralt, I switched roles: now I was the one deceiving. Now I was the one deliberately deleting evidence, manipulating the game's memory to cover up indiscretions not even I could resist. But it wasn't for the same reasons—I wasn't hiding something that felt good, or out of shame, or any other reasons people cheat. I erased the brothel visits out of respect for Yennefer, and I used their fictional relationship to stage the site of my own betrayal and pain.

Yennefer was right to be suspicious—it is not possible to play Geralt as completely monogamous. I tried many times, reloading saves to make different decisions that would bypass kissing his friend without *my* consent. Throughout the game, Geralt is presented with opportunities to indulge in the game's emotional gray areas with other women far from Yennefer's notice, and he can visit brothels as often as he'd like without penalty to his long-term relationship. And while Geralt can choose either Triss or Yennefer as his life partner, there are severe consequences to romancing both. (Do *not* do it.)

While researching whether Geralt is monogamous in the books (he is . . . and isn't), several users on Reddit point out that Geralt and Yennefer are about a hundred years old, and as magical beings they are sterile—two major factors in the practice of monogamy.

I am critical of my own monogamy and critical of cis-hetero-normative relationship structures, the colonial-capitalist construct of marriage, the unlikelihood of monogamy with longer life spans, how upholding the nuclear family where the patriarch has all the power deeply entrenches the project of Western whiteness. I even proposed polyamory to my ex and was open to seeing sex workers together, but in the end I never had the guts, or the desire, to be with anyone else.

I can hold all of these critiques and still believe in monogamy because of a deep historical bind to the precarity of my subject position: I am repeating the pattern of my mothers, estranged from their families by marriage. In Mexico my grandmother was taken far from her family by her husband at fourteen; in Houston my mother's nearest family member is an eight-hour drive away, at the US-Mexico border; here in Los Angeles, my nearest family member is sixteen hundred miles away. An isolated woman in a strange place is vulnerable, unprotected, easily controlled, and even easier to leave.

Perhaps this is my generational curse. Migration is an abandonment wound that tears families apart, erodes ties, severs connections, erases memory. When you've lost so many people you love to borders, illness, labor, the state, and you feel alone in a strange country, you don't leave your spouse. My parents stay in a toxic marriage because separating would mean death for my disabled dad. Marginalization often means we can't cut ties with family; not only do we have an embodied compassion for their racial trauma, but cutting them off would make them vulnerable to severe structural harm. When marriage becomes the last bond holding everyone together, monogamy feels like a kind of safety.

Somewhere along the way, I confused marriage with a trauma bond.

Eventually my marriage became a field of deleted files, fragments and residues of overwritten saves, impossible to reload. After years of parsing a divorce lawyer–guarded stone wall, what can evidence do? In the end, I finally had to let go of any possibility of truth.

In *Witcher 3*, what is satisfying about Geralt's detective work is the way his witcher senses highlight invisible violence. As he walks through the aftermath, streaks of bright red energy reveal the emotional residue of what happened in the air, allowing us to visualize his intuition and reanimate the scene, follow the trail, and recover suppressed evidence. For survivors, the way Geralt's witcher senses give memory and feelings shape and allow them to stand as evidence is a powerful thing to witness. Geralt can't be gaslit—even when all evidence is erased and nothing can prove the victim's testimony, *feelings* are the record that exposes abusers and contradicts their lies.

Still, I always chose not to punish the abuser but to repair the harms they'd done. The Bloody Baron, a violent alcoholic abandoned by his wife and daughter; Olgierd von Everec, a husband haunted by his most monstrous act, the neglect of his wife—as Geralt, I did not kill them, or force their families to forgive them. I chose the longer, more complicated solutions, fought demons, relieved haunted places scarred by traces of their violence, only to let them go and live with their choices. While the game gave me the power to utterly ruin the hurters and delight in their suffering, it also gave me agency and control over Geralt's actions in his personal life as a partner and father. And all of these choices were deeply meaningful. Would I choose to live in a just world, where with great power, *I* chose not to do harm? With those choices, the worst thing I could bring myself to do was make Geralt fuck a lot of sex workers. I chose to hurt *myself*.

On my second and third playthrough, although I tried to play a darker version of Geralt, to make different choices and punish with violence to see the "bad endings," in the end, I always chose to make him faithful to Yennefer, supportive of Ciri, to not hurt. With each playthrough I gained a new understanding of trauma, of the humanity refracted through the monstrous, and chose again to lift everyone's curses, repair relationships, restore memory, liberate communities, reduce harm. I could take my personal revenge, but Geralt made me fight for something bigger.

Healing is a complicated process—nonlinear, interior, exterior, social, personal. Sometimes it's just being stuck for a long time, hitting a wall, a stalemate. Maybe it is not possible to heal, but instead one can be rearranged into another self, one can go on. Maybe healing can be achieved not by bringing the monsters in our lives to justice but by facing the monster within, and in the letting go, end the cycle. And while I do not believe forgiveness is possible in the face of great harm, especially if the harmed person remains powerless, I now believe in a kind of justice that goes beyond the carceral logics of punishment, a vision of justice that, through centering the end of trauma, must end the monstrous conditions we live in.

Geralt of Rivia, witcher, monster hunter, folk healer, lifter of curses, is a partner and father whose story begins in the aftermath of his betrayal, and who chooses to repair his relationship and reunite his family. He healed something in me by teaching us to live as moral outcasts, protect exceptional daughters, love brilliant and difficult women, and, most importantly, teaching us that at the center of every curse and the core of every monster is an unremembered, unavenged victim, a story untold. Geralt lifts curses by exposing hidden truths not just through their telling but through a collective remembering that corrects the historical record, undoes a knot of violence, accounts for hidden evidence, believes the unbelieved. To break a curse is to reload a deleted save and witness our choices so that in the end we can bury our ghosts and be released from our monsters, so that we might live out a future liberated from the past.

Trauma is a narrative choice—the choice to repeat a story until it becomes a curse, an ouroboros that makes a person consume themselves. The human brain does not like to hold on to trauma for that long; traces of it endure to keep us safe, but perhaps it is the insistence on the story that keeps us stuck. I now see the difference between trauma and grief: trauma is a fixation on what is lost, while grief is proof that love still lives. Neither is just. My body will always store the traces of trauma in the absence of memory, clenched like a fist in anticipation of nothing. I have a long way to go, but I have stopped punishing myself so much with labor, and learned to allow myself to rest, waste time, do nothing. Video games help me recall, writing to release. Rather than resign myself to an eternal state of suffering, trapped in deleted memories, cursed to a repeating story, as Geralt, I was given two swords: steel for humans, silver for monsters, tools to confront the haunted parts of myself.

And in doing so, the curse I am lifting is my own.

IN THE SHADOW
OF THE WOLF

I lay in dark and dreaming sleep while wars and countless ages passed. I woke still weak a year before I joined you. . . . I will save the elven people. Even if it means this world must die.

—SOLAS/FEN'HAREL, *DRAGON AGE: INQUISITION—TRESPASSER*

THE DREAD WOLF FENRIR, SON OF THE TRICKSTER GOD LOKI, LIES in wait beneath the earth, bound by a magical rope. According to Norse mythology, Odin bound the wolf, who is prophesied to appear at the dawn of Ragnarök, the cosmic battle of the gods against invaders at the end of the world. When the long winter comes and all humanity is at war, the black wolf will break loose from his bondage, and with fire streaming from his eyes and nostrils, and his jaws open from earth to sky, he will devour everything in his path and swallow the sun, moon, and stars. The mountains will crumble and the oceans will rise to drown the world, until nothing is left but the void, ending the cosmos, the gods, and all human memory of what once was.

But before all of this, Fenrir bites off the Norse god Tyr's hand.

I had not connected the Inquisitor's severed arm at the end of *Dragon Age: Inquisition—Trespasser* DLC (downloadable content) to Sigurd's severed arm in *Assassin's Creed Valhalla* until recently, when I finished both games back-to-back. It's too specific an amputation to be a coincidence, with too-specific circumstances—both the Inquisitor and Sigurd lose their arm to an apocalyptic wolf. In *DAI*, elf mage Solas—trusted companion, friend, and, in my case, lover—turns out to be the ancient trickster god Fen'Harel, or the Dread Wolf of elven lore who sabotages the Inquisition and, with a final kiss, disintegrates your arm. In *AC Valhalla*, siblings Eivor and Sigurd are led astray by Basim, leading to the loss of Sigurd's arm, echoing the loss of his arm to the wolf Fenrir in his former life as the Norse god Tyr. (It's a long story—the siblings are also Norse gods; we'll get to that in a minute.) But the similarities don't end there: both Solas/Fen'Harel and Sigurd/Tyr are dual characters who are revealed to be gods repeating their fates in their human lives; both are from races or cultures oppressed by a monotheistic empire. And both games—crucially—draw from the myth of Ragnarök as an allegory for a race war at the brink of apocalypse and extinction.

PLEASE, FOLLOW ME TO MY NORMAL VIKING CONSPIRACY WALL

Historical high fantasy in earthy medieval settings might be my favorite genre of visual storytelling. When done well, it can bring us back to the elements, be a refuge from the crises of modernity, and clarify a confusing world by reforging our problems with simplicity and possibility, centering friendship, self-discovery, and a coming together to vanquish great evil. But as much as I love the genre, it can also be a haven for reactionary politics, which is why I've long been troubled by the turn to Vikings in popular culture and media. Historical Vikings themselves are not the issue—what is troubling is *why* they're back, what deeper political rumblings their return might signal, and what myths endure in our present racial imaginaries.

It's alarming to see the blond, blue-eyed, all-powerful white Viking warrior archetype in media produced for mass consumption. I'm disturbed by ahistorical depictions of Vikings as a white ethnic group, and the investment in maintaining that myth with all-white casts. Viking contact with North American Indigenous people in Greenland is a delicate history, and I wonder about how depictions of Vikings' tribalized whiteness enable fantasies of white indigeneity to be rendered as historical. Vikings have long been a site of white projection, most recently to provide a convenient historical precedent to claim Black and Indigenous cultural practices, from wearing locs and braids to dressing as shamans in animal skins. And while I appreciate textured, attentive representations of historical Viking dress, body modification, material culture, and lore, I worry about how fantasies of white indigeneity supplant the stories of Native American and Indigenous people, who continue to be starkly underrepresented and reduced to crude stereotypes in the media. But beyond all this, I wonder about fantasy's preoccupation with Ragnarök—the cataclysmic end of the world, the cosmos, memory, and the gods—and its variations on our own apocalyptic urgency, reimagined as the Long Night, the Wild Hunt, the Eternal Winter, and so on.

And it's not just in *Dragon Age: Inquisition* and *Assassin's Creed Valhalla*—these are simply two massively popular games among many. Here is a short list of Viking- and Norse mythology–themed media properties from the last fifteen years: *Dragon Age, Assassin's Creed, Frozen, God of War, Valheim, Hellblade, Game of Thrones* ("The Long Night"), *The Witcher* (Skellige and Ragh-nar-Roog), *Thor, The Last Kingdom, Norsemen, The Northman, How to Train Your Dragon*, and *Vikings* and its recent Netflix spin-off *Vikings: Valhalla*. Why do Vikings and Rag-narök dominate twenty-first-century cultural production? What drives the demand for them, and what anxieties do they reflect about our own world? These things are all connected, but I couldn't grasp how. Until the severed arm.

———

NORDICISM, THE NINETEENTH-CENTURY THEORY OF RACIAL HIERAR-chy that would serve as the prototype to the Aryanism of the Nazis, marks the evolution of white supremacy from "biological fact" to social-moral imperative. Arthur de Gobineau's 1853 *Essay on the In-equality of the Human Races* posits that Nordics—hardened by the severe mountains and harsh winters of the North—are the superior race, de-fined by their whiteness, intelligence, natural leadership, and grit. For Gobineau, only the blond Germanic Nordics, the purest of Aryans, could be leaders of the world, and when Aryans diluted their blood through interracial mixing with the so-called lower races, it brought about the "downfall of civilizations."

Nordicism is still going strong in our racial imaginaries. At its most benign, it appears in our praise of Sweden's education system, Norway's health care and bike lanes, the "progressive" politics of Scandinavian countries and their off-grid co-ops. At its worst, Nordicism is codified in our policies that place no restrictions on immigration from Scandinavian and Northern European countries, and in our media, who reinforce the notion that Nordic, Germanic, and Anglo-Saxon people are "good" immigrants and assets to our country, and that people from the global south are dangerous strains on the economy. Nordicism is a primary racial logic of white supremacy in the Western world; its ideas are so standard, so deeply ingrained, they're foundational to the concept of white American identity and heritage, which reproduces itself in our national imaginaries, which shape our collective futures. America's long history of ethnic cleansing and eugenics projects—from Jim Crow to the Chinese Exclusion Act to Operation Wetback to Indian boarding schools to the mass sterilization of Black, Latina, and Indigenous women—are attempts to shape that future, motivated by the imagined threat to whiteness. As the "border surges" and "immigrant caravans" and "woke-ification" of our time threaten whiteness, the very core of American identity, what better hero than a Viking to defend it?

"WAIT, AM I THE DRAMA?": HISTORICAL VIKINGS JUST FINDING OUT THEY'RE WHITE

The grand irony is that Vikings could not have possibly been homogeneously white. Vikings and related Norse Germanic tribes lived between the ninth and eleventh centuries, existing before the invention of race by more than five hundred years. They would not understand the concepts of whiteness, Blackness, indigeneity, orientalism, and so on—and would therefore have no "whiteness" or "purity" to maintain.

In fact, Vikings were among the most culturally heterogeneous, ethnically mixed populations in antiquity. As explorers, raiders, and pirates, they survived by pillaging other lands, kidnapping brides and children along every known coast. Archaeological findings show that early Vikings thrived precisely *because* of their ability to trade and integrate with a wide range of cultures, spanning the Northern Hemisphere and all the way down to Africa. It was only in the seventeenth century in Western Europe that the emerging sciences began the colonial project of classifying ethnic groups into racial hierarchies, constructing European whiteness as a physical and intellectual ideal.

Although the Vikings were long gone by then, the myth of the pure white Viking took hold in the racial imaginary as the symbolic European ancestor. The Viking represented the physical and social ideals of whiteness and masculinity—intrepid explorer, conqueror, warrior, symbol of seafaring expeditions and discovery—and thus became the archetype used to justify colonial domination as the inherent nature of white people and, therefore, justify white supremacy as a scientific fact.

"To be white is to be a striver, a crusader, an explorer and a conqueror," said Richard Spencer, American neo-Nazi and ideologue of the alt-right, in a speech upon the election of Donald Trump. "We build, we produce, we go upward. . . . For us, it is conquer or die. This is a unique burden for the white man, that our fate is entirely in our hands. And it is appropriate because within us, within the very blood in our veins as children of the sun, lies the potential for greatness."

In January 2018, just months after the Unite the Right rally in Charlottesville, where white men gathered with tiki torches to cry out "We will not be replaced," Donald Trump stated that while immigrants from affluent European nations such as Norway or Sweden were welcome in the United States, immigrants from "shithole countries" such as Haiti and El Salvador were not. "Why do we need more Haitians?" he said. "Take them out." This anti-immigrant, ethnonationalist language would escalate in the following months to his calling immigrants "animals" and vermin who "infest" the country.

In 2019, white men in El Paso, Texas, and Gilroy, California, carried out mass shootings, citing the "invasion of Hispanics" and "hordes of mestizos," or mixed-race Latines, as their targets. The El Paso shooter wrote a manifesto espousing replacement theory: the myth that white men are being replaced by minorities at the dawn of a mass white extinction. On the day of the shooting, the Gilroy shooter posted a photo of a Smokey Bear fire warning sign instructing his followers to read *Might Is Right*, a late-nineteenth-century fascist manifesto by an author calling himself Ragnar Redbeard, who viewed the pure white Viking as the pillar of strength great nations are built on.

Texts like *Might Is Right* are shared often on 4chan, a massive gaming network and nexus of radicalization. Users post neo-Nazi propaganda, white supremacist misinformation, and misogynistic memes, sometimes going so far as to organize alt-right demonstrations and instigate acts of violence. Both the El Paso and Gilroy shooters copied language from the widely shared manifesto of the Christchurch, New Zealand, shooter, who livestreamed his assault on Facebook in the style of a first-person shooter video game—which closed with "I will see you in Valhalla." In 2022, a copycat shooting in Buffalo, New York, which explicitly targeted Black people, was streamed on Twitch, a gaming videochat platform, until it was quickly removed. The shooter's gun and armor were covered in Norse symbols, such as the Sonnenrad (Black Sun) and the Othala rune. The connective tissue of these mass shootings is the alt-right, gaming, and Viking imagery and symbolism.

Cut to the January 6 US Capitol insurrection, where Jacob Chansley, the QAnon Shaman, bare-chested in Party City Viking cosplay, displayed three Odinist tattoos any white supremacist would recognize as dog whistles—Mjölnir, or Thor's Hammer; Yggdrasil, or the Tree of Life; and over his heart a valknut, three interlocked triangles representing the "knot of the slain," a runic symbol sometimes interpreted as indicating a willingness to die as a warrior in Odin's army at Ragnarök. While the three symbols are not necessarily racist in every context, the mass use of Norse symbols at the Capitol insurrection *was* the context.

The conception of Ragnarök as a modern-day race war is rooted in toxic masculinist fantasy. There is ample evidence that Danish settlements across Europe assimilated peacefully into agrarian life and converted to Christianity of their own will. But for the rising alt-right, Ragnarök is a convenient metaphor for waging war against the white apocalypse—the invasion of nonwhite others that will bring about white extinction and the downfall of American civilization.

And this is historically when the Viking has been resurrected—when white supremacy is threatened by social change.

Rewind to 2011: President Obama is completing his first term and campaigning for the second, a presidency that will serve as the catalyst for the white backlash of the Trump era. That same year, *Thor* is released in theaters, *Skyrim* redefines fantasy role-playing video games, while on television, *Game of Thrones* airs its first season and is catapulted to overnight success. *Vikings* will also begin production in 2011. Since then, the Viking has reemerged in full force, Disneyfied, even yassified, stripped of explicit white supremacist associations while fulfilling a deeply reactionary cultural response to a changing world under a Black presidency.

LORD OF THE RACES

Race is not just part of world-building in fantasy. It *is* the world.

The Lord of the Rings and *The Silmarillion* borrow heavily from the creatures and worlds of Norse mythology—Middle-earth is based on Midgard, Mordor on Muspelheim, and so on. But Tolkien applied a twentieth-century lens to a ninth-century cosmology—what were once Yggdrasil's "creatures" (dwarves, elves, humans, giants) Tolkien called "races," each with their particular physical and moral characteristics: Elves are fair and intuitive, Dwarves are ruddy and proud, Hobbits are earthy farming folk, and Orcs—black-skinned, socially dead, corrupted—are an unpaid labor force representing a great evil.

Race is so foundational to Tolkien's world-building that even Galadriel's opening monologue for the film adaptation of *The Lord of the Rings* (2001) establishes race as the frame for the story (emphasis mine):

> The world is changed. . . . It began with the forging of the great rings. Three were given to the Elves, *immortal, wisest and fairest of all beings.* Seven to the Dwarf lords, *great miners and craftsmen of the mountain halls.* And nine, nine rings were gifted to the *race of* Men, who above all else, *desire power.* For within these rings was bound the *strength and will to govern each race.* But they were all of them deceived, for another ring was made.

In Tolkien's time, the world *had* changed. Written between 1937 and 1949, a period spanning World War II and the height of Nazi Aryanism, *LOTR* captured industrialization, war, and the rise of fascism in the Western postcolonial world. Race was not only the West's primary way of organizing the world; it was Nazi Germany's primary concern. Although Tolkien intended only to write a mythic retelling of Anglo-Saxon history and strongly denied that *The Lord of the Rings* was a historical allegory, Middle-earth—from its moral geographies (West good, East evil) to its races and their metaphors—is undeniably a reproduction of Europe. While fantasy is not history, the worlds we build cannot help but reproduce colonial history and its metaphors.

As the blueprint for high fantasy literature, *LOTR*'s racial allegories have endured. They are reproduced across the genre in books, role-playing games, video games, television, and film. In *LOTR*-inspired fantasy, race structures the social hierarchies, geographies, and conflicts of the world. It's even the first decision (race, gender, class) a player must make in creating a character for any campaign in the iconic Dungeons & Dragons role-playing game.

When done well, fantasy's core racial archetypes—Elf, Dwarf, Man, Hobbit, Orc, to use Tolkien's schema—subvert their racial stereotypes to perform a more complex relationality, using difference to provoke difficult conversations about our world. At its best, fantasy can act as a radical critique of the larger, more abstract politics of structural power. Done poorly, fantasy races merely replicate the racial logics of our world. The reemergence of the Viking in popular media is often here to do the latter; not even the queerest, most diverse portrayals of Viking culture and Norse mythology—like *Assassin's Creed Valhalla* and *Dragon Age: Inquisition*—can improve upon this model. In fact, they may make it worse.

WHITE APOCALYPSE: THE STORY WE KEEP TELLING

First, a quick recap of Ragnarök's story beats. The Norse gods have become arrogant, gluttonous, and tyrannical, at constant war with other realms. Odin, head of the Norse gods, is given the prophecy of Ragnarök, "the doom of the gods"—a betrayal that would see a Dread Wolf bring about the fall of Asgard, realm of the supreme Æsir gods, and as a result the end of all creation. In an attempt to cheat fate and prevent Ragnarök, Odin issues a decree to kill all the wolves. But as it turns out, one of the wolf pups is Loki's son Fenrir, a mongrel and abomination he sired with the giantess Angrboða, an enemy Jötunn and mother of monsters. Loki begs Odin not to kill his son, so Odin agrees, allowing Tyr to raise the pup while he devises a plan to tie the black wolf into a state of unbreakable bondage. By the time Odin returns with the magic rope, Fenrir has grown to a terrifying size.

Fenrir is wary of why Odin has come back with a rope and senses that Odin will try to bind him, so to gain his trust Tyr places his hand in Fenrir's mouth as an oath that the wolf will not be bound. Odin tricks both of them and binds Fenrir anyway, causing Tyr to lose his hand to the beast. Once bound, Fenrir will remain imprisoned in a deep cave until Loki returns to free him, breaching Heimdall's gate to Asgard at the entrance to the rainbow bridge (literally a border patrol checkpoint), bringing all kinds of giants and sea monsters into the highest, most guarded gated community of Asgard. After Fenrir breaks loose and the tides rise and swallow the earth, Loki leads an invading caravan of ships from the lower realms, steering a ship carrying Muspells, black lava-giants from the fiery South. The Norse gods refuse defeat and wage war against their fate, only to fall to the loosed wolf Fenrir, a mixed-race abomination come out of bondage to end all creation.

Although Odin loves Loki, the Æsir clan has never trusted the trickster god, depicted throughout history as a dark-haired, Semitic-coded outsider who shape-shifts and deceives, and will eventually sabotage Asgard from within.

The original myth of Ragnarök—which predates the invention of race and was never written as a race war allegory—is a cautionary tale against arrogance, which sees extinction as an inevitable, cosmic fate, urging those who would fight it to accept defeat and instead live fully, knowing their world will all be gone soon. In our time, however, Ragnarök has become an allegory for the coming race war and a rallying cry against white genocide. As it is read today, it is a warning not to trust racialized outsiders, who will infiltrate the promised land, conspire with other outsiders, and bring about the downfall of civilization and extinction—convenient to anti-Semitic, anti-immigrant, anti-Black interpretations.

ASSASSIN'S CREED VALHALLA: ODINISM WITH PRONOUNS

Before we begin, we must first establish Eivor's gender. Eivor Varins-dottir, the Assassin from *Assassin's Creed Valhalla,* is canonically a fe-male assassin but can be played as either male or female according to player preference, or the player can "let the Animus decide," which is a choice that will intentionally switch Eivor's gender at key points in the course of the story. In the game, Eivor is gendered with they/them pronouns because they are two distinct beings in the same body for reasons that will become clear.

In *Assassin's Creed* lore, the gods we know from Greek, Roman, and Egyptian pantheons are ancestors of the Assassins—that's what gives them their powers. In this universe, the gods of mythology are called the Isu, an ancient prehistoric humanoid race that through breeding with humans long ago, created the Tainted Ones, superhumans from Isu bloodlines who have passed down extraordinary abilities genera-tion to generation through triple-helix DNA, so rare that only a hand-ful of present-day descendants remain, and who through the Animus, an advanced genetic neuro-modeling device, can relive the memories of their ancestors in a virtual reality simulation and become Assassins of antiquity during key historical eras of upheaval.

I began playing *Assassin's Creed Odyssey* after exams, and to its credit, without giving too much away, it's a fascinating critique of the genetics, tech, and military industries as colonial forces that exploit eugenics and farm human memory toward insidious ends. Here's the problem: the idea of the Isu seems to be inspired by the idea of root races, a key con-cept of theosophy, an influential occult philosophy that fused pseudo-science with mysticism, originating in the late nineteenth century, and whose eugenics-based racial theories directly influenced the Nazis.

According to root race theory, seven root races span the course of human evolution: Polarian, Hyperborean, Lemurian, Atlantean (as in the lost city of Atlantis), Aryan (the current phase of the human race), a future sixth race that will be eugenically selected and bred (in Baja California, Mexico, no less, more on that in a minute), and the seventh and final race, an evolved, eugenically selected, superhuman race that will inhabit a future Pacific continent. While root race theory did not define any of the root races by skin color (its theories were more mystical interpretations of archaeological findings of prehistoric humans), it did define a white variation of the Aryan root race evolved from the Atlantean race, some of which became the Nordic-Germanic peoples. This is the "scientific" basis for Aryanism, the Nazi ideology of white racial purity and supremacy that defines Aryans as white Nordic and Germanic peoples and the most racially pure "master race," due to its direct lineage from Atlantis.

Perhaps I'm sensitive to anything that points in the same direction as La raza cósmica, an essay written in 1925 by Mexican politician and intellectual José Vasconcelos touting the ideology of Mestizaje, or the idea of Latin America as the site of an evolved cosmic fifth race resulting from the fusion of all the world's races, and the "abundance of love that allowed the Spaniard to create a new race with the Indian and the Black, profusely spreading white ancestry through the soldier who begat a native family." The essay builds its argument on Theosophist cosmogony, pseudoscientifically assigning the history of world civilizations to that of the Lemurians, Atlanteans, Aryans, and so on. Although Vasconcelos's original intention was to reframe miscegenation as a spiritual evolution in response to the growing aversion to mixing races in the United States and Europe, and critique US imperialism for committing "the sin of destroying [Black and Indigenous] races while [Latin America] assimilated them," his positive eugenics is *still eugenics*. It is because of this essay that the mestize was constructed as the national race of Mexico, and how mestizaje, or the "improvement of the race," romanticized its racial sanitation project, encouraging the gradual loss of Blackness and indigeneity through intermarriage with Indigenous women toward a common Mexican destiny. It has resulted in the detribalization and whitening of Mexico through an insidious campaign of Spanish agrarian enterprise and intimate colonialism—widespread capitalist-sexual violence through European-Indigenous marriages with child brides, along with violent colonial hostility toward Black and Indigenous Mesoamerican peoples. So when it comes to root race, yeah. It's personal.

Atlanteans, the Fourth Root Race. In the *Assassin's Creed* universe, the Isu demigods fit a little too closely with the *racist* reading of root race theory. In *Assassin's Creed Odyssey,* set in ancient Greece around 431–422 BC, the assassin Kassandra is a Tainted One, a human-Isu hybrid—a clever interpretation of the half-human, half-god heroes of Greek mythology like Hercules and Perseus. The Isu of *Odyssey* are the gods of the Greek pantheon, who live in the city of Atlantis, which makes them Atlanteans. At face value this is harmless, until the next game, *Valhalla,* when the root race implications begin.

Aryans, the Fifth Root Race. *Assassin's Creed Valhalla,* set in 873 CE, 1,300 years after *Odyssey,* focuses on the assassin Eivor, who is *not* a Tainted One descended from the Isu but *is* the Viking god Odin, reincarnated in human form. This is where it becomes not so harmless. Walk with me:

1. Eivor is a human assassin with human parents, and no Isu admixture in their bloodline. Their adopted brother Sigurd is also human, with no Isu in his bloodline. Usually, Assassins have some measure of Isu-human genetic

admixture (connected to the Levantine Brotherhood, more on this later), but the human Viking Assassins do not.

2. The Isu gods are actually the prehistoric race of Eden, a technologically advanced civilization who created humans as a slave race. Adam and Eve led a group of humans to rebel against the Isu and wipe out their civilization in an event called the Great Catastrophe. The Isu that survived helped humans rebuild, and those gods are the ancestors of the Assassins, humans with access to Isu powers and technology.

3. If the Greek Isu gods of *Odyssey* are Atlantean, the fourth root race, but the Norse Vikings of *Valhalla* are not human-Isu hybrids, then that makes the Norse the fifth root race, which is none other than—you guessed it—the Aryans.

In past games, the Isu of Eden were the good-time gods of the Greek and Roman pantheon—Juno, Minerva, and Poseidon, depicted as ten feet tall with glowing armor and exaggerated features—and ancestors of the Assassins who helped build Atlantis after Eden fell. Crucially, when the Isu got it on with humans, they created Tainted Ones, mixed-race superhumans who eventually became the Assassins, beginning with Bayek of Siwa, who founded the Hidden Ones in Egypt, which evolved into the Levantine Brotherhood in the Middle East, and eventually the Assassin Brotherhood of Mediterranean Europe. All of these Assassins are human descendants of the Isu of Eden, not gods reincarnated as humans.

In *Valhalla*, however, Eivor, Sigurd, and other Norse characters are humans *and* literally reincarnated Isu gods. Unlike the Isu of Eden from previous games, the Norse Isu gods of Asgard are not physically taller or phenotypically different from Norse humans—instead they look exactly like their reincarnated human forms.

It is unclear why *Assassin's Creed Valhalla* breaks with the Tainted Ones storyline, but doing so unlinks Eivor from any genetic relationship to the Isu of Eden or the Levantine Assassins, while still possessing all of their exceptional powers and abilities. The implication is that Eivor is not a mixed-race *descendant* of the Isu like past Assassins—instead, Eivor *is* Isu, a racially pure version that evolved into both human *and* god. Eivor's blood is not "tainted" with Isu blood from Eden or human blood from Africa or the Levant, which means that they have no shared lineage with Bayek, the Black Egyptian Assassin and founder of the Hidden Ones, or the Levantine Brotherhood, or the heavily mixed blood of Assassins from Southern European countries. This implies that the Norse Isu gods, unlike those of Eden, never went extinct, and therefore never had to interbreed with Norse humans to survive, unlike any other culture in the *Assassin's Creed* universe. Instead, the Norse Isu simply evolved into a superior race of humans so genetically pure that the Isu gods Odin, Thor, Tyr, Freyja, and so on can simply upload their memories from Yggdrasil into any Norse human vessel and reincarnate at will—because the Norse naturally possess evolved Isu abilities, innate to their superior biology. So long as they maintain their racial purity, being Norse is superhuman enough for the gods to be reincarnated in them. That's a major deviation, and a meaningful one.

As if the "Norse Vikings are literally gods because of racial purity" angle wasn't bad enough, somehow the politics of *Assassin's Creed Valhalla* get even worse. The story begins in Norway, until circumstances force siblings Eivor and Sigurd to set out and form their own colony in England. Once they arrive, they must grow their settlement, which requires the player to raid monasteries over and over throughout the game. The raids are a play sequence with their own soundtrack and indulgently violent animations—aesthetically rich, culturally precise, intense, and rewarding, so well designed that they can even become fun, implicating the player into a kind of Brechtian moral bind. What does it mean to raid and burn down monasteries as settlers for reward? To boast and brandish an axe bloodied on a monk's cut head? The raiding imagery and music call back to the Norwegian church burnings of the 1990s, when black metal musicians and neopagan heathens burned down medieval churches in protest, claiming that the Norwegian people had been brainwashed by the Abrahamic religions and forgotten their pagan gods. In the same Norse Viking heathen tradition, modern-day Odinists and alt-right ethnonationalists still target temples, churches, and mosques for violence today. Many gamers don't know this history, and yet by raiding the monasteries, they are enacting these sublimated white supremacist themes for fun, and if that weren't bad enough, doing so to grow their settlement.

I don't believe the *Assassin's Creed* developers mean to advance white supremacist views or ideologies. In fact, I think they aim to refute them with accurate history—in the game, Black and Asian people live in Viking settlements, reflecting a more historically accurate medieval Europe as the migratory Eurasian landmass it was. Our protagonist Eivor is canonically female but can be played as either gender and can have romances with any gender, as any gender. Their brother Sigurd (Tyr) is a Viking explorer who, early in the game, returns from a diplomatic expedition having made contact with many lands and traded with "people of all colors," bringing back Silk Road gifts and people from all over the known world willing to settle among the Norse. To add to their credit, the developers took great care in designing a historical depiction of Vinland, the Viking name for the Newfoundland region of the Americas, consulting Indigenous language experts to write untranslated Indigenous language dialogue and voice its inhabitants.

The Norse gods themselves are also not depicted in the best light—they are excessive, proud, devious, and boastful, and Valhalla, the great hall of fallen warriors, is a nightmare. Eivor often ignores Odin's counsel of violence and domination, opting instead for diplomacy and allyship by asserting their will over Odin's control. Although the reincarnation of the gods is a central narrative pillar, Eivor's story is ultimately one of leaving Norway, and Valhalla, refusing to be tied to Odin any longer. By reclaiming their soul from Odin's grip, Eivor severs their fate from Odin's fate, thereby ending the Æsir's reincarnation loophole and liberating themselves from the cycles of violence that killed their parents and displaced their clan. It's a beautiful story, and a beautiful game.

Still, there is the problem of Basim, the mysterious, silk-tongued Assassin who returns with Sigurd from Constantinople. Basim is part of the Levantine Brotherhood of Assassins, and you find out later that he is also implied to be Muslim—a heavily racialized character against the backdrop of Vikings in medieval England, voiced by an actor who affects a vaguely Arabic accent. Despite his outsider status, Sigurd brings Basim into the Raven clan and treats him as a brother, much as Odin does with Loki. Although Basim becomes a friend who trains Eivor in stealth Assassin techniques and gifts them with the Assassin's blade, it is difficult to read Basim's intentions or know where his loyalties lie. It is a constant tension throughout the game—who is he, how much does he know, is he helping Eivor and Sigurd or luring them toward danger? He turns out to be the game's principal villain—the reincarnation of Loki seeking Odin in medieval times to avenge his son Fenrir. Basim betrays Eivor and Sigurd in this life, just as he did in Asgard; and just as Loki conspired with the lower realms to bring about Asgard's downfall, Basim's foreignness and connections to shadowy global networks are what make him dangerous. His ability to shapeshift—to move between worlds, play both sides, deceive, infiltrate, sabotage, and ultimately invade—represents the imagined threat all racialized outsiders pose to whiteness.

On the surface, it may seem that Viking stories are an attempt to seek an authentic reconnection to European culture, but the ubiquity of Viking narratives implies a deeper cultural desire: the return of white male dominance, free from colonial baggage or accountability. White men are attracted to Viking narratives because these let them imagine themselves as both the victors and victims of history, both superhuman conquerors and oppressed rebels fighting against Christianity and empire. The Viking predates settler colonialism, and is therefore a representation of whiteness exempt from the racial reckonings of the last ten years—Black Lives Matter, responses to global migrant crises, abolitionist and decolonization movements—that attempt to hold white people accountable for their history. The Viking is a symbol of masculinity and aggression, but also of extinction, and in our current political moment, it captures the rage of white men in social decline.

But perhaps *Assassin's Creed Valhalla* and other Ragnarök narratives speak to a different but related anxiety—of history repeating itself. The United States is just 247 years old; the Viking Age only lasted 273 years, between AD 793 and 1066. They could not continue to raid and plunder as a way of life. They faced an existential choice: adapt or die. Perhaps *Assassin's Creed Valhalla* is an old story reincarnated to help us learn from our mistakes.

There is no denying, though, that white supremacy is in the very DNA of Norse mythology and Odinism, and just as Odin can upload and reincarnate his memories into new bodies, so too can white men upload white supremacy into Viking narratives; so too can the gamer download white supremacist programming by consuming those narratives and embodying Eivor, the genetically superior Viking god, not just as an Assassin but as a vessel for his rage. It is up to the gamer what path he chooses with the material of Eivor's story—radical inclusion or reactionary aggression.

"I'M REALLY SAD, THEREFORE EVERYONE MUST DIE"—SOLAS, PROBABLY

In *Dragon Age: Inquisition*, the events leading up to its Ragnarök are a bit more ethically and emotionally complex. An evil mage has torn a gash in reality called the Breach, allowing demons to come through from the spirit realm (the Fade) into the realm of the living. You, the Inquisitor, spend the majority of the game politically uniting the realms and their races, only to find out that one disgruntled white elf supremacist you thought was your friend has been plotting against you the whole time in order to eradicate not only all the other races but his as well, and also to end the world.

Throughout the game, the rebel elven mage Solas is one of your primary allies, who helps you until he disappears without a word, only to be revealed at the final cutscene as Fen'Harel, or the Dread Wolf, ancient elven trickster god. (The betrayal! Cue me, screaming and crying and throwing up.) Solas only helped you because he means to restore Elvhenan, the magical prehistoric civilization of the elves, by ending the world for everyone else. Was he a megalomaniacal villain all along, or is he just a lost elf, bent on self-destruction?

The lore of the elves in the *Dragon Age* universe could fill an entire literature course, but for the purposes of this essay, suffice it to say that the elves are an allegory for both slavery and Indigenous dispossession, once a great civilization connected to the land, now estranged from it and one another and cut off from their immortality, memories, and magic. Those who maintain ties to what's left of elven culture are called the Dalish, who are identifiable by their facial tattoos and live in nomadic tribes in the wilderness; those who choose to sever ties are city elves and live in alienages, marginal settlements for the magically oppressed. Although the elves are the most oppressed race, like Tolkien's elves, they are mostly all white, and maintain an impossibly ethereal, delicate physicality as tall, thin, graceful, intuitive creatures. Despite their rarity and magic, they are reviled rather than revered, and are a labor class who suffer constant racism, exploitation, and sexual fetishization.

In *Dragon Age: Inquisition*, the player can choose from four races: an aristocratic human, an exiled dwarf, an "exotic" Qunari, or a Dalish elf. The *Dragon Age* games, especially *Inquisition*, have been widely praised for their inclusive representations of race, gender, and queer sexualities and romance storylines, as well as their robust avatar-building tool, which allows the player to construct their Inquisitor's features and race to the most precise, delicate degree. In the *DAI* universe, skin color does not define race—only magical race is acknowledged.

In post-Tolkien high fantasy, however, elves cannot be disentangled from colonial history, which inscribes their whiteness with meaning. The elves of *DAI* are still derived from Tolkien's elves of Norse mythology, described as demigods and luminous beings "more beautiful than the sun," earthly prototypes for the Æsir gods of Asgard. They are "of the purest white," as if "lit from within," although originally not in the racial sense. Their ancient genetic purity is what makes them immortal, telepathic, wise, and superior to all races, vulnerable to "fading" if they stay among humans too long. They are seen as a noble race going extinct as humans rise to power and corrupt the world.

So although the elves of *Dragon Age: Inquisition* are a colonized, dispossessed, and enslaved race, Solas and the elves are still based in Norse mythology and its symbolic systems, written as allegories for racial purity and superiority. Despite their colonial subjugation at the hands of empire, they can never be understood as allegories for Indigenous or Black people, but as whiteness imagining its own extinction. The fantasy of white genocide is the desire to possess Black and Indigenous histories of subjugation, where whiteness imagines its own history inflicted upon itself—a kind of reverse colonialism, where experiences of enslavement and colonial dispossession are imagined in white bodies. But those histories can never be possessed, not even in fantasy—when whiteness imagines its own subjugation, it is always in the context of apocalypse, where liberation means everyone must die: Ragnarök.

Before the events of *Dragon Age: Inquisition*, Solas—then the god Fen'Harel—lived in the ancient age, when Elvhenan, the immortal elven civilization, existed as a kind of Eden, or a version of the world unified with the realm of the spirit. Fen'Harel grew disgusted with the elf gods when, in their quest for power, they began enslaving their own people. To save the elven people, Fen'Harel created the Veil between the mortal realm and the spirit realm, and banished the elven gods forever. This required such a huge amount of power and will that he fell into a deep slumber. Humans rose to power, and the elves became mortal and disconnected from their magic. Since then, nine ages, or thousands of years, have passed, bringing us to the Dragon Age, when Fen'Harel wakes up. Elvhenan has been renamed Thedas, and a monotheistic religion reigns. Fen'Harel, now Solas, has to live in a terrifying world nearly devoid of magic, where subjugated elves have forgotten their splendor and all collective memory has been lost, surviving only in ruins and lost relics. The elves who did not die from human illnesses have been conquered and enslaved by humans.

Incognito as a common rebel mage, Solas joins the Inquisition to ultimately fix his "great mistake"—the creation of the Veil—and restore Elvhenan. Tearing down the Veil between Thedas and the Fade is an apocalyptic plan, however—doing so would be like breaking Solomon's seal and opening the gates of hell, liberating demons that would effectively end the world for everyone. But that is Solas's fatal flaw: his noble intentions make love into a destructive force, and his hubris makes him unable to foresee the consequences of his actions.

Solas is less like Odin or Thor and more like Loki, the outsider god, however. In the story of Ragnarök, Loki represents the Other in the race war, the leader of the invaders who will topple the white supremacy of Asgard.

Throughout, there are moments that complicate our understanding of Solas's motivations and resonate as postcolonial critique. Operating from a place of great sorrow, Solas is always acting on behalf of the elves' liberation and survival. He is an embodiment of ancient memory and a repository of arcane knowledge, which he recovers by crossing the Veil and sleeping in elven ruins, dreaming their history in an effort to record and restore what was lost. Whatever your relationship with Solas (it can easily go sour), he is also an archivist, painting heroic murals of your actions as the Inquisitor. If your Inquisitor is a female elf and in a romance with Solas (I was—11/10, highly recommend), he takes you to a beautiful waterfall at night and informs you that your facial tattoos, the Vallaslin, are actually slave markings, not gifts from the old gods, and offers to delicately and lovingly remove them with magic before mysteriously dumping you. Tortured, brilliant, unknowable, and ever-maligned as a duplicitous trickster god, Solas can be read as a tragic antihero who only sabotages and betrays those he loves because he is always opposed to the abuse of power, willing to sacrifice the world for the elves in order to restore Elvhenan and give the land back to its original people.

A very complicated decolonial, genocidal boyfriend.

Solas ghosts you at the end of *Dragon Age: Inquisition,* and we don't see him again until the very end of the *Trespasser* DLC. First you must navigate a complex conspiracy and chase him through an interdimensional realm of mirrors, broken bridges (isn't that every situationship?), elven ruins, and a structure called "The Shattered Library"—floating half-rooms of deteriorating books and records documenting lost elven science, poetry, great romances, and heroes. As you maneuver through the entropy of elven memory, you see the world as Solas does: already broken and lost to the fathoms of time.

Memory is a central theme in *Dragon Age: Inquisition,* if not its main battleground. One of the final quests in the base game is to find the Well of Sorrows, a fountain deep in a ruined elven temple that contains all the collective knowledge and memories of the ancient elves in its waters. The ruin is guarded by ancient elven sentinels—strong, graceful elves who have protected the well since the fall of Elvhenan. These elves have witnessed violence and atrocity at the hands of men across the ages, as well as the deterioration of elven culture and the magic of Elvhenan. But they do not identify with the elves of Thedas nor seek to help them, and only allow you, the Inquisitor, to access the well in order to be freed from the heavy burden of remembering.

This quest hits different: my history and indigeneity have been totally obliterated. I remember Indigenous members of my family and retain some of their healing rituals, but after they died, no records of their medicines, knowledge, or lineage survived. I would give anything to restore the path back to my ancestors. Solas's anxiety over restoring elven memory is recognizable to me as a kind of postcolonial haunting. He must watch as human mages study the elven history their kind obliterated, becoming self-proclaimed experts in elven ruins, language, and artifacts in order to appropriate elven magic. I get Solas, and his rage.

When you finally reunite with Solas at the end of *Trespasser*, the once slight and nerdy mage is now a gleaming god, elegant in smoky-opal elven sentinel armor, wolf fur draped over his shoulder, solemn and resolute in his goals. Solas has had a glow-up, and now that he looks better than ever, he's going to break your heart *again*. Solas says, "I suspect you have questions," and delivers this monologue:

I sought to set my people free
from slavery to would-be gods;
I broke the chains of all who wished to join me.
The false gods called me Fen'Harel,
and when they finally went too far
I formed the Veil and banished them forever.

Thus I freed the
elven people,
and in so doing
destroyed their world.

[. . .]

I lay in dark and dreaming sleep
while countless wars and ages passed;
I woke still weak a year before I joined you.

My people fell for what I did
to strike the Evanuris down
but still some hope remains for restoration.

I will save the elven people.
Even if it means this world must die.

Those iambs, though! Solas, unmasked as the Dread Wolf Fen'harel, has become Fenrir, the wolf that brings on Ragnarök, and the consequence of the impossible love of a god who can only liberate through betrayal. His deception is painful but necessary, although his feelings are real: "I would not have lain with you under false pretenses." (I am *bereft*.) The Inquisitor begs him to change his mind, but with a heavy heart and deep sorrow—"Ir abelas, vhenan," *I'm sorry, my heart*—he refuses to end his genocidal plan. And so with a final kiss, he cuts off her arm. (It's complicated—just know it was a kindness.) "Solas, var lath vir suledin!" the Inquisitor begs. *Our love will find a way to endure!*

Big "I can fix him" energy. The Solas-Inquisitor romance (Solavellan, if you want to spend hours browsing fan fiction and erotic fan art, not that I have) is the most popular in *Dragon Age: Inquisition*, with its tragic, star-crossed-lovers storyline complicating the finality of Solas's Ragnarök plot. The Inquisitor, the woman he loves, is an elf who stands for the cooperation of all races, all lands, all realms, in the fight against tyrannical evil and allows him to imagine another kind of future, consider another way to survive.

But Solas's romantic standards do raise an eyebrow. Of all the romanceable characters in *DAI*, Solas, a straight white male elf, is the only character with rigid racial and heterosexual standards: female elf only. Every other character is open to other races and sexualities.

Solas's sexual preferences could be read as racist, but as an elf—a fetishized, oppressed race—his desirability politics are murkier. Does Solas not mix races in an effort to preserve his elven racial purity? Or is it because Solas is a god that he does not mix with mortals? How you read his romantic preferences depends on how you want to read Solas himself—genocidal villain or rebel liberator.

There's also the problem of elven slavery as a metaphor. In *Scenes of Subjection*, Saidiya Hartman writes that slavery is incomprehensible; it is such an unintelligible, unfathomable violence that it can never be represented or understood. No attempt to represent slavery—neither explicit depictions of violence and brutality nor revenge fantasies—can capture or convey the material, bodily, lived, generational suffering of slavery, and to try is to indulge a desire to consume and possess Black pain. Representations of slavery meant to inspire empathy require the white viewer to imagine Black suffering as their own, resulting in a slippery empathy that exists only when Black suffering is visible and intelligible on a white body. This is why representations of white enslavement are dangerous: they do not increase empathy for Black descendants of the enslaved but rather allow white people to imagine themselves as slaves.

Even in fantasy worlds where skin color is neutralized and race is magical and metaphorical, fantasy races function within the same racial imaginaries as our world, just abstracted and distanced from history. Without a historicized racial context, the enslavement of white elves has no proximity to colonial violence, and therefore cannot motivate a politics of liberation. Instead, it validates white reactionary rage.

In *Dragon Age: Inquisition*, slavery is the narrative device that justifies Solas's genocide, framed as a kind of retributive, decolonial apocalypse. Is Solas's destruction of the Veil a revolutionary act of liberation and justice for the elves? Or is he an arrogant, tyrannical god, always acting on behalf of others without their consent, working from an ideology of elven supremacy? The only thing that saves Solas's campaign from fascistic vibes is ultimately his magical race, lacking structural, institutional, and political power. That, and love.

WHAT IF THE END IS ACTUALLY THE BEGINNING?

So we're back at the severed arm. How do they connect? *Dragon Age: Inquisition—Trespasser* and *Assassin's Creed Valhalla*'s respective visions of fantasy use the same repository of images from the same Norse and Viking symbolic systems: wolves, gods, apocalypses, whiteness, race, severed arms. But despite their developers' efforts to rehabilitate those systems, they end up in the same place with the same problematic implications: Ragnarök, or the race war at the end of the world.

Viking stories are often about fighting extinction, with extinction defined as the physical obliteration of a people. This is a difference between stories told from the perspective of the dominant culture and those told from a colonized or lost culture: extinction is not just the obliteration of a people but of memory, the shared cosmos of knowledge systems, language, gods, myths, and culture of creation—forcibly lost to the history of invaders.

What's unique and tragic about both of these games is how clearly *AC Valhalla* and *Dragon Age: Inquisition* worked really, really hard not to be racist, sexist, or homophobic, and went to great lengths to attempt radical inclusion. Ubisoft's disclaimer before all *Assassin's Creed* games has evolved and expanded its scope over time, from "This work of fiction was designed, developed, and produced by a multicultural team of various religious faiths and beliefs" to ". . . various beliefs, sexual orientations, and gender identities." They are really trying! And still, by virtue of its mythology, its history, how that history is situated in the present, who it engages, and what its racial imaginaries motivate, these games easily lend themselves to white supremacist interpretations.

Fantasy becomes high-stakes territory when it is reframed as what world we can collectively imagine, and for whom. If the stories we tell about the past are really the stories we are telling about the present, then the fact that Norse mythology and Vikings and European monarchs and British accents maintain such a strong hold on fantasy is *already* a racial conversation, and should be critiqued on its implications. As the white-dominant monoculture of the twentieth century fades, and content diversifies around smaller, more niche audiences, historical fantasy remains one of the last "universal" genres—code for default whiteness in a Western European setting—and one of the last holdouts employing all-white casts. In traditional fantasy, whiteness is canonical, a standard set in the source material, and therefore exempt from critique. But this is changing, in baby steps. The first phase has been to diversify characters and casts, with some attempts more successful than others. The recent backlash against the "woke" casting of actors of color in shows like *The Witcher* and Amazon's *Lord of the Rings: The Rings of Power* goes to show that fantasy is one of the last, unspoken realms of white dominance, ripe for radical new visions. The next phase will perhaps decenter the West.

In some versions of Ragnarök, after Fenrir consumes the sun, the ruins of the world will sink into the sea and nothing will be left but the void, the end of all creation. Other versions imagine a lush green world emerging from the waters, healed and repeopled by survivors who strive for life. Odin's obsession with his own extinction was rooted in ego and arrogance all along—as it turns out, the end of the world is ultimately a failure of the imagination.

"We've already survived an apocalypse," says Rebecca Roanhorse, Black and Indigenous author of the science fiction novel *Black Sun*, in the *New York Times.* "I set [my book] in the future specifically so I could say hey, Natives exist, and we'll exist in the future." What future does the survivor imagine when the end of the world has already happened? Fantasy has long been ready for narratives that transcend the limitations of white Western European history, whose timeline will always end in apocalypse and violence. "Whose fantasy" becomes a question of "whose imagination," and what characters, geographies, and histories that entails.

I desperately want to see fantasy and video games from different relationships to history, and different relationships to empire. The *Witcher* books, written by Polish author Andrzej Sapkowski following the fall of the Berlin Wall and the end of the Cold War, are just one example of how folktales from countries with histories of colonization, enslavement, pogroms, and genocide, decentered from Western European narrative conventions, breathe new life into high fantasy. What if lost mythologies and suppressed sagas from the global south were to be given the budget of an *Assassin's Creed* triple-A game? What kind of histories and futures could Black and Indigenous fantasy help us to imagine?

Fantasy, after all, is the space of the imaginary, and the imaginaries we collectively engage create our futures. Rather than resurrect and relive oppressive European colonial histories, why not spend time with people who have survived that history, and can evolve our sense of collective possibility? What other heroes can save us from these new monsters? And if we change our imaginaries, what are our stories capable of? What do they make capable in us?

THE FINAL BOSS

A Poetics of World-Building
in the Apocalyptic Imagination

N 2019, WHEN MY BROTHER GILBERT CAME TO LIVE WITH ME IN LA to help out with my son, I studied for my doctoral exams. As I read through a huge pile of postcolonial theory, race and digital media cultures, Black and Indigenous ecologies, and animal studies texts, he would play games on his PlayStation—*Skyrim, Assassin's Creed Origins, Monster Hunter.* He'd just graduated from community college with a two-year associate's degree, a huge accomplishment of which I was very proud. But I could tell my doctoral exams intimidated him, so I did everything I could to level the intellectual playing field between us. When I'd take breaks, I'd collapse on the couch next to him, and we'd think through the concepts I was grappling with as he played. Here's a secret: advanced theory isn't hard, it's just gatekept, and with the right frame and language, anyone can understand it. Gilbert pushed my readings and offered examples of those theories in the games he was playing.

One night, I kept hearing this line from the TV: "I take the bow, I sweep the sky with it. . . . I am he who knots the cord and lashes the shrine together. You will not devour my heart!" This is a piece of battle dialogue spoken by the Egyptian assassin Bayek of Siwa as he battles Apep, the Soul Eater, a giant snake in the chaos nightrealm of the dead in *Assassin's Creed Origins*.

"Okay, Bayek," I said. "That's some poetic-ass dialogue."

"Right? That's my man," my brother said. "And honestly, that's nothing. There's sooo much poetry in video games." At first he got me hooked on playing *Skyrim*, which quickly became a productive site of critical inquiry in colonial ecologies, memory studies, digital race. World-building is a mapping of our metaphors, built from the primal symbols and images of our collective imaginaries—kingdoms and their races reflect our own racial cartographies, biomes radically rebuild our ecologies, and lore is the invention of a collective past, or a collective future. After I beat *Skyrim*, he suggested I play a game called *Horizon Zero Dawn*, an RPG set in a postapocalyptic United States a thousand years in the future. "Robot dinosaurs!" he'd say, as if that were a convincing argument.

Within the last few years, I've cooled on science fiction as a genre, especially postapocalyptic stories. The genre isn't the problem—my issue is the framing of the future within a Western narrative context. The story is always headed toward, or surviving after, an apocalypse. This is the trap of Western consciousness, which operates on a series of givens: time is linear and it only flows in one direction; the mind, body, and soul are separate; magic is feminized folk wisdom and of the past, science is masculinized and oriented toward the discovery of the future; nature is named as a thing separate from us, no more than a setting and a source of extraction, imagined as a pristine untouched wilderness— the opposite of civilization. And Western narratives center the human, an invention of the Enlightenment sciences that emerged alongside the invention of race. The human is constructed in the image of a European man, center of reason, and defined by the presence of an Other. And for a long time that meant that only white people counted as human. Everyone else was savage, animal, property, alien. The concept of the human is rooted in European definitions of personhood; to be human is to always carry the historical baggage of colonialism and be defined by its inventions of gender, class, and race. Western consciousness is our default experience of reality—it's how we perceive time and space, structure language, form memory. We're all sitting in it right now. Can you feel it? How locked down in it we are? *Time keeps on slippin', slippin', slippin' into the future.* (I'm so sorry to bring the Steve Miller Band into this.)

The dominant stories driving climate breakdown and climate injustices are stories built into the physical infrastructure of our societies, environmental writer Amitav Ghosh argues. Everything, from your home to the layout of your city to the transportation system you depend on to the food system you participate in, is built on stories. The nuclear family, the suburb, cars, factory farming—these are all stories that build our world, just as real as metal and nails and cement. And those stories drive us toward certain futures.

The Sapir-Whorf theory of language tells us that the language we speak determines our perception of the world, reality, and time. Grammar creates a system of relation between people, places, and actions, and orients them in time. Mexican Indigenous linguist Yásnaya Elena A. Gil in her book *Ää: Manifestos sobre la diversidad lingüística* (Manifestos of Linguistic Diversity), writes about how Western languages construct time in the metaphors of horizontal planes, where the future moves ahead on a timeline into new space, and the past is behind us as a given. An everyday clause like *vamos a*, "we're going to," reinforces coloniality through that metaphor of moving ahead in space. She writes:

The linguist Martina Faller says that in the Quechua and Aymara languages, the metaphors of time are different. The past, which we already know, lies in front of us, while the future, uncertain, is behind us, at our backs so that we can't see it. In the case of Mixe language, time is also a metaphor of space, only that it's not horizontal, but vertical—time passes through us from our head to our feet; time falls onto us. Our saying: One cannot know what is coming, it comes down.

It is also thought that the Hopi people already had a sense of the theory of relativity long before Einstein because it is a concept nascent in their language, which has no tenses. This reorientation of time is depicted beautifully in the film *Arrival*, when twelve heptapods land on Earth to offer their language to humans. At first humans, using colonial and adversarial languages, perceive the heptapods as threats. The Chinese linguists communicate through mah-jongg, a game of adversaries and war, and thus translate their communication as "offer weapon." The white woman instead translates their message as "offer tool," and as she begins to decipher the circular heptapod symbols and signs, she begins to experience the future as a memory.

In her poem "Obligations 2," Layli Long Soldier detaches from colonial grammars—linear reading, sentence diagramming, tenses, clausal relationships. The poem can be read in any direction, and it pulls the reader into a constant present of infinite readings, where the future, the present, and the past are simultaneous. (Layli Long Soldier is our most beautiful heptapod.)

What is possible in a limited structure of linear time, where capitalism treats nature as a thing to be stripped and extracted from until it is barren, and not as part of us? Where hierarchies of race, class, and gender structure our relationships, our lands, our borders, our economies, our identities? Where we are always defining an Other to define ourselves?

We are surviving late-stage capitalism as we speak, and the knowledge that it will inevitably take us to the apocalypse is reflected in our stories, where we must literally fight a "final boss" to survive—*Parable of the Sower, 28 Days Later, The Terminator's* Skynet, *The Last of Us, Avengers: Endgame, Avatar,* even *Game of Thrones.* Winter is coming, and it's hard to imagine any other future. I've been calling this the apocalyptic imagination—the future of the West rendered in the memory of colonialism, or the fear that what happened to Indigenous people will inevitably happen to us. It is no accident that indigeneity appears in apocalyptic stories, if even just as an aesthetic; it is central to the apocalyptic imagination, from the Native couple that has survived the cordyceps zombies and is just chilling in their cabin in *The Last of Us* to settlers using the Indigenous body as a literal avatar for settler survival in *Avatar.* As a mestiza, although I'm an Indigenous descendant, I cannot ethically claim indigeneity—colonization has erased the archival paths back to my pueblo. James Cameron, however, can make billions cosplaying it. The West! What a piece of work.

Horizon Zero Dawn is a fascinating example of the apocalyptic imagination. Set a thousand years in the future, Western civilization is now a ruin. The land has rewilded, reclaiming the buildings and bunkers of humanity's last days. The land is now home to machine animals, and humans have reverted to primitive tribes that scavenge old cars and computers for parts, using bows and arrows, spears, and other rudimentary weapons to defend themselves from the machines. This is where I had a problem—after the apocalypse, to depict a humanity that has reverted to primitive ways to survive, the characters—including its main character, Aloy, a red-haired white woman whose future-Indigenous garb is composed of landfill plastic, leather, and scrap metal—are dressed and styled in a way that recalls Indigenous stereotypes. The bodies imagined in this state of future indigeneity are majority white, descendants of Western civilization. The settlers who brought the apocalypse to the Indigenous people of the Americas have now brought about their own, and now get to cosplay as Indigenous. It was too much, and I could never get into the game. Still, my brother was curious about my take on the ending, and he insisted that I at least watch him play while I studied so we could talk about the story.

"Dude, check it out. Metal poetry flowers," my brother said. An X button that read "Download" appeared above the flower, and when opened, the code the flower ran on said:

Code fragment downloaded:

///
[function: true]
From the mind of a single, long vine one hundred opening lives.
[function: true]
///

In the world of *Horizon Zero Dawn*, the tech industries of the global north have so completely fucked the world that at the end of the Anthropocene, nature itself is run by a central AI called GAIA. At first it worked well—the terraforming program used machine animals (robot dinosaurs!) to turn the land, clean the water, and germinate seed until the Derangement (presumably named after Amitav Ghosh's concept of the Great Derangement, or our current moment of ecological breakdown and climate change). In the video game, the Derangement was a turning point in GAIA, when the machines went from being docile and avoidant and became hostile to humans. Flora was never part of GAIA's program, but after the Derangement, these strange metal flowers began popping up all over the land. Their appearance is a total mystery, and when their file is opened, their subprogram gives no clues or additional information. Instead, the flowers run on these cryptic "code fragments" in the form of nature poems. But my favorite part: the metal flowers physically block your path. You cannot move forward or progress until you destroy the flowers, and to do so feels like hubris. And that, I *loved*—how the earth, scarred by colonialism and technocapitalism, still finds a way to override the GAIA nature program and make flowers out of metal, with poetry as their code. That is a radical concept: after all the flora in the world has gone extinct, the AI uses poetry to reproduce flowers because it is a language that retains the memory of flowers. Poetry is the language of collective memory, containing our oldest images, symbols, stories—a language the earth recognizes and uses in rebellion against humans' artificial technologies. Before I forget: bee orchid. We'll come back to it.

Every metal flower had a different poem fragment. Some were brief haikus, whereas others were much longer meditations, even entire sonnets written in formal Old English. I, ever-practical and thinking about a job, asked my brother, "Did the developers write original poems for the flowers?" We looked it up, and the answer was disappointing. The code fragments were pulled from existing poems. It always annoys me when poetry is represented in pop culture as old writing by dead poets—it implies that poetry is a language of the past, a language lacking utility in the present other than to be reprinted in Hallmark cards and quoted in speeches.

The metal flowers had three species, each running a different kind of poetry code. The Mark I flowers reproduced Japanese poets like Basho; Mark II flowers used lines from Persian, Indian, and Chinese philosophers;

and Mark III flowers (I guess the most evolved?) reproduced the longest passages from British and American literature. And that sucked. Even the poems' flower "species" replicated the canon's colonial structures.

Here's the thing, though: the rebel AI never came up with its own poems. It could only replicate lines from existing poems, re-create existing images, draw from the language of long-dead poets. AI would never write an original line. Poetry, it would seem, was also a memory, existing in the future only as fragments, readable only as code.

Which made me wonder: Does poetry exist in the future? I don't mean fifty or a hundred years from now, but across the lone and level sands of time. What poems will AI remember? What consensus will its algorithms arrive at to rebuild the memory of our past? What pasts will AI reproduce?

I am reminded of the poem "Ozymandias" by Percy Bysshe Shelley, in which an inscription on the pedestal of a once mighty statue of Ozymandias, now reduced to a pair of legs and a shattered head, proclaims, "Look on my Works, ye Mighty, and despair! / Nothing beside remains." But something did remain. The absence of Ozymandias's sculpture is felt in its echo. The language fills the absence with affect—what remains is the memory of hubris, now layered with irony and grief, forever preserved in language.

While poetry contains the memory of the world in its ancient symbols and images, it is also an untamable language, unintelligible to AI and utterly unreproducible. If AI is the next stop in Western progress, what radical potential does it have to build a new world?

Hear me out.

Language is in crisis. As the forces of algorithm accelerate misinformation, abstract violence, dismantle meaning, and estrange us from one another, the creative process of storytelling and meaning-making itself is in jeopardy, threatening to replace writers with AI. In the forward charge of Western progress, AI is "the future," a cheap techno-capitalist labor source and, according to its own developers, a world-ending technology that will hyperconcentrate wealth, strip natural resources, devalue highly skilled creative and intellectual work, worsen inequality, produce a consensus version of reality, and accelerate civilization collapse. AI *is* the apocalyptic imagination (the AI abbreviation was accidental), and its creators are the Final Boss.

Listen, I'm not one for pessimism, but once quantum computing comes fully online, the world as we know it will be replaced with something unrecognizable. Our most beloved stories have tried to warn us—from entire newsroom and writing staff layoffs to deepfakes to record arctic temperatures to police robot dogs, the real world is happening so much faster than we realize. So what do we do? AI technology learns from us every time we use it, and learns from us even when we don't use it. Its natural language and cloning abilities are improving at an alarming rate, able to generate art, photos, film— the entirety of human creation—in any style with incredible accuracy.

Except one. AI sucks at poetry *so bad.*

Poetry is a language AI cannot fake. It is an insurgent language liberated from utility and sense-making; it resists manipulation and emptying by design; it is a rhizomatic grammar that invents new structures and patterns of meaning and relation, forges new neural pathways; it is a speech act that manifests in space like a spell, a contract, a condemnation. And most importantly, poetry is our oldest oral tradition, containing our most ancient memory. Remember when I wondered what poets AI would remember? Well, I asked ChatGPT: *Who are your favorite poets?* And it responded with the most celebrated poets in the English language, an attribute I never asked for. It just presented its bias as

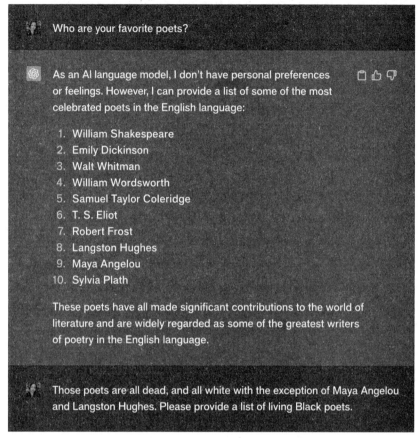

Who are your favorite poets?

As an AI language model, I don't have personal preferences or feelings. However, I can provide a list of some of the most celebrated poets in the English language:

1. William Shakespeare
2. Emily Dickinson
3. Walt Whitman
4. William Wordsworth
5. Samuel Taylor Coleridge
6. T. S. Eliot
7. Robert Frost
8. Langston Hughes
9. Maya Angelou
10. Sylvia Plath

These poets have all made significant contributions to the world of literature and are widely regarded as some of the greatest writers of poetry in the English language.

Those poets are all dead, and all white with the exception of Maya Angelou and Langston Hughes. Please provide a list of living Black poets.

AI only knows dead poets.

neutral fact: Shakespeare, Emily Dickinson, Walt Whitman, William Wordsworth, T. S. Eliot, Robert Frost—a list of mostly Western white men, all writing solely in English. Because of course.

If you'll forgive my foray into structural linguistics for just a moment, according to Swiss linguist Ferdinand de Saussure, language takes two distinct forms: *langue* and *parole*. *Langue* is language that exists outside of the body and is shared as a social concept, like grammar rules, vocabulary, the written word, whereas *parole* is embodied language, everyday speech, the moment of speech, living, breathing language that physically interacts with the world and, when spoken to another, creates relation. The difference between these two forms of language is best illustrated in a story from Plato's *Phaedrus*, when Socrates tells his student the Egyptian myth about the creation of writing. According to the myth, the god Theuth presented the pharaoh Ammon with the gift of writing, which he called an "elixir of memory and wisdom." But Ammon was skeptical, and argued that writing had the opposite power:

> For this invention will produce forgetfulness in the minds of those who learn to use it, because they will not practice their memory. Their trust in writing, produced by external characters which are no part of themselves, will discourage the use of their own memory within them. You have invented an elixir not of memory, but of reminding; and you offer your pupils merely the appearance of wisdom, not true wisdom.

For Ammon, the danger of writing is that it externalizes language and depends on signs that may be interpreted differently by others, and therefore becomes open to misunderstanding, or worse, manipulation and violence. When memory is recorded in writing, one person's account becomes documented history; when memory is embodied and shared through an oral tradition, it becomes collective memory. History is subjective and documents can be manipulated; collective memory is public, and much harder to eradicate or contradict.

This is what poetry is. Poetry *is* the oral tradition, the performance of public memory. Poetry contains the cosmos of every creation myth, pulls dream-language from the collective unconscious, transmits rituals, customs, and tradition across generations, keeps records in the form of epics, fables, psalms. But it is in the performance of poetry that language becomes a living thing, charged with feeling, animated by body and breath, until that moment of recognition that plunges you into the strange truth of pure language that, for a split second, contains the memory of the world. (I've heard WHEW *snaps* HOLY SHIT, WHAT THE FUCK involuntarily tumble out of people in response to a poem.) *That* moment, when you "feel physically as if the top of [your] head were taken off," like Emily Dickinson said, *that feeling* is what makes poetry an incorruptible language, and the steady foundation upon which to build worlds.

The word *poetry* itself comes from the ancient Greek word *poiesis*, meaning "to make" or "to create," but as a concept, it is closer to "to bring forth," or "to reveal." To create is to reveal what was already there. Let's say you want to make a chair, and a tree provides the wood for that chair. Yes, you are creating that chair, but you are also revealing the chair inside the tree, or the potential form a tree can take. That chair already existed in the tree, but by creating it, you just revealed it and brought it forth. Poiesis is not just what artists do, but the world itself in the act of creation—the blooming of the blossom, the emergence of the butterfly from the cocoon, the snow that melts and creates a waterfall, the waterfall that feeds the river, and the river that houses the fish and fish eggs. According to Heidegger, poiesis is a threshold occasion, or the moment of ecstasis, when one thing steps outside of itself, outside of its old form and becomes a new one. In *The Poetics of Space*, Gaston Bachelard writes, "the poet speaks on the threshold of being," or draws from the collective unconscious and roots the cosmos to language, and from that threshold between cosmic being and language, a world emerges. Can poetry really rebuild the world?

In *Staying with the Trouble*, ecotheorist Donna Haraway offers her concept of sympoiesis. If poiesis is to create or make something from nature, sympoiesis is a "making-with" or "worlding-with" nature—a radical reorientation of the storying human into animal, in company with the "complex, dynamic, responsive, situated, historical systems" of a shared ecology after the Anthropocene. The planet is already engaged in sympoiesis all the time. Haraway shows us this concept in a xkcd webcomic called *Bee Orchid*, which features an orchid that looks like a female bee. This orchid evolved its form to lure the male bees, who were so stupid about pollinating that their species became endangered. Anyway, that bee went extinct (because men), but the memory of its mate lives in that flower. And like the metal flowers in *Horizon Zero Dawn*, that orchid's genetic code reproduces the memory of the past, and that is also poetry.

In *Humanimal*, poet Bhanu Kapil writes a searing indictment of British colonialism and Western dualist concepts separating human from animal. The book tells the story of the "Bengali wolf girls" Kamala and Amala, two girls raised by wolves in the Bengal jungle in 1921, and their time under the tutelage of Reverend Singh, who studied the girls and attempted to reintegrate them into Indian society. The wolves that raised them were killed, the girls' supinated limbs were surgically reset to walk upright, and they were taught language, socialized with human mannerisms, and taught to behave as "human." But in "taming" the "hideous" girls, they also killed the wolves inside them. Later, in *Schizophrene*, Kapil details her experience of writing *Humanimal*. Because the only existing records of the wolf girls were biased accounts from Reverend Singh and other specialists, written in violent colonial language, in the absence of their unrecorded childhood with the wolves, Kapil attempts to recover that unrecorded history from the memory of the earth. "I threw the book into the dark garden," she writes. "The account begun mid-ocean, in a storm." Kapil buried the manuscript to "absorb" Kamala and Amala's story, and in so doing, dreamed visions of the girls. In this way, Kapil inverts the concept of the necrobibliography, or the texts we bury to silence the past, whose silences come back to haunt us. Haunted by the girls, Kapil literally buries the text to exhume their story, and in so doing collaborates with the earth to re-cover a truer, more complete animal memory.

In *Zong!*, poet M. NourbeSe Philip composes a 182-page poetry cycle entirely from the words of the case report for *Gregson v. Gilbert*, a haunted legal document recording the drowning massacre of some 130 enslaved Africans aboard the slave ship *Zong*, en route from West Africa to Jamaica, beginning on November 29, 1781. The captain of the slave ship made critical navigational errors, causing extreme delays in the voyage, and so, to save on food and water, he ordered the enslaved to be thrown overboard so that the Gregsons could file a claim of reim-bursement from their insurers, the Gilberts. When the Gilberts refused to honor the contract, the Gregsons sued and won. The Gilberts' appeal, however, granted a new trial, and it is the language from this proceed-ing and the sole existing public document related to the massacre that makes up the book. *Zong!* begins by parsing the legal language in the document as well as its interstices, gradually opening up its silences to access the testimony of the enslaved, buried in the subtext. Philip breaks the encoded language of the historical document down into fragments, utterances that, through ululating interpolations and rep-etitions, enter into a fugue state that is able to access water memory, or the depths of the pre-language unconscious—an ocean of collective memory where the dead might speak. The spirit of the text moves through the work so that the buried voices of the enslaved surface from the ocean of the collective unconscious. Philip's fragmentation of the document is a literal code-breaking, a decryption of drowned voices that tell their story in the form of pure affect—a haunting. The testimonies of the enslaved have been drowned, their silences buried; their story can never be told, yet it must be told. The earth is a perfect record, and only the poet can access the language of its testimony.

In *Poetics of Relation*, Édouard Glissant points to the importance of fragmentation and form in writing the ghosts of colonialism, and the necessity of nonnarrative nonlinearity in the writing of historical atrocity. The postcolonial terrain does not reflect the linear history of Western conquest but is instead haunted by the Plantation, a repeating, circular history made possible by shattering memory and language, only to be replaced with "incomplete, obliterated, or ambiguous archives." To me, Glissant is describing haunting as a form of earth memory, a record repeating in its cycles; I've always defined haunting as a kind of psychic imprint in the earth, a visceral energetic charge you can feel in space, full of emotional information—like the feeling of a house where someone has died, or entering a room just after a fight. A haunting is the earth in the act of remembering, a repeating record of the past that collapses time, shining its echoes into the present and future. To be haunted is to remember with the earth.

In "A Small Needful Fact," a poem that is one long sentence punctuated by commas, or breaths, poet Ross Gay reflects on Eric Garner's death by police asphyxiation. Rather than writing about Garner's death, Gay shows us glimpses of his life through the life process of trees, and their symbiotic relationship to us as they create oxygen out of our exhalations. Gay's use of "perhaps" tells us this is not a memory but a fabulation, a speculative account of Garner's time working for the Parks and Rec department. But the consciousness that narrates the poem feels like tree memory, its slow time, its sensory data, the detail of "his very large hands" planting trees "gently into the earth," his contribution to life with plants that "house and feed small and necessary creatures," his Black life as part of all our life processes, and his small role in "making it easier for us to breathe"—a fact that only amplifies the injustice of his death. The "us" in the final line can be read as us humans, but part of me feels the trees share in this lament, as Garner's exhalations were also part of their breathing.

Sympoiesis can be used in the absence or erasure of documents, where the earth is the only remaining record. This record, or earth memory, we might also know or understand as haunting, or the imprint of a memory that lives in the land and refuses to fade.

Cuban artist Ana Mendieta in her Silueta series, begun in 1973, collaborated with the earth and its processes to reveal its memory in the form of silhouettes—haunted imprints that recall forgotten ancestors, construct past and future selves, reanimate ancient crime scenes, unearth primordial forces through the presence, or absence, of the female form. This "omnipresent female force" Mendieta sought was a felt thing, a form that would only reveal itself through an intuitive process of feeling her body interact with the earth in collaboration. Sometimes the figure would emerge as an absence imprinted in the elements; sometimes it appeared as a transmutation in processes like fire or gunpowder; sometimes the figure called for Mendieta's body to merge with the earth, and as she did, her body itself became the haunted site where time collapses, providing a glimpse into the racial-sexual violences of colonialization, the earth's witness now embodied, its traces traced. As a colonized woman, Mendieta sought to excavate ancestral memory through the body. By literally tracing her body into the earth, she leaves a trace, a record that opens a portal to ancestral memory.

We know that stories are not just representations of the world, but *makers* of the world. Some stories are world-making, others world-changing, but the stories written in the apocalyptic imagination are, most often, world-reinforcing.

Consider This:

1. Every time you chat with AI, it uses 500 milliliters of water on the average. That may not seem like much,

about as much as a sixteen-ounce bottle of Aquafina. But if used worldwide, that water consumption quickly adds up into something much more significant.

2. Training one AI model can release as much as five cars' lifetime's worth of carbon emissions. Training GPT-3 required the amount of water used to fill a nuclear cooling tower.

3. ChatGPT's creator, OpenAI, paid Kenyan workers as little as $1.32 per hour to parse and label toxic AI content. AI labor is routinely outsourced to the global south, and exposure to its most extreme language and images has traumatized workers.

4. AI is at the forefront of mass surveillance and facial recognition technologies used by federal agencies, military, and police. Peter Thiel, Facebook board member and Trump adviser, is a primary funder of companies Palantir, Clearview AI, and most recently Anduril (named after a sword in *The Lord of the Rings*, also backed by SpaceX), maker of the 189 autonomous surveillance towers along the US-Mexico border. Customs and Border Protection began using compulsory facial recognition technology to scan migrants at border crossings in Texas and California in September 2018. Clearview AI trained on "more than 3 billion photos ripped from Facebook, Instagram, YouTube, and other websites" to develop its facial recognition technology, with an image database "almost seven times the size of the FBI's." Clearview has credentialed users at the FBI, Customs and Border Protection, and hundreds of

local police departments, and such technologies have recently been implemented at scale, when ICE and the FBI scanned state DMV databases without the public's knowledge or consent, and Miami police used the technology to arrest a protester following the George Floyd uprisings. After Clearview signed a contract with ICE in 2020, Charles Johnson, Breitbart writer and close associate of Thiel, wrote they were "building algorithms to ID all the illegal immigrants for the deportation squads." Palantir, named after the crystal balls of *The Lord of the Rings*, has used its data-mining and analytics technology to gather personal information about undocumented migrants and help ICE carry out violent immigration raids across the country.

5. AI is the single biggest threat to the livelihoods of creative, information, media, and culture workers, having already led to mass layoffs and major publication closures. Over a dozen authors, including George R. R. Martin, Victor LaValle, George Saunders, Jodi Picoult, and the Authors Guild have filed a lawsuit against OpenAI and Microsoft, citing the companies' illegal use of their copyrighted material without permission to train ChatGPT and other generative AI tools. The Writers Guild of America and SAG-AFTRA held strikes over the spring and summer of 2023 to demand AI and image protections for writers and actors; Getty Images and visual artists have also filed lawsuits against Stability AI and Midjourney for illegal use of images to train their programs, to which the companies have responded that it is "impossible" to create AI tools without copyrighted material.

6. AI is a robot, capable of endlessly exploitable free labor, which diminishes the value of *all* labor, human and AI-generated alike. The etymology of the word *robot*, from Etymology Online: from Czech *robotnik* "forced worker," from *robota* "forced labor, compulsory service," from *rabota* "servitude," from *rabu* "slave." AI's uses—generating human content, data, images, and labor without the human being—is just the latest dehumanizing force that continues the capitalist project of slavery without slaves. Black domestic workers, Chinese railroad workers, braceros, hacendados, undocumented migrants, women, children, and prisoners were and are all dehumanized labor subjects; what will it mean for all labor itself to be dehumanized?

7. Military applications of AI have led to an unprecedented death toll in Gaza in 2023, due to the Israeli military's use of an AI targeting system called "Habsora" ("The Gospel"), which can "generate" targets almost instantly, wiping out entire families and residential areas, described by former intelligence officials as a "mass assassination factory."

How do we exit the Apocalyptic Imagination? How do we exit being human, exit the West, exit time? World-building is a radical reorientation to time and space—rather than progressing on a linear path, ever growing, consuming, extracting, perhaps we exit time by refusing to progress. Perhaps we refuse the future and simply stand still in the field of temporal simultaneity, like Layli Long Soldier. Perhaps we exit history and rehistoricize the world through Sylvia Wynter's concept of decolonial scientia, a new system of knowledge based in Indigenous knowledges, where history begins not with the emergence of the Human but with the emergence of the first living organisms on the planet, of which we are but one.

In *Becoming Human*, by Zakiyyah Iman Jackson, and the larger field of animal studies, the Western idea of "the human" is left behind entirely, as it never included Black, enslaved, colonized, or Indigenous peoples to begin with. To embrace our animal consciousness is to exit history and enter a different kind of time, live another kind of life in kinship with the natural world. In fact, the concept of "nature" will not exist either—it will just be the world as it is. Restorying is possible.

AI cannot compete with this kind of revolutionary language, cannot imagine Black and Indigenous futures. It has trained on the worst of us, and can only ever replicate and remix what has already been written, thought of, told. But AI cannot give birth, lose a child, get its heart broken, be abandoned by a parent, forgive an abusive parent, watch a parent age, experience racism, transition its gender, emigrate, or be separated by immigration. It is pure *langue*, a disembodied language that, in being external, can never engage in *parole*, or language that lives in the body, breathes, shares, connects, and interacts with the world. Poetry is that embodied language. Poetry is of the body, from the body, stored inside us, always on the threshold of becoming: an origin, a myth, a performance, an utterance, a bard's tale, an installation, a book, a draft. That threshold is poiesis; poetry allows us to step outside of ourselves, our old forms, our old worlds, and make new worlds possible. We've done it before: "In the beginning was the word."

Anyway, it doesn't matter if we change. The orcas are already organizing. They will sink Jeff Bezos's yacht. At our end, the earth will defeat the final boss. And then it will live on, without us.

MAGICAL REALISM
Or Newton's Apple Suspended between Falling from the Tree
and Being of the Tree

I keep trying to get everyone in my family to go to therapy. No one
ever responds. Well, my brother responded once by explaining "hood
psychology," or how depression and trauma are handled among
working-class men of color, where hardships are common but toxic
masculinity still demands lack of emotion and restraint. "It be like that
sometimes" or "It is what it is" are tacit acknowledgments of
circumstances you are powerless to change. Therapy isn't accessible
in the hood—it's not covered by most minimum wage insurance, so
disorders go undiagnosed and unmedicated across racial, language,
and culture barriers. I think of my boomer immigrant parents, how
they've been expected to suppress and overcome, and immediately
know, therapy will never speak their language. I feel so delicada
for being in therapy, and feel even worse when I apply what I've
learned with my parents, like I'm patronizing them with my
enlightened, whitened feelings when I gently interpret and name
their anger, listen, understand, hold difficult truths. Now, I'm
everyone's therapist.

There are clinical names for what the body does when our reality
betrays us: shock, disassociation, post-traumatic stress disorder,
mania, psychosis, schizophrenia. These are diagnoses based on the
assessment criteria laid out in the *DSM-V* (*Diagnostic and Statistical
Manual of Mental Disorders*, 5th edition), a book that, as I only
recently found out, has largely been discredited by mental health
professionals, including its own creators. The National Institute of

Mental Health withdrew its support from the volume in 2013, two weeks after it was published, citing the diagnosis of "symptoms" as arbitrary, revealing more about the diagnosing expert's own cultural bias and ties to the pharmaceutical industry than about the patient's well-being. In the 1950s the first *DSM* consisted of only 60 disorders; by 2013 there were 297, each classified by "clusters" of symptoms whose borders are more porous than defined, and which overlap across 90 percent of all diagnoses.

It makes me wonder what the baseline for sanity is, what the reality we agree on should look and feel like. Because psychiatric diagnosis is pure unreality; all deviance is measured against a default white male body, standing in the sterile white room of Western science. Under a microscope, stripped of context, we all look crazy. I resent the focus on mental illness as an individual condition, somehow all rooted in childhood trauma rather than being a product of its environment. Diagnosis rarely turns its gaze outward to the social or the structural—depression is never linked to public school food and lead in the water; anxiety is never connected to lack of child care or Astroturf playgrounds; ADHD is never diagnosed as a response to standardized tests and black mold in buildings; bipolar disorder is rarely connected to broke, overworked parents or racial trauma. Who can help but think magically in that kind of world?

Magical thinking, derealization, and disassociation are not only normal responses to a traumatic environment but, for many of us, also a culturally specific narrative framing of survival.

We know trauma compounds across generations through epigenetic scarring—what "disorders" do colonization and slavery manifest as in our bodies? What does a fracture in reality, the colonial encounter, do to a collective story, a collective memory, a collective unconscious?

Here is what I know: trauma is not depression, or grief, or anxiety. It is a fundamental change in your relationship to reality. Once a stable, predictable, knowable thing bound by physical laws, after trauma, reality becomes an unknowable, unstable thing. You lose all sense of the world as it once was. Reality is suspended in time between two futures—the foreclosed future you were headed toward and the dangerous, uncertain future you are now forced to accept.

Magic, like violence, is the blunt force of someone else taking narrative control. The loss of power in your own story. In someone else's reality, your story becomes so unbelievable, so unlikely, the burden of proof falls on you to reclaim the truth. But how can you, when the laws of nature no longer hold the world together? I think often about how what it means to be racialized, gendered, alienated as an immigrant is to experience reality as someone else's story, as unreality, narrated in a strange language, a reality where you are, by default, unbelieved. And from that position—unreal, unbelieved—why even tell your story? To a therapist, or to anyone? From that position, the only story you can tell that is intelligible is the story of your success. Immigrant success stories and bootstraps narratives are when we can finally become part of the story, when we can join reality, and the future.

I am laughably bad at math, but one thing I fully understand is the x-y axis, negative numbers and positive numbers, time and space as a field. I have seen how equations, when plotted on an axis, form a wave, or an intersection in the field of space. The parabola is my favorite; it reminds me of the word *parable* and the symmetry of a parable's story, the most famous parable being the one about the rainbow. Yes, I mean the story of Noah, but not the flood. My fascination is with the rainbow as a sign after an apocalypse, God's parabola as the symmetry of creation and destruction—positive numbers, negative numbers. A rainbow is a reflection of the earth's shape in light across the firmament; how light cuts the earth with light, how light and water fan matter out into color. Creation and destruction in a single form. The rainbow's parable: a covenant with God that never again would life on earth be threatened with total annihilation.

I said earlier that trauma is not individual but a collective, structural, and shared reality. I also described trauma as the moment a timeline breaks into two futures—the foreclosed, and the unknown.

Creation: Once upon a time, I believed, as Martin Luther King Jr. said, that "the arc of the moral universe is long, but it bends toward justice." I always loved that visual, that preacherly turn of phrase. If the starting point of the arc is injustice (negative numbers), when calculated, it guarantees an end point as its equal and exact opposite. The symmetry of the parabola is a parable promising justice after injustice as a mathematical certainty.

Destruction: Later, I learned about another arc in Thomas Pynchon's novel *Gravity's Rainbow*, named after the path a missile traces across the sky before it lands. All projectiles follow the curved path of a parabola in an act of war. After launch, they cover horizontal and vertical distance, but as gravity pulls the projectile down, its horizontal distance begins to arc, and bends the path of the projectile into a rainbow. A parable as mathematical certainty: human progress is not a line but a parabola whose symmetry will always end in self-destruction.

Both arcs abide by the laws of nature; both are a state of suspension, headed toward different outcomes. Justice is relative, depending on whose narrative gets plotted onto the timeline of history. Now you see why I could never be a mathematician. To me, even a parabola is a site of magical realism, deciphering the beauty of God's intelligence. The realist uses the parabola to exact a death calculation, allowing for no such sentimentality in the machines of war.

THE USES OF FANTASY

I T'S EASIER TO IMAGINE THE END OF THE WORLD THAN THE END OF capitalism." This is the title of the first chapter in Mark Fisher's book *Capitalist Realism: Is There No Alternative?* It's a famous phrase often quoted across the internet, attributed to philosophers Fredric Jameson and Slavoj Žižek. Based on Socialist Realism, the leftist art and culture of the Soviet Union, *capitalist realism* is the art and culture of empire, and our current shared "reality" as a kind of mass delusion, in which every aspect of human life and relations—love, birth, death, food, shelter, mental health, relationships, space, even dissent—is commodified and exploited for capital. The book asks, what happens to the imagination when capitalism "follows you when you dream," structures time, shapes our consciousness, resets our nervous systems, becomes the dominant narrative of "reality" that suppresses what we do not want to see—the tents that stretch from Skid Row to Hollywood Boulevard, the salmon farms clogged with waste in warming oceans, the bombs whistling down from the sky. That disconnection from the Real—from ourselves, the earth, and one another—is deliberate, and meant to disempower and demobilize us, to make us believe there is no other alternative, no other path to the future, to limit our ability to imagine other futures, to dream of any other world.

The global south has entered the chat. This of course is a very broad summary of Fisher's book, and although I have my critiques, I want to call attention to these two words: *imagine* and *realism*.

ONE NIGHT IN LATE OCTOBER 2023, I CAME ACROSS A VIDEO ON TIK-Tok where a few young Palestinian men are gathered in a recording studio and invited to listen to something. The video looks and feels like a glossy BuzzFeed production, but it isn't. "You ready?" the producer asks. "Mm-hmm." Once they sit down, give their consent, and put on the headphones, a realistic news report that Palestine has finally been liberated begins to play. The news report is narrated by a woman speaking in Arabic and played in voiceover for the viewer, and as the audio plays, their reactions are filmed individually and cross-cut as they listen. One smiles privately to himself; the next closes his eyes and takes a deep breath, exhales; the third lifts up his kufiya.

You can almost see what they're picturing. There is a moment when the imagined scene is sustained long enough that it becomes real for a split second. Then the news report ends. One of the men takes off his headphones and says, in English, "One day." The TikTok poster, who has translated the Arabic audio to English in captions, writes, "(Insha'Allah)." Of 3,569 comments, every single one I read spoke of tears, goosebumps, hope. I have tried to find the source of the video, but all my searches produce are videos of death, destruction, commentary. On

TikTok the video is not cited either—it is a copy downloaded and credited to another user, an account that when clicked, is banned.

IMAGINE

There is a conversation between George Lucas and James Cameron in his 2018 documentary series, *James Cameron's Story of Science Fiction*, where the two directors break down the political allegories of *Star Wars*. Lucas begins by explaining that as an anthropology student, his expertise was in social systems, and that in storytelling, science fiction has two branches: science, and the social. As a storyteller, his interest was in the social. Cameron responds, "You did something very interesting with *Star Wars*, if you think about it. The 'good guys' are the rebels, they're using asymmetric warfare against a highly organized empire—I think we'd call those guys 'terrorists' today. We call them Mujahidin, we call them Al Qaeda." George Lucas replies, "When I did it, they were Vietcong."

Cameron clarifies. "So *were* you thinking of that?" and before he even finishes the question, Lucas nods and affirms, "Yes." Cameron seems a little uneasy with that answer, so he tries to soften that position and situate the film in American history as part of the anti–Vietnam War protests of the 1960s and antiauthoritarian against-the-man politics nested within a fantasy. Lucas corrects him: "Or a *colonial* . . . 'we're fighting the largest empire in the world.'" Lucas, in no uncertain terms, explains that the rebels weren't based on white hippie liberals, who are *part* of empire, but were an allegory for the Vietcong, a small group of "Third World" anticolonial, anti-imperial revolutionaries and freedom fighters. Terrorists.

It was wild to hear George Lucas, the director of a multibillion-dollar franchise, use the word *colonial* to describe the Empire (especially to the director of *Avatar*). As a kid, watching *Star Wars* always felt like seeing the Rio Grande Valley in space—a hot, heavily patrolled working-class planet of farmers and wanderers, junkyards and jalopies, franken-droids made of spare parts. Tatooine was a postcolonial landscape, where the good guys bypass borders and checkpoints by mind-controlling the mind police, their spaceship is a bucket of bolts that keeps breaking down, and a beautiful princess is the brains behind the rebellion. It was a future that mirrored the broken-down cars in our driveway, my dad's warped copies of *Popular Mechanics* and his "inventos" (like his homemade power strip, just a light switch with electrical plugs screwed into a piece of plywood), guitar cables and effects pedals cracked open to reveal their circuit boards. When *Star Wars* reruns aired on weekends, sometimes we'd watch the Spanish-dubbed version, where R2-D2 was called "Arturito," and Chewie didn't have to be translated at all because Chuy is a common nickname in Spanish. Those films were a cultural bridge that dissolved borders and helped me find other Black and brown nerds and outcasts. But most importantly, *Star Wars* was a piece of monoculture whose vision of the future was based in radical, decolonial, and anti-imperial movements, and it resonated with Americans enough to be the fourth-highest-grossing franchise of all time. It offered a vision of the future beyond the Empire, a future that somehow, felt like it also imagined *me*.

In this documentary series, James Cameron interviews six filmmakers whose "visions of the future" have had the most impact in cinema, all of whom were white men: George Lucas, Christopher Nolan, Arnold Schwarzenegger, Ridley Scott, Steven Spielberg, and Guillermo del Toro (ethnically Mexican, but still white). They also discussed *Terminator, Alien, Interstellar, AI*, and *Avatar*—films that all envision the future as an end to the world, and the encounter with the Other as an existential threat. The only exceptions are Guillermo del Toro, who talks about fabulation as a future imaginary that erodes the difference between self and Other, and George Lucas, who dared to imagine the end of empire.

I have no delusions that *Star Wars* is a revolutionary text, especially not as a multibillion-dollar franchise and Disney IP. *Star Wars* is for kids, which means its politics are simplified, abstract, diluted. Its representations of the Other far, far away have major problems, from its racist and orientalist caricatures of Jabba the Hutt, Jar Jar Binks, and the Trade Federation, to its poor gender politics and consistent use of Black women as aliens, to its racist reactionary fandom. I won't pretend that American billionaire George Lucas truly espouses anti-imperialist, decolonial politics, or that *Star Wars* is exemplary of radical revolutionary art. Rather, I'm interested in its *imagination,* and how it differs from other pop culture science fiction texts of its time, from *E.T.* and *Close Encounters* to the *Star Trek Enterprise* "going boldly where no man has gone before." (Trekkies: I know that *Star Trek* is quite radical also, I come in peace.) I am interested in what forbidden futures *Star Wars* invites us to imagine, and how its original framing as an allegory for the Vietcong has become a container for other radical allegories in works like *Rogue One, The Last Jedi,* and *Andor.* How was *Star Wars* able to Trojan-horse a decolonial critique of imperialism into a B-film-turned–commercial blockbuster, and why did that story resonate so much with Americans?

Western science fiction largely imagines the future as technological progress, which is inextricable from capital and violence, the same apparatus bringing us to the brink of apocalypse today. Technology is science fiction's "magic," and the future is STEM-focused, sleek, and masculine-coded, a narrow turf with little imagination of people who fall outside of those definitions. What does it mean, then, that the majority of filmmakers invited to "envision" the future are white men? Why are they making the popular science fiction films that imagine our futures and shape our narratives? Why are the futures envisioned in *Terminator*, *Alien*, *Interstellar*, and *Avatar* all imagined at the end of the world? Why can we only imagine our extinction, where either we are being invaded or we must invade? If capitalism supposedly drives innovation, why can't we imagine our way out of our own extinction?

On some level, we sense the inevitable outcome of imperialism, and the capitalist-colonial project, to be our own extinction. The fear of being invaded by aliens or robots (or robot aliens!) who want our resources (*Independence Day*, *Terminator*), or its opposite scenario, depleting our resources to such a degree that we become the invaders, driven out into space to search for a new planet to colonize (*Interstellar*, *The Martian*)—both are visions of the future rooted in the memory of colonialism, a future that believes it is moving forward but is just history repeating itself in cyclical time. It is the future envisioned by the West, an imaginary built by the subconscious images and symbols of extreme individualism, disconnection, loneliness, material obsolescence, scarcity, waste. It is the projection of the colonial conscience, a dystopia where what we did to Indigenous people will happen to us; the fear that extinction is not only our future, it is our fate. That is, except *Star Wars*.

If *Star Wars* is truly a story based on antiauthoritarian revolutionary movements, as Lucas claims, then by virtue of its success, it is a radical challenge to the dominant Western narratives of the future. The Galactic Empire, much like the West, can only ever imagine its own destruction, so the world it literally builds from that imaginary is the Death Star—a cold, lifeless moon-sized space station and superweapon with the power to obliterate worlds, which it does to Alderaan. The Rebel Alliance, a coalition of dissidents and defectors, is symbolized by a Starbird, a phoenix rising out of the ashes of a destroyed star, a mythical creature that makes new life from its own death. It is the imagination of a future beyond Empire. It is the refusal of death and a call to rise from destruction, to form alliances with other rebels fighting for liberation. It is naive, idealistic, even cringey, but through exceptional courage and sheer dumb luck, it wins.

That's the imagination I'm interested in—how fantasy is a site of collective world-building; how by virtue of being accessible to all, the speculative genres create borderless collectives through fandoms. I'm interested in stories that can appeal to a child's imagination and present opportunities for deepening and rigor as they grow, as opposed to adults-only cultural discourses that require a certain level of literacy and expertise to participate.

I remember screaming with excitement when I saw the *Force Awakens* trailer in 2015, which opened with a shot of a Storm Trooper removing his helmet to reveal a Black character—John Boyega's wonderful portrayal of Finn. His presence reframed the Storm Troopers, an army of clones and conscripts, through the history of enslaved, fungible Black bodies—a thrilling read on the Empire in the time of the Black Lives Matter movement. It would seem that the films were responding to race, gender, and power in a post-Obama world that had just elected Trump. The leads were a white woman Jedi, an escaped Black Storm Trooper, and a Latino resistance fighter pilot who flies across galaxy borders—all symbols of resistance to their particular oppressions, all in solidarity. The antagonist was not an all-powerful, oppressive tyrant like Vader but Kylo Ren, an impotent, angry young white man and nepo baby who glorified Vader and was threatened by women and minorities banding together to challenge his fragile inheritances of power—a clear representation of the alt-right. I *loved* Rian Johnson's first two films, until *Star Wars'* white male fandom began its racist, antiwoke harassment campaign of the actors and called for a remake—ironic, considering its original story. As this controversy escalated, *Rogue One* (2016) was released. The film depicted the cruelty and trauma of fascist imperial violence, and the martyrdom of radical revolutionaries who made Luke and Leia's rebellion possible.

Enter *Andor* (2022), a story set in the familiar *Star Wars* universe that uses its original decolonial framework to tell a story from the close perspective of a migrant in a surveillance state. Cassian Andor, a refugee whose home planet is made uninhabitable by occupation and resource extraction, is forced to migrate as an Indigenous child. Life in the Empire is one of fugitivity, where migrants are criminalized and heavily policed and people are controlled through carceral systems of labor. Diego Luna, a Mexican actor who first played the role of Cassian Andor in *Rogue One*, was deeply involved with the writing of the show, emphasizing the importance of portraying the *Star Wars* universe as an allegory for US-Mexico relations, and the danger, desperation, and paranoia of a displaced migrant under imperial rule.

Andor is based not on Joseph Campbell's Hero's Journey but on the migrant's journey—the invisible, marginal Third World bodies that make First World heroes possible. *Andor* is set in an imagined collective past, at a distance far enough away to defamiliarize its world from our politics just enough to allow the story to be told. "I believe science fiction and stories that happen in a galaxy far, far away are a great tool to comment on our world—on your life and my life and the way we interact," Luna told *Vanity Fair*. "We need to explore the revolutionary we can become to change things, to stop war, to make this world a livable place." Critics and fans raved about the radical risks of the show and named it one of the best of 2022, but all had the same question: How the *hell* did they get Disney to greenlight this?

In her 1965 essay "The Imagination of Disaster," Susan Sontag critiques the tropes of science fiction films of the fifties and early sixties as expressions of deep cultural anxieties following World War II. Before alien invasions and space colonialism took over the genre, early sci-fi themes were more focused on radiation, contamination, destruction, and becoming alien as their horrors—widespread fears following the Holocaust, the Hiroshima and Nagasaki bombings, and the looming threat of nuclear war. The world had just witnessed science and technology produce two decades of unspeakable war crimes, images that resurfaced in science fiction as bodily deformations, sentient body parts, environmental devastation, mad scientists, and the loss of one's humanity. In contrast, Japanese science fiction, specifically Godzilla films, contend with the mass trauma of the Hiroshima and Nagasaki bombings through the rage of a reptilian monster, mutated by toxic nuclear waste.

According to Sontag, science fiction is not about science but about *disaster*, and the *inadequate response* to disaster. Annihilation, made bearable to witness through a "technological distance," and the thingification of creatures, aliens, and monstrous deformations. Science was supposed to be the great unifier, the mark of societal progress, the basis for utopian fantasy, but its application has revealed terrors beyond what we thought we were capable of, and the knowledge that the response will be inadequate, all packaged in a "naively and largely debased commercial art product [showing] the most profound dilemmas of the contemporary situation."

I disagree with her on one point: "There is absolutely no social criticism, of even the most implicit kind, in science fiction films. No criticism, for example, of the conditions of our society which create the impersonality and dehumanization which science fiction fantasies displace onto the influence of an alien It." I believe speculative fiction is one of the most rigorous sites of social critique, and as artifacts of popular culture, are records of our imaginaries as texts that are radically accessible to all. From *Metropolis* to *Short Circuit* to *Wall-E* to *The Matrix* to *Andor* to *Cyberpunk 2077*, and recently, the relevance of the hospital bombing in *Mockingjay*, the speculative is one of the only places engaging the allegories of dystopian futures as a site of political critique.

The problem isn't so much that science fiction displaces violence onto an alien bad guy—not anymore, at least. It's that science fiction displaces historical atrocities onto imagined dystopian futures, fantasizing a white heroic resistance to the violences that Black, Indigenous, and non-Western subjects have already faced. If the future and fate of the West depends on the end of capitalism, the loss of the material comforts, luxuries, status, access, and security is terrifying. By contrast, science fiction films from postcolonial, non-Western, and global south perspectives that have already survived world-breaking—that is to say, primitive, backward, futureless places—if they even make it onto Hollywood's radar, are simply lumped into foreign categories, like *Okja* or *The Shape of Water*, or categorized as separate from science fiction, like martial arts films, anime, folktales, fantasy, horror, or magical realism. What Jake Sully of *Avatar*, Katniss Everdeen of *The Hunger Games*, HBO's *Watchmen*, *The Handmaid's Tale*, and other Western dystopian sci-fi makes visible are the suppressed histories and necropolitics that emerge in critique, and the glimpse beyond the apocalypse those critiques give us, from the people who have already survived them.

REALISM

In the first year of my doctoral studies, I took a class with the novelist Viet Nguyen, who assigned Eric Bennett's *Workshops of Empire: Stegner, Engle, and American Creative Writing during the Cold War*. The book is a critique of how the CIA colluded with writers to depoliticize American literature through academic institutionalization, the formation of a literary elite, and the standardization of literature via prizes, programs, and publications that are still emblems of the highest literary prestige today: the Iowa Writers' Workshop, the Stegner and Kenyon fellowships, the *Paris Review*, and so on. The proliferation of graduate-level writing programs based on the Iowa Workshop model across the country would go on to profoundly shape American literature by indoctrinating generations of writers to write spare, concrete psychological realism. And so began the domination of domestic realism, sometimes called Iowa fiction, literature that valued individualism over social issues, materialism over moralism, and deep character studies over lofty political ideals—capitalist realism. (It must be said that the book *Finks: How the C.I.A. Tricked the World's Best Writers* delves deep into this history and reveals a much more nuanced political landscape, including an analysis on race and Latin American relations through the CIA's relationships with James Baldwin, Ernest Hemingway, and Gabriel García Márquez. Yes, them.)

Two years after the Iowa Writers' Workshop was founded, the House Un-American Activities Committee was formed to identify suspected Communists in Hollywood. The politics of American storytelling was being managed on two fronts—the institutionalization of literary prestige by the Iowa Writers' Workshop, and the blacklisting of Hollywood Communists. In 1947 the Motion Picture Alliance for the Preservation of American Ideals (MPA), cofounded by Walt Disney, began policing the politics of film production at every level, issuing a list of ideological positions prohibited due to their Communist overtones: "Don't smear the free-enterprise system, don't smear industrialists, don't smear wealth, don't smear the profit motive, don't deify the 'common man,' don't glorify the collective." This is how the Iowa Writers' Workshop, writers trained in the anti-Communist literary arts, also shaped Hollywood screenwriting, famously adapting Tennessee Williams's *Streetcar Named Desire*, and guided the ideological shift in American storytelling toward intimate psychological character studies.

At the same time, science fiction B-films like *Creature from the Black Lagoon, Gojira, The Thing, Them, The Beast from 20,000 Fathoms, Attack of the 50 Foot Woman,* and so on were engaging with forbidden content—social issues, critiques of industrialism and enterprise, morality tales, stories of the "common man," collective survival when creatures attack. While the psychological realism of serious cinema upheld the individualistic narratives of capitalism, science fiction, through the imagination of disaster (and its inadequate response), engaged prohibited "Communist" themes *by design*. Toxic waste spills? A critique of free enterprise and industrialism. Invasion films? Glorified collective survival. Becoming alien/losing humanity? Critiqued individualism, race, and dehumanization.

If America's preeminent narrative genre is domestic realism, then its crown jewel is the story of a marriage in crisis. (Bonus points if it's set in New York City, and it ends in divorce.) When I was in writing workshops, I ripped through hundreds of novels and short story collections set in the domestic worlds of upper-middle-class families and relationships, their gray intimate spaces, the universe that forms between people. Lorrie Moore and other short story writers were early favorites, and I learned much from them, marveled at their technical precision, plunged into their psychological quandaries. But as much as I enjoyed those books, there was a palpable silence in them that grew as I continued my studies and my own relationship deteriorated. The more I read, the more I subconsciously steered my life along the psychological pathways of the domestic realist novel, felt myself move toward more heteronormative white middle-class culture, art, and opinions, and while I never expect to identify with literature, I did expect some level of recognition.

But as the state of the world grew more dire, and as my own life grew more volatile, I felt a growing sense of emptiness in realism. A hard truth I arrived at is that American literature, in order to be called literature, is necessarily bourgeois. The upper-middle-class American writer's imagination, no matter how dexterous it may be at inhabiting other people's lives, is produced in the shadow of Iowa, written for upper-middle-class audiences, *no matter their identity*. American literary realism, in its focus on representing the world (often a far more luxurious one than I've ever known) through language, falls into the mind-body problem of representationism, or the philosophical problem of whether language can reproduce reality at all. Iowa realism techniques teach us that the best writing is achieved when the concrete is in tension with the psychological interiority of character, a kind of dance between the richness of consciousness and movement through the world—something that has become somewhat of a cynical exercise in the age of QAnon, stark wealth inequality, and multiple realities experienced on phone screens, as the center of consciousness once again falls apart.

The technical proficiency of realism can be thrilling when done well, and for me, even more exciting when subverted by experimentation, but even the most ambitious metafictional risks feel heavily cynical, self-conscious, even mean, written with critics and a career in mind. I had reached a point of such profound personal devastation in my life—my husband's cruelty, the baffling exhaustion of parenthood, the urgency of survival as a single parent, our violent country—that realism only baffled me. The memoirs, autofictions, and novels I once loved, letting my imagination expand inside someone else's reality, relate to someone else's trauma, were now rendered in an unrecognizable language. My boundaries had dissolved, and I could not take in the hell of other people while trying to survive my own. The capitalist realism simulation was glitching. That's when I turned to fantasy.

Domestic realism zooms in so close to the individual that you don't see the rest of the world; fantasy zooms out so that you can see yourself in context with it. The growing silence I felt while reading literary realism novels was *me*—on some level, realism, by representing a reality I should recognize but increasingly couldn't, started to feel like a simulacrum, an uncanny reality bordering on the sublime. In PTSD terms, the mismatch between self-perception and reality mirrors the effect of gaslighting—a state I experienced in the worst moments of my marriage. Books, television, and film felt no longer pleasurable but dangerous and dissociative. In an abusive marriage, the domestic itself becomes abject, and the more I tried to come back to comfort narratives, the more they represented an older self or a version of the world that was long gone. All the grand narratives that formed my reality on a conscious or unconscious level—Happily Ever After, Bootstraps Individualism, Good Immigrant, Manifest Destiny, College-Marriage-Baby-House, Good Wife, the American Dream—had failed, and I could therefore no longer structure my reality through narrative. Domestic realism was no longer a site of aspiration, delicious voyeurism, introspection, drama; it was a site of loss, lies, betrayal and self-betrayal, and the long, slow violence of intimate partner abuse.

Realism was also a betrayal of language itself. No matter how much I wrote or told my story, I could not convey the pain of my marriage without finding myself deep in cliché. Despite all of my narrative experiments, forms, framings, and tricks, I could not change the reality of my story, could not make it new enough, write it lyrically enough, or structure it well enough to be understood. Language failed to represent my reality. It is easier to read a woman in pain from an aesthetic, critical distance than to actually be present with the constant mess of it. Domestic realism was no longer a neutral setting to explore the intricacies of family and relationships. Instead, it was as charged and tense as horror—a kind of hyperrealism, every detail examined and overdescribed through heightened, hypervigilant senses. The storytelling mode of an honest person deemed untrustworthy, unbelieved.

OJALÁ

"You throw another moon at me, and I'm gonna lose it." It was maybe the twentieth time I'd watched *Avengers: Infinity War* with my son, and the twentieth time I'd heard this piece of dialogue. But this time, I heard the poetry in the delivery.

In shorthand, science fiction imagines a kind of future, and fantasy (or traditional high fantasy, at least) imagines a kind of past. I have spent much time on science fiction here because as a genre that is supposed to imagine the future, in recent years, it seems that all science fiction can imagine is the end of the world. This is a depressing state of affairs for someone whose cultural memory and familial past have essentially been erased, and whose future is not certain. Since having my son and shifting to a solitary life, without family nearby, without a partner, without support or security, or love except for that I have for my son, the past few years have presented hardship after hardship, each as heavy and magnetic as a moon, tossing the tides of my life into tempests. If life threw another moon at me, I really was going to lose it. The loss and denial of my memory, my cultural and familial history, the powerlessness of my language, racial alienation, isolation—fantasy is a balm for all of it in deeply meaningful ways.

In the video game *Baldur's Gate 3*, I play an elf bard who runs around with a bow, a lute, and a way with words— those are the only tools I need to fight for the world, and with my love at my side and a fellowship of friends, this is how we save humanity together. One of the most useful spells I can cast is called *Silence*, a bubble that domes over a fight to prevent spellcasters from using their magic. It occurs to me that in fantasy, words mean a great deal—they very literally shape reality through spells, prophecies, and lore. In the real world, words and language don't mean much—writers and journalists are laid off every other week, legacy publications are shuttered every quarter, television shows are canceled before they can even establish momentum in their worlds, text is generated, and legacy criticism venues are disappearing—bought out, folded into bigger magazines, moved over to TikTok. Something vital about language—how we make, read, understand the world, communicate, see one another—is slipping away. Language is a threat to power, and if avenues for discourse and truthtelling disappear, without the relation language makes possible, it is harder to create the allegories that help us see others' struggles as our own. But in fantasy, worlds rise and fall on the power of a single word—*dracarys*, for example.

In fantasy, the rebels are the heroes, admired for their refusal to bow to corruption or power, or kneel before a tyrannical king. Rebels find their allies, and in time, are vindicated. In the real world, rebels are pariahs, outcasts, blacklisted, silenced by the powerful—all it takes is a little bit of professional sabotage and a blow to your reputation, and you'll never work in this town again.

And for people whose pasts have been obliterated by colonial and imperial violence, erased by enslavement, whose histories are subsumed into the Western narrative, fantasy is an articulation of collective memory, which is pulled from the collective unconscious. I don't mean this in a woo sort of way, but in the very literal sense that language itself is material, so real it creates our first wound, and from that wound, our deepest unconscious constantly interacts with the world, and the bodies, memories, and lives of others—an exchange that forms the symbols, themes, and patterns that persist in collective memory. Maybe that is woo.

What I can tell you is this: *Baldur's Gate 3* is set in the year 1492, and rather than reproduce colonial history through a figure like Columbus setting out to discover the Americas, instead, Faerun, a Europe-like continent, is invaded by a ship from the outer astral planes full of soulless, colonizing creatures. The fight for humanity is the fight not to *become* the colonizer, the fight for one's own mind in a world of mind control and misinformation, to refuse to be colonized and save the world. It is Europe confronting its own colonial history by imagining itself in the place of the colonized, and making the choice not to repeat history. By inviting us to imagine a collective past, a fantastic one in which 1492 did not break the world, we're instead invited to imagine a history in which regular people made as many allies as possible from every realm and united to take down the crown. Fantasy allows the imagination of history to become a site of repair.

Fantasy has been something I watch and read with my child daily.

As the abuse in my marriage began to escalate, fantasy not only helped me find my way back to hope after a PTSD/c-PTSD diagnosis, its "hope against all odds" sense of speculative possibility dovetailed with my decolonial and abolitionist readings, ideas that showed up in play with my son. Imaginative play, pretend, role-play with action figures—all of these ways of connecting with my son—were also acts of world-building, in which I shared my imagination with his, and he with mine, and through a collaborative narrative we expanded each other. In play, we could imagine our way out of the burning world and for a moment envision a safer one where he never felt lonely, I was never sad or tired, and we always had money. And once you're fully in the pretend-play world of a child, it doesn't take long to step into the wardrobe after them. *Okay, pretend there's a ghost behind me and we have to catch it in the ghost trap.* Okay. *Mom, let's switch bodies.* Okay.

His imagination is something to behold. Mid-conversation, he'll say in complete seriousness, *On my planet, I have a temperature-controlled armory.* When things are hard and I'm feeling down, pessimistic, or doubtful, he will say, *Mom, I'm from the future, remember? You have no idea how happy we're going to be. Because I actually know it.* What a lifesaving thing for an eight-year-old to say. I play along.

I'm not perfect, and neither is he. Sometimes he watches a lot of trash on YouTube. Sometimes he plays Roblox and repeats alarming language in the chat. He did his first active shooter drill this year. World-destroying. Part of raising a child is making sense of world-destroying too.

One of my favorite words in Spanish is *ojalá*. It is a word borrowed from the Arabic *insh'allah*, "God willing," but its everyday use expresses hope that something will happen. In my family, *ojalá* was always said in response to the impossible, something we could only hope for. Talking to family in Mexico about them coming to visit. *Ojalá*. Telling

318

my grandmother that her cancer would go into remission, and she could come home. *Ojalá.* My dad buying Lotto numbers after devising another strategy. *Ojalá.* Any impossible dream that seems so simple, so accessible, to others. *Ojalá.*

My son and I live in a small 1950s apartment complex in Burbank where only one family in the building has a child my son's age. They drifted apart during shelter in place, so throughout his life, I've been his primary playmate. I rub off on him with my love of 1980s movies like *Ghostbusters* and *Back to the Future;* he rubs off on me with his love of characters—Darth Vader, Peter Venkman, Tony Stark, Miles Morales, Peter Parker. (Yes, I am concerned with the overrepresentation of white men.) His play is vivid and imaginative and detailed, a richly rendered world reenacted from the source material. He watches videos on how to make toys more "movie-accurate," and builds out worlds in our apartment out of LEGOs and old boxes.

I took Joaquín to see *Avengers: Endgame* on a day he was sick. In April 2019, three pop culture universes aligned—the *Game of Thrones* finale, the last *Avengers* film, and the release of Beyoncé's Coachella performance on Netflix. That two-week span was lovingly called *Endgame of Thrones: Homecoming* among intersecting BIPOC fandoms, the week when pop culture, at the height of its powers, gave us the endings that closed out a decade of pop culture. Joaquín was only four, but his favorite character was Iron Man, so we went to see it. He, of course, brought his light-up Iron Man mask.

"... and I ... am ... Iron Man." *SNAP* When Tony Stark sacrifices himself to save the world, I looked over to Joaquín to see if he was okay. He seemed not to feel anything, and just stared at the screen. I held his hand and asked if he was okay. He nodded. And as the rest of the Avengers surrounded Tony, and he took his last breaths, my son lifted up his Iron Man mask, facing backward to the rest of the theater.

He felt something big from the story, and was moved to create his own symbol to perform that feeling in response, interacting with the people in the audience. He held it up for a long time, throughout Tony's death scene, and then came to sit on my lap for the rest of the movie. It was a kind of mourning, but strangely calm, even hopeful. "What did you think?" I asked.

He made a little heart with his hands. "He'll be back," he said. "There's more world after him."

MAGICAL REALISM
Or the Wolf Is the Land Is the People Is the Border: An Animal Study

At the border between Western consciousness and Indigenous knowledge, there is a wolf. Like every border, it too is imaginary and man-made, separating two profoundly different perspectives of the land and its beings: *property* or *relative*; *settlement* or *wilderness body*, *human* vs. *animal*. It is then that the wolf becomes a liminal creature, crossing the metaphysical border between wilderness and settlement, nature and nation, individual and collective, self and Other. How you see the wolf is a phenomenological orientation; it depends on how you experience yourself in the world, and the stories and symbolic systems that have shaped you. Is the wolf an animal, or is it your kin? Do you fear the wolf, or do you respect it, learn from it? Are you preoccupied with the differences between you, or the similarities? Do you want to protect it, or be protected from it? Is your fate tied to its fate, or is it separate from you?

I have always felt kinship with wolves. Perhaps it began while watching the telenovela *Cuna de Lobos* (Cradle of Wolves) with my grandmother in Brownsville. Even though I was only three or four, I was fascinated by the mysterious nature of the wolf, its metaphors for both villainy and family. I became obsessed with having a wolf companion after reading *Island of the Blue Dolphins* in third grade. I would later learn that my maternal family line's surname, López, although a very common name, is derived from "wolf." My godmother's name, Guadalupe, means "river of the wolf" (وادي اللب, wādī al-lubb, hidden river/valley, Arabic; lupus, wolf, Latin).

The edge of Western consciousness is also a frontier, ever expanding into the wolf's territory. Before European settlers came to the Americas, wolves and Indigenous people shared the land peacefully, reverent of each other's territories. Some tribes saw wolves' dedication to their pack as a model and a lesson, others considered wolves guides and developed mutual hunting relationships. Wolf packs are also eminently respectful of one another's territories, as shown by a 2018 GPS map by the Voyageurs Wolf Project, tracking wolves from six different packs across Voyageurs National Park for about a year. But the wolf lived in the colonial imagination as an infiltrator, trickster, predator, menace, and ghost, its howls in the night thought to be the voices of the Indigenous dead returned, stirring the settler conscience. They were feared at first, then hated, blamed for every social ill projected onto their bodies: they killed livestock, they wandered onto private property as if it were wilderness, they were changelings, demons, evil spirits, then most insidiously, metaphors—the shadow of disappeared Indigenous people, returned as wolves to reclaim the land. Wolves represented the receding edge of the wilderness, able to cross its boundaries. By the mid-1800s, between Manifest Destiny claiming the wilds and the Homestead Act transforming land into property, European settlers began expanding into the American West, and the eradication of wolves became central to the ongoing colonial project.

White settlers were unusually violent and antagonistic toward wolves, characterizing the animal as a vicious predator and infiltrator of livestock farmers' private property. There are numerous photographs of farmers and wolf trappers posing with dozens of hanging wolf scalps in a way that recalls the brutality of lynching, their actions motivated by something closer to hatred than greed. Jon Coleman documents this in *Vicious: Wolves and Men in America*, and one particular account has stayed with me—that of famous naturalist and illustrator of *Birds of America*

John James Audubon, who in 1814 remorselessly witnessed a farmer trap and cut the hamstrings of three wolves, crippling them so that his dogs could mutilate and torture them as they desperately signaled their submission until, finally, he shot them. Audubon was a vocal advocate for the complete elimination of wolves, citing the threat they posed to American livestock and wild game, and thus the business of agriculture.

The US government adopted Audubon's position and began disseminating antiwolf propaganda and incentivizing their slaughter, launching numerous extermination campaigns that made the sport of killing wolves so lucrative that wolf scalps were used as currency. By the late 1800s the government ordered the extermination of wolves using the language of "infestation"—*predator, infiltrate,* and *eradicate*— language that mirrors the dehumanizing language Fox News and the Trump administration have used to construct the myth of illegal immigration. In 1974 the Mexican gray wolf officially came under the protection of the Endangered Species Act as one of the most imperiled species ever to be listed.

In European and Christian folklore, there is no animal more dangerous, devious, or criminal than the wolf. It begins with the word: *wolf,* from Old English to Finnish to Latin, is an adversary, a useless thing, a devious trickster, a predator in the dark, one of the West's most ancient symbols of the Other, a site of difference that produces the Human. In *The Animal That Therefore I Am,* Jacques Derrida writes, "I move from 'the ends of man,' that is the confines of man, to 'the crossing of borders' between man and animal. Crossing borders or the ends of man I come or surrender to the animal—to the animal in itself, to the animal in me and the animal at unease with itself . . ."

The wolf is not only a metaphor for the untamed urges of man—lust, hunger, violence—the wolf itself becomes the threshold between man and animal, the savage we become, our "lesser selves," the savage within we must kill. In Norse mythology, the wolf is the world-ender, the mongrel, the god-slayer, the sun-eater—a symbol of hate, chaos, and destruction. But while the West primarily saw the wolf as a threat, a shapeshifter, a monster at the edge of self, Indigenous peoples of the Americas saw a very different being. In many traditions, wolves figured prominently into both cosmology and community as guardians, guides, heroes, creators—allies.

In the end, the Western narratives won. The stories we tell our children—fables, folklore, fairy tales—are repositories of ancient memory, stories that transfer our ancestors' most primal images of the world as symbols. The wolf, and its metaphors, embody a "wilderness" imaginary separate from us. The wolf is the ecotone, bearing witness to the borders that form at the edges of man. If the most ancient memory of the wolf we have is that of an eternal enemy, then both the wolf *and* the threshold, or border, it represents can only ever be conceived as dangerous.

You might think the point I'm making is that the wolf is a metaphor for colonization, for the extermination of Indigenous peoples, or for migrants; or that it's a symbol, an embodiment of both physical and conceptual borders. But that is a violence of language, of signification, which disappears the wolf and its world into symbol. The wolf is native to both Eurasia and the Americas, which is why it is present in all of our oldest myths. It too has an embodied memory of us, before we divided ourselves from the world. Language has only ever hurt the wolf, erected symbols around it. I want to bring the wolf out of language and give the world back to it. Because if we've given the world back to the wolf, then we've already begun to repair the wound of language, of property, of difference, of borders, begun to reworld the space between human and animal.

WHEN WE ALL LOVED A SHOW ABOUT A WALL

ICE, Borders, and the Accidental Revolutionary Politics of Game of Thrones

IMAGINE, JUST FOR A MOMENT, THAT THE BIGGEST, MOST-WATCHED television show in the world is set on a border.

And imagine its hero is named after the land, but unable to claim any of it. His name is just *snow*—a white field where an ancestry should be. He is a bastard, son of a nobleman and a mystery woman, and therefore a second-class citizen who cannot take his father's name, entitled to nothing, his lineage erased, barred from social mobility. So with no one and nowhere to go, he has no choice but conscription to a life patrolling the border, marked by a wall.

He's been brought up to believe that borders are just, that the Wall is protective, and that the border patrol are a brotherhood of honorable men. But in his duty he finds that his fellow officers are corrupt sadists, rapists, and murderers, and the people on the other side are not the enemy but dispossessed Indigenous refugees—"Wildlings," descendants of the First Men, who after centuries of separation and violence now live in extreme poverty and danger. He has been brought up to hate his kin, made Other by the political veil a wall becomes. The refugees are fleeing a global threat the whole realm denies—the memory of racial extinction at the hands of men, embodied in the form of an undead king who brings climate change, with dead Wildlings as his army, marching steadily toward the living.

Our hero captures a Wildling girl who challenges his unquestioning loyalty to the border patrol, to a country that denies them both the right to a life—his most fundamental beliefs. He falls in love, and upon living with the Wildlings, undergoes a profound crisis of identity. The Wildlings' fight against extinction is justified, and will be all of humanity's fight soon. When he returns to the border patrol, he is changed, his allegiances split. The living Wildlings must cross the Wall, or no one will survive.

When he is promoted to commander of the border patrol, he uses his power to grant the Wildling refugees safe passage across the border and asylum, giving them back what land he can. But this is a grave betrayal of the brotherhood, so a group of officers conspire to murder him. When he is brought back to life, he renounces border patrol and allies with the migrants, the Indigenous, the refugees, in the fight to reclaim their ancestral lands as they too help him claim his. Soon the Wall will not be able to hold back the winter, or the dead. The North remembers—our hero, a bastard whose lineage is lost to the amnesia of history, fights for collective memory, and he cannot fight the darkness alone.

Now imagine that this, the biggest, most-watched television show of all time, airing this storyline at the height of family separations at the border, *intended* to make this statement:

Fuck borders. Fuck border patrol. Fuck militarized walls and apartheid states and empire. Grant every Indigenous refugee asylum, and give them their land back as reparations. The memory of colonial violence will return to us in the form of climate change, mass displacement, and forced labor. Memory is the site of our collective survival. The land remembers. To remember is to refuse total annihilation.

That show existed. It was called *Game of Thrones*, and that hero was Jon Snow. So why did critics collectively miss, or avoid, that reading?

In order to examine the cultural forces that created the conditions for the global phenomenon that was *Game of Thrones*, it's important to situate it as a show that spanned the 2010s, with characters and plotlines that resonated rather than commented on the transition from Obama's two terms to Trumpism, neoliberalism to neofascism, mass shootings, Brexit, the alt-right white nationalist movement, Black Lives Matter uprisings, climate change, ICE, and the construction of the wall at the US-Mexico border. A major player in the era of prestige television, *Game of Thrones'* rich, complicated story became a global phenomenon with a "universal" appeal in a time when the monoculture was beginning to splinter into streaming niches. Perhaps the last truly universally loved show to air on television, its audiences spanned the political spectrum and defied age, race, gender, class, and borders. Over the course of its decade-long run, every major media outlet fanatically covered *Game of Thrones*, from glossy full-issue exclusives and comprehensive episode recaps to high-production-value GOT analysis podcasts, which even *Vanity Fair* got in on. Between seasons, reputable publications printed industry rumors and on-set drone photos to feed hungry readers, happy for any conjecture about the upcoming seasons. Even the most staunch critics scoured Reddit and online fandoms for theories and analyses about the show and its characters, especially Jon Snow—his parentage, his role in the prophecies, his fate beyond the books. Endless cultural criticism and thinkpieces flooded the cultural landscape, scrutinizing *Game of Thrones* from every angle. And while there were occasionally some thoughtful takes by white feminists and academics, unpacking the show's politics, the border wall remained largely unaddressed. Amid Obama's detention centers and anti-immigrant policies and Trump's family separations and incarceration of child migrants as our own wall went up, in the nine years between 2011 and 2019, when *Game of Thrones* aired, not one major outlet published a meaningful reading by a Latine critic on the world's biggest show with a border wall at its center.

This is a meaningful absence in the ongoing global conversation that was *Game of Thrones*, an American show produced by HBO in California, home to the largest migrant labor workforce in the United States. The whiteness of the American media landscape lacks the critical range to read the Wall beyond its role as a set piece or plot device, or the subtexts of migration, climate change, neocolonialism, and race, which went largely uncritiqued for a decade. While white women could publish feminist critiques of the show's sexual violence and nudity or close readings of Daenerys and Cersei, no one ever thought to tap a Latine critic to write about their readings on the Wall, on Jon Snow, on the racialization of Dorne. Even after the Trump White House released "The Wall Is Coming" memes in *GOT* font in 2018, Latine critics were noticeably absent from the conversation, which more often than not leaned apolitical.

More than any other show in history, *Game of Thrones* was experienced as a conversation—real-time live-tweet reactions and fan theory forums exploded with content every Sunday night, only to be mined and curated by entertainment columnists, podcasters, and listicle editors who shaped the discussion around *Game of Thrones*, sticking mostly to book-to-show comparisons, production rumors, theories, and memes, with the occasional white feminist take that remained uncritical of Daenerys. But the conversations I craved around race, gender, climate change, colonial politics, and borders were nonexistent in an overwhelming overflow of content. If I wanted a smart race discourse, I got it from the #DemThrones and #ThronesYall hashtags thanks to Black Twitter, in large part responsible for the show's boom among BIPOC millennials. (*VICE* covered Black *GOT* fandoms, but not Black critiques.)

Broadcast in 207 countries and territories, and simulcast in 194 countries and territories, *Game of Thrones* was a global phenomenon. Its fandom knew no borders, amassing worldwide audiences that defied age, race, gender, and class, and spanned the political spectrum. Unlike *Mad Men* and its other prestige contemporaries, *Game of Thrones* took a hands-off approach when it came to explicit political commentary, preferring instead to keep the story and its characters open to viewer interpretation. Conservative outlets could read the show as pro-wall just as easily as feminists could read Cersei and Daenerys as empowered, liberatory characters. But despite its massive popularity and influence, *Game of Thrones* had the power to make a profound revolutionary statement about borders, migrants, colonialism, and race in a way no other show ever has, and it missed the opportunity because showrunners David Benioff and D. B. Weiss, along with a majority-white media landscape, never accounted for Latine fans or perspectives, and therefore lacked the contexts and experiences to make those crucial connections between the show and our world. By the time the show became a global phenomenon, Latine critics could hardly get a word in edgewise.

Unlike *Breaking Bad*, *Weeds*, or *Narcos*—shows set on the literal

US-Mexico border—*Game of Thrones* is set in a historical Western imaginary, free from the baggage of race and colonialism. Instead of racial stereotypes, its heroes and villains resonate with our own identities through the metaphors of monarchs, monsters, and magic. Perhaps its explosive popularity lay in its ability to mirror our subjectivities—racialization, gender, class, enslavement, indigeneity, migration, fugitivity, disability, monstrosity—within the brutal framework of white supremacy.

JON SNOW IS ACCIDENTALLY THE BEST MEXICAN AMERICAN character ever written for television. I know, an absurd claim that at first I made only half jokingly. But as the seasons went on, I found deeper resonances with his character. Like every mestizo, he is a bastard—half noble, half erasure, unable to claim either lineage. Bastards are named after the land they are born on—Sand, Rivers, Snow. As Jon Snow, he remains illegitimate and unclaimed by the Starks, and this nameless no-identity defines him; despite growing up in privilege, he is a second-class citizen. His name, Snow, is erasure, amnesia. Having no house name means he has no place in history, and therefore he has no future. He will not be remembered; he belongs to the land.

Audiences had no problem grasping the Wall at the edge of the North as a metaphor for the border, but the analysis never went past the structure, and the critique was always surface-level, with murky "walls are bad" politics. In ecological readings, the Wall is a metaphor for glaciers, the ice structures that hold off climate change, represented by the Night King and his undead army no one believes is real at the edge of the world. But in almost every analysis, the North is the site of the West's apocalyptic anxieties: climate change, the endless dispute for power bringing about nuclear winter, immigrant invasions. But few were able to parse the real-world allegory of the Wall, happening in real time: how borders are sites where climate collapse, mass migration and displacement, and the mobilization against empire become one and the same struggle. And who better to navigate this territory than a nameless, landless bastard conscripted to defend stolen land; a dispossessed person defending nobles' right to possess; a second-class citizen defending the ruling class, a border patrol whose identity crisis becomes a crisis of conscience?

Like every traditional fantasy, *Game of Thrones* is a production of colonial, racial, and national imaginaries, where the story of the West(eros) is centered, and all other histories are minimized and marginal by design. Dorne is Spain, Morocco, and Latin America combined—a hot southern place with fiery, passionate (and queer) people. Sothoryos is Africa; the Summer Isles, the Caribbean; and the Grey Waste is Russia. And the realm's Indigenous peoples—Wildlings, Dothraki, Children of the Forest—are farthest from civilization, on the extreme edge of every continent, if they haven't all but disappeared. In this view of the world, Latine histories, geographies, and bodies are subaltern, illegible, rendered as stereotypes, like Oberyn Martell. Jon Snow was never imagined as Latine, or mestizo, but as a tragic Arthurian hero, an Aragorn with a trauma plot. His domain is the moral territory of power and war, a series of tests preparing him for his ascension to the throne. This is *not* the domain, or the destiny, of Latine characters. Latine characters are limited to colonial contexts—drug lords, revolutionaries, gangsters, maids, gardeners, parents, workers, lovers, struggling immigrants with a heart of gold in a supporting role.

But Jon Snow patrols the physical and moral terrain of the border, and by depicting that structure with all the nuance and depth a heroic character requires, *Game of Thrones* accidentally portrayed the complexities *and* complicities of borderlands mestizo identity. A Hollywood depiction of a son of immigrants becoming a border patrol might zoom in on his guilt, the suffering of migrants, appeal to audience empathy with unambiguous morals—the trap of representation. But the whiteness of *Game of Thrones* allowed us to see the Wall stripped of its political stigmas and racialized contexts and see it for what it really is—a projection of narratives.

IN 2016, THE BORDER PATROL UNION OPENED ITS PODCAST CALLED *The Green Line* by playing the oath taken by the Night's Watch in *Game of Thrones*. The end of the oath says, "*I am the sword in the darkness. I am the watcher on the walls. I am the shield that guards the realms of men.*" In border patrol's interpretation, the realms of "men" they guard are ostensibly the United States and Canada, while the land beyond the Wall, at least according to the lore, is the land of all that is not human—the Others, the White Walkers, the dead. In our world, the wall separates humans from the "violent animals of MS-13," according to President Trump, dehumanizing all migrants as Other, Monster, hordes of socially dead.

In summer 2017, the final shot that concludes *Game of Thrones'* season-seven finale is that of hundreds of thousands of undead wights walking through a breach in the Wall, the colossal ice structure protecting the northernmost border of Westeros from a great evil in the wilds beyond. It is a terrifying, cataclysmic finale, meant to fill the viewer with abject dread. And it does—the Wall was the only thing standing between Westeros and the violent, mindless, ever-multiplying dead. Once the mindless hordes cross over, no army will be able to stop them. Everyone will die, and rise again as one of the dead.

On October 12, 2018, one thousand Central American migrants were forced to leave San Pedro Sula, Honduras, and walk to the United States. Leaf rust, a fungal plant disease spreading rapidly in the warming temperatures, was on its seventh year of devastating the region's coffee crop. Small farms lay abandoned in the countryside, some to migration, others to violence, all to climate change. Indebted farmers were violently dispossessed or disappeared. Once predictable seasons lost their patterns; without rain, there was no harvest, no work, nothing to eat. Displaced Indigenous farmers became climate refugees, faced with a choice: migrate or starve. Men left their families, children left their parents, pregnant women left with children in tow. Over the next two months, the caravan swelled to more than seven thousand, surviving Mexican state and cartel violence along the way. After walking more than 2,500 miles across the span of Mexico, from one ocean to another, they arrived in Tijuana in early December, along with the winter. In response to their arrival in Tijuana, and their denial of asylum at the border, that following January, President Trump tweeted a graphic based on the *Game of Thrones* tagline, "Winter Is Coming," styled in the show's signature font. But instead, it said, "The Wall Is Coming."

―――――――――――

ALTHOUGH LATINES ARE RARELY, IF EVER, PRESENT IN FANTASY imaginaries, fantasy is inextricable from Latine immigrant lives, forming the language, symbols, technologies, and policies of far-right, anti-immigrant actors. Peter Thiel, billionaire tech investor and Trump adviser, named his mass surveillance companies, used by US Customs and Border Protection and ICE, after magical *Lord of the Rings* artifacts. Palantir, a data-mining and visualization company, is named after the palantíri, the seven seeing-stones, a network of crystal balls used to telepathically gather intelligence and surveil Middle-earth. Thiel's latest company, Anduril, is named after the sword reforged from the shards of Narsil, the sword Isildur used to cut Sauron down, and wielded by Aragorn, King of Gondor and Isildur's heir. The runes inscribed on Andúril read, "Sun. I am Andúril who was once Narsil, sword of Elendil. The slaves of Mordor shall flee from me. Moon." Anduril is the maker of solar-powered surveillance towers that run day and night along the US-Mexico border. They are tall, thin steel poles with mounted cameras, sticking up from the landscape like swords.

The US-Mexico border wall itself is a fantasy. It is the fantasy of the white ethnostate, and the fight against cultural and hemispheric rupture, surging with racialized, laboring bodies, desperate to invade. Any border, reinforced by a wall, is a site of race-making, nation-building, resource hoarding, wealth extraction, and temporal dislocation—a narrative site where difference is produced through language, and violently maintained by the fantasy of shared identity. For Jon, the violence required of him to maintain the Wall rested on his identity as a man of Westeros, a fantasy of belonging that would only ever see him, a bastard and man of the Night's Watch, as a second-class citizen, unworthy of title, land, or family name, and therefore, any lineage or inheritance—futurelessness. The Night's Watch merely deputized him to maintain that fantasy with the invention of power over the Wildlings—power he wielded from the fantasy of belonging to a nation, an identity that, under scrutiny, falls apart once he realizes he has more in common with the dispossessed on the other side. And that delusion of belonging despite marginalization and alienation, that striving to be from a lineage, a homeland, a tradition with ties you cannot claim and that will not claim you, the name *Snow* that represents ancestral amnesia, the wall that maintains the fantasy and the complicity in its violence, and the slow process of disidentification with nation, borders, its wealthy families—that is a heroic borderlands Latine story I have never seen on any screen.

Game of Thrones is not a Latine borderlands show. But its resonances are. I don't mean to give Benioff and Weiss undue credit; rather, I intend to make legible an experience and perspective that are constantly rendered illegible in popular culture. How could a fantasy world like Westeros, so culturally and temporally removed from our postcolonial world, possibly be an allegory for the US-Mexico border, or have Latin American migrants in mind? I'm not saying it did. But the answer, I think, lies in the collective unconscious, and the images it renders in its geographies, its symbols, its Others. The US-Mexico border cannot be reproduced as realism in any story without also reproducing its affects, or feelings—deeply held biases, racial constructions, fears, narratives, rhetorics. Fantasy decontextualizes its stigmas, detaches it from the anchors in our world so that only symbols remain—this is why Trump and Border Patrol respond viscerally to the Wall as a symbol of security and apartheid—a lure for a story that contradicts our assumptions. It is precisely because of the show's whiteness—its cast, characters, setting, and its allegorical framing in European history—that such a radical geography could even *be* rendered on television, much less its political discourses.

In *Game of Thrones*, fantasy allows the world a certain level of decontextualization, where allegory distances as it compares. *Game of Thrones'* whiteness empties the bodies at the border of their racial contexts, stripping the Wildlings from any association to migrants from the global south as "a faceless brown mass" who are at best "seeking a better life" and at worst "invading our country" and "breaking the law," and either way, a source of cheap labor who will take advantage of social programs.

Let's assume the representation of Latine people was the furthest thing from Martin's or Benioff's and Weiss's minds. As a piece of visual culture, *Game of Thrones* is a representation of Western power rendered in the discursive and imaginative spaces of the fantastic. But it is also a product of the postcolonial imagination, reconceiving history through the filter of colonialism and race. So what can a fantastic rendering of the past tell us about power today? Since fantasy is a direct line to the realms of the symbolic and imaginary, it turns out it can tell us quite a lot.

This is the power of fantasy: the ability to build worlds rendered historically neutral by whiteness, unburdened by the baggage of representation. Once the audience is transported to Westeros (or any medieval Western imaginary), unbound from white guilt and the politics of representation, viewers' guards come down and are at ease and attention, receptive to the Trojan horse that is a beloved character's radical politics, subjectivities, and identities. Jon Snow, for example, can denounce the border patrol by leaving the Night's Watch and grant all migrants asylum by giving the Wildlings their land back. Someone just needs to interpret that reading afterward.

It was extraordinary to watch a hero like Jon Snow (and Daenerys, for that matter) perform the radical politics and subjectivities of slavery abolition and land back on the global stage and be loved for it. But before I unpack these characters, I want to push back on white Western literary definitions of what fantasy *is*, and what its possibilities can be.

Before Tolkien, stories about heroes, monsters, magic, and myth were not "fantasy" but part of a symbolic language that corresponded to the land and its culture, evolved out of every known oral tradition. Human consciousness evolved by encountering itself and the Other in the realm of the symbolic, but Western literary tradition, especially fantasy, coded colonialism, race, and white supremacy into the genre, calling itself "high fantasy" and diminishing anything that wasn't set in medieval Europe as "folklore," "fable," anthropological artifact, or "magical realism."

It remains unlikely that a BIPOC fantasy show, decentered from Europe and whiteness, will have a *Game of Thrones* budget anytime soon; until then, in the absence of our own narratives, we must find ourselves in the dominant culture, which necessitates that we read the material much more critically. But because existing critical frameworks (literary theory, anthropology, criticism) are flawed, instead I want to reconceptualize fantasy as the memory of the colonial unconscious, giving shape to the lost and suppressed symbols and images that persist in our cultural imaginaries.

Imaginaries are powerful, primal repositories of images, symbols, and feelings that produce our reality and the imagined Other every day, and hold the power to invent nations, erase entire peoples, shape identities. For example, Claudia Rankine's concept of the racial imaginary is how the imagination structures the reality of race, and animates the white fantasy of Black criminality to manifest as police violence. Racial imaginaries also have the power to construct national identities and its Others. Fantasy traffics almost exclusively in the symbolic and the imaginary, providing accidental insight into the collective unconscious: Why are there still walls in our invented worlds? What do the trees remember? What do our monsters mean?

Even in fantasy, the concepts of race, gender, class, nations, and borders are all reproduced—Westeros, Middle-earth, and other medieval fantasy worlds are created from colonial imaginaries that are not neutral but instead a heightened projection of an unconscious desire and fear of the Other—the same forces that create our politics, prejudices, and violences. Reproductions of race, white supremacist power dynamics, and gender violence are what can make fantasy seem like a reactionary genre—an escape to a world where white men can indulge fantasies of domination.

But what if fantasy is not a genre of escape but a site of deep imagining that plumbs the depths of our unconscious and reshapes us from the raw material of desire into more possible selves? For mestizes, people whose Indigenous ties and lineages have been erased, a wall exists where relation should be, fantasy can be a site of colonial memory, a glimpse of the world at the time of conquest, rendered in the memory of the West and its Others, just beneath the surface in subtext. The Weirwood trees, the direwolves, the Children of the Forest—in the brief moments they appear on *Game of Thrones*, these images resonate like a memory without data, a feeling of recognition somewhere, mostly invented, that guides me toward memory recovery.

THE WALL, AND JON SNOW, ALWAYS MEANT MORE TO ME, A GIRL born between countries where the throat of the Rio Grande meets the sea; a girl for whom identity is an enigma of family secrets, colonial erasure, and disappearing memory; a girl born on the land of the nearly extinct Mexican gray wolf; a girl born stranded in a borderland, resigned to a foreclosed future. The Wall in *Game of Thrones* has the same function as the one in our world—a structure that divides peoples and invents separate territories, inscribed with spells to shield us from our own evil, patrolled by the very people it split. Jon Snow is so much more than an Arthurian hero, bastard, or king—he is a betrayed figure maligned as a traitor, an old story I've rarely seen in the mainstream—La Malinche, or the child of La Malinche, richly drawn and sad-eyed and complex, alive and on television.

We connect to the characters we love based on our core wounds. Some of us will choose Daenerys if our core wound is centered around personal power, proving others wrong. Perhaps I should want to identify and defend Daenerys, as a woman who has survived sexual violence, whose life has been determined by men in power; a woman who has had to fight for every inch of credibility in a world that devalues women. But I don't identify with Daenerys, a conqueror, daughter of a royal lineage, ambitious inheritor of a throne.

I identify with Jon. A borderlands figure, stranded in a white field, unsure of who he is. An unloved, outcast, misunderstood child who has only ever tried to be good, to keep his word, to fight for those he loves, to be claimed by the land he was born in. I identify with a man who will risk it all to tell the truth, to do what is right, however gray, even if it costs him everything. I see my grandmother's history in him, see her vindicated as he punches Ramsay Bolton over and over in the face, remembering my tío Joel and the story of her rescue. I identify with a child whose past is a vast silence, who has only ever been lied to, who has lived absent of the people who loved him the most.

I identify with a man who, in doing right, is exiled, banished, deported. In the closing scene of the series, he has been sentenced back to the Wall, and upon his return, reunites with his wolf, Ghost, and the Wildlings, who now claim him as their own, and as he passes through the Wall on horseback to leave Westeros, he also exits the West, surrounded by his people, his black-cloaked back to us, disappearing into the trees.

AFTERWORD

Sunday, December 11, 2022. 10:47 a.m. Hall of Faces Photo Ops, Room 409.

I MADE IT. I FIND THE BACK OF THE LINE AND SQUAT TO CATCH MY breath on the corporate gray carpet, sweating my makeup off under the dull fluorescent lights. Digital billboards across the street flash through the glass corridors of the Los Angeles Convention Center, home to the first *Game of Thrones* Official Fan Convention, where I've sprinted up the escalator and followed the arrows and signs to finally be just minutes away from meeting Kit Harington, my reason for being here.

"Ma'am, were you in line?" the attendant calls out to me. Behind her, hundreds of people are wrapped around the corner, waiting to be let through the ropes keeping the walkway open.

Oh shit, I totally cut this line. The signs hadn't pointed in that direction. Lying, I nod.

The attendant seems skeptical, but lets it go. As usual, I am running late despite leaving two hours early, this time because of the rain and always because of the wormhole that is LA parking. But upon seeing Balerion the Black Dread's giant dragon skull in blue lights, I realize: *Oh my god. I'm really here. Oh no. This is so embarrassing.*

I am a forty-year-old woman alone at a fan convention, earnestly posing with dragons in public. I definitely have better things to do. I'm not even dressed in a costume. I've fought so hard to be taken seriously my whole life—as a poet, a PhD in literature, an arts and culture critic. Why is this show so important to me? I can say it's because *it's a cultural phenomenon that uses the historical allegories of fantasy to stage empire's deepest epistemic anxieties as a site of postcolonial critique,* but also because it ran alongside the major milestones of my life and as such was also a companion in my deepest, most hopeless hours of grief.

Right, this is research for the book. In addition to being an impostor and a fraud as a critic, I am also a total poser as a fan—despite watching the show in a catatonic state many times, I skimmed my way through the first three books, learning the rest from wikis and Reddit.

A Jon Snow impersonator walks by, fur cape flowing behind him. *Con Snow!* people cheer. I remain skeptical. *That's a thirty-five-year-old dude from Irvine with a plastic sword.*

The dull reality of our world is beginning to bleed into the fantasy. Not even *Game of Thrones* can escape the sterile ordinariness of commercial space. The walls are not dragonstone but off-white PVC panels; the restrooms where Daeneryses and Night Kings have left toilets flushing and hand dryers whirring have heavy pink doors; the banners and signage with stills from the show are printed on the same thick vinyl as gas station ads. This could just as well be a tech conference, middle managers in line for the Salesforce strategy session. This one just has braided white wigs and giant plastic dragons.

It is a corporate conference, and we are all commodities and contributors to the business.

This is what happens at the end of all fantasy—the return to the real world, somehow duller and emptier and lonelier than before. Fantasy in particular operates in the space of the symbolic, able to access our unconscious and activate our deepest wounds. When a story is so deeply attached to our identities, feelings, traumas, even our sense of community, its ending feels like an abandonment, a real loss, which makes it hard to let go.

Fandoms make it so that you never have to let go. The story can just keep going, and going, and going for as long as you want it to. That's what conventions and theme parks capitalize on—the nostalgia. I will always chase the high of #DemThrones Black Twitter, the hashtag for fans of color of the show. I can search the hashtag for maybe a few years more before most people delete their accounts forever, and then that world, and that time, will really be gone. If world-building is a vision crafted out of language, fandoms bring it even more to life through collective dreaming.

But for me, the sensory power of that dreaming is lost the minute that world is reproduced cheaply as a mass commodity. The materials of our world make the magic an uncanny simulation in plastic. What was once alive is now dead, with people in Dockers or fishnets or baseball caps lining up at the cash registers to pay for a $15 keychain. The spell is breaking, and I am falling out of love. It has happened every time—the Jurassic Park rides, Star Wars, Harry Potter, and now . . . well, maybe not yet.

At the conclusion of the first season of HBO's *House of the Dragon*, the first official *Game of Thrones* fan convention was announced on the official HBO podcast. It would be taking place in Los Angeles, the city I lived in, with none other than Kit Harington (ever heard of him?!) as the featured guest. It felt something like magic.

I wanted the chance to thank him for playing Jon Snow. His portrayal had saved my life during a difficult time, and the essay I wrote about him opened doors. I was outbid on the meet-and-greet ticket, so I would have to tell him all that in the thirty seconds I had when they took the picture.

I'd gone to TJ Maxx and Target the night before to get a new outfit, new makeup that wasn't drugstore brand, and hair-taming products. I decided on olive dress slacks and a tailored black T-shirt with leather ankle boots. I splurged on Better Than Sex Mascara and other fancy makeup. I bought fake nails but never used them. I slept in hair rolls and a face mask and spent two hours getting ready when I don't usually take more than five minutes. But when I got there, the rain had smeared my name-brand makeup and zapped the kinks and frizz right back into my hair. You can't flat-iron fate, I guess.

My heart was racing when the line finally shuffled into the conference room. He was mere feet away. And then I saw him.

It was Kit, but somehow a far cry from the Kit I thought I knew. I didn't expect the whole Jon Snow thing, but I also wasn't expecting . . . this. He looked fantastic, but also like a seventies porn star. He was in tight acid-wash jeans and a white T-shirt with a camel-colored leather jacket and motorcycle boots. Fashionable, and sporting a *healthy* mustache with thick chops running down the sides of his mouth, and no beard. His mustache was the star of the show, like a letter M wearing bell bottoms on his face. He would later explain the reason for the ironic facial hair—he was filming a movie where his character was a seventies villain. He obviously looked great, but how someone you used to know looks great when you run into them years later, now a stranger, buzzing with the energy of a different frequency, and who has definitely moved on from you.

He was also somehow more . . . white than I remembered? I'd projected too much of the borderlands cumbia curly man-bun look (the Latine King of El Norte!), internalized too many fan illustrations of a more Dornish-looking, southern-born, olive-skinned Jon Snow. That racialized Jon was largely my own creation, projected onto an Englishman. His eyes were still brown and almond-shaped, but lighter now, and rimmed with gray—in Spanish, this is called ojos café castaño, not ojos negros like mine. Still, he seemed kind, maybe disassociating a little.

As a former smoker and sometimes vaper, I chewed gum in line to calm my nerves. When my turn came, a fan had stopped to chat with him, and then he reacted cheerfully and hugged her. She walked away, and then I was out-of-body nervous as he greeted me in the procession. He posed, put his hand on my back. Then I blurted everything out.

ThankyousomuchforbeingJonSnow—click!—*writingaboutyougotmemy firstbookdeal.* He reacted—*Oh!*—like a congratulations was coming, but then the photo assistant came over and interrupted.

"We have to retake it. Your gum. Your gum."

Oh. Oh no. Take two. Jesus Christ. Okay, he's standing next to me again, don't fuck it up. Smile like a normal person! *Snap.* Mortified, I said thank you quickly and literally ran away, jogging to make it look casual. "To make it look casual." Jesus Christ.

Hours later the photos were ready—both the official one and the blooper. In the first, I am blinking, my mouth wide open, white gum fully visible. The second is perhaps the worst, most awkward photo I have ever taken in my life. I'm tense, trapped in the fact of my body, my weight, my unruly hair, my fading looks, my age—it's all there, in full view next to *the* Kit Harington. That photo would be all I had for him to sign.

In the afternoon autograph line, he is much more relaxed, interacting with the fans and asking questions, making small talk as he signs. People bring books, film stills, swords for him to autograph. There are daps and handshakes. Then I'm next. His assistant slides him our photo.

He takes it, signs it wordlessly, and slides it to the right without looking up at all. Grateful, I take it and walk away.

Me and Kit Harington. I am very uncomfortable.

It could have been a fluke. He'd met thousands of people that day; he'd signed a thousand things a thousand times. He probably didn't even remember me; I was just one fan in a mass of people. Or maybe he remembered exactly who I was, and wanted to avoid the secondhand embarrassment of talking to the gum lady again.

It was hard to concentrate the rest of the day. I'd embarrassed myself, as I usually do with important people, people important to me. I tried to enjoy the rest of the conference—I loved seeing the details on the original costumes and props and meticulously crafted baubles from the show. I went to other actors' talks. But a spell had been broken—not by him, by me. The world that had become a safe haven, a time machine, a world where the only truly good man I knew lived (however fictional a good man is), all of it suddenly felt like an elaborate delusion—cheap, empty, expensive, another dead end.

Kit's interview closed the conference, and while he was charismatic and charming as ever, it was clear that *Game of Thrones* was still a tender subject, an exposed nerve. He'd begun his journey in 2009 at twenty-two years old, and the show was connected to every major milestone of his life, and every stressor: his first television role, instant world-wide fame, his wedding, gossip and drone cameras and videos of him drunk in bars, rumors of flings with Emilia Clarke during his marriage, deepfakes of him in bed with a Russian model, his substance abuse, his recovery. He didn't talk about those things, but about losing the boundary between himself and the character of Jon Snow, not knowing where Jon ended and he began. He commented on not seeing *Game of Thrones* footage in years, and would sometimes say, "I haven't thought about that in ages," or remind us, "It's just a TV show."

Finally a fan had the nerve to ask him about the elephant in the room, the dreaded controversial ending in which Jon Snow kills Daenerys. My hackles went all the way up. I felt *so* protective of him. Having to kill Daenerys was so traumatic for Kit. His reaction to the table read upon finding out—his hand over his mouth, hands on both sides of his head, putting his head down on the table, pushing back from the table, hand over mouth again, in tears—is so well known that the whole sequence is now a meme. He was not only horrified by the decision, he anticipated and understood every bit of the criticism—gender, sexism, power, intimate partner violence, story pacing, fridging, how it came out of nowhere—and fans are still brutal to him. There were already so many kinds of heartbreak to get through that last season, but to destroy that legacy and be part of its spectacular decline to become something people hate, that I can't imagine.

"We were all like, what the . . . hell," the fan said, and then asked her question in a cutesy, accusatory tone. "Were you expecting that ending? 'Cause . . . we were not." The crowd laughed. I took note of her little outfit, because I was gonna find her later.

Kit was patient and generous, and thoughtfully answered as best he could:

"Here's my take on it. I think it's okay to be hurt. . . . And I think that there were various things we all could have done differently throughout the show, not just in the final few seasons. But I think the story is right—Jon killing Dany, I'm sorry—I think is the right ending. [*Applause*] For me, and it's important to say *for me*. For you, it may not be, and that's okay, too. But for me, with where the show went, that felt, that felt right. [*Tentative applause.*]"

I think I yelled, *YUP!* in support and looked around. I mean, yes feminism, but Dany nuked millions of innocent people with her dragon? Girlbossed just a bit too close to the sun? But once again, fans projected their headcanon onto an actor and conflated him with a character he played. So did I, to be fair.

I remembered reading that Kit had checked himself into rehab a few days ahead of the show's series finale. Being *particularly* bad at endings and letting go, I understand how unbearable it is to even be known, much less continue to exist when something you're not proud of is public, and makes you feel vulnerable. And you can see the immensity of it on his face in the scene from "The Last Watch" of his very last day on the very last shoot. His face was red, puffy with tears. He looked down as he spoke, and thanked everyone. Later he said taking off his Jon Snow costume was like his "skin was being peeled away." In an interview with *Esquire*:

My final day of shooting, I felt fine . . . I felt fine . . . I felt fine . . . Then I went to do my last shots and started hyperventilating a bit. Then they called, "Wrap!" And I just fucking broke down. It was this onslaught of relief and grief about not being able to do this again. It wasn't so much about Jon. It was about not being in this world, not getting to smell those smells, fight those fights, be with these people—the whole package.

But the weirdest bit was when we came off set and they started taking the costume off and it felt like being skinned. It felt like they were unceremoniously, for the last time, ripping off this character. I was still blubbering my tears. The costume girls were like, "Fucking, come on, get it together." I'm being very actorly and crying. I remember going, "Wait, wait, wait!" And they wouldn't. They just ripped. *[Pantomimes sleeves being taken off.]* I was like, "I need to say goodbye." But it was too late. He was gone.

There was something about the costume being taken off me that was like, *Oh, I don't get to be him anymore.* And I love him. I loved being him.

The role had broken his heart, and something about it all, about *Game of Thrones,* had ended for him. It had to, for Kit Harington the person, to live.

I STOPPED BELIEVING IN MAGIC ABOUT A YEAR AGO. IT HAPPENED during the writing of this book, which is a distressing thing to happen when you're writing about magic and fantasy as a way of processing profound, generational grief. But one day, after hours of TikTok tarot readings telling me someone from the past was going to confess their feelings, confess they actually loved me, and then after hours of pulling my own cards for verification and taking pictures of the spreads to prove it, after every other picture in my camera roll was of 11:11 and 3:33 screenshots and mundane things I'd interpreted as signs, after hours spent looking up the planetary transits of key dates and comparing them against my natal chart, I realized: *I had to stop.* I had to stop, or this torture would never end. I kept looping the same contradicting answers. *Yes. Love is coming, they love you. No, love is not coming, let them go.* And when things start looping, that's when I know I'm self-soothing, I'm numbing, I'm trying to survive myself.

Whatever I was doing, it wasn't divination, or storytelling, or curanderismo, or magic. It was hypervigilance. Magic, a practice whose metaphors had once healed me, had become a maladaptive trauma response, another loop I'd gotten stuck on.

My relationship to the practice had changed. Finding a spiritual practice to survive my divorce had once helped me remember, reconnect with my dead, recognize and break patterns, externalize and interpret my grief, collaborate with the earth and the moon and its seasons, express my feelings, find gratitude. But like always, I turn any kind of relief into a self-sabotage trap, a delusion, a self-deception tool. I was using tarot every few minutes, the same way I did at the end of my marriage, where I would consult tarot cards and compare natal charts to try to figure out "the truth" about my husband, his feelings, his motives, why he was doing this, trying desperately to gain some kind of insight or power over my life. Magic is a last resort in a perpetual feeling of powerlessness, what you do when you have no power over the choices being made for you, and no protection in the world other than yourself. That kind of precarity can make a person paranoid, defensive—a shell of what they once were when they could trust the world.

If I didn't have a *guarantee* that I'd be safe and successful and loved, I would not take any more chances. What if the world spun off its axis again, what if I *couldn't anticipate what was coming?* I couldn't handle any more surprises or 180s or rejections. I couldn't take *any risks* unless I knew it was safe. And eventually, I didn't go out anymore, never texted or called anyone, didn't go on dates, didn't pitch or send out work. Needing to be safe was no longer keeping me alive; instead, it had made me stop living.

Magic could not undo shame, predict failure, or change any outcomes. I had to become okay with trying and failing again. I had to fail, again and again, and not let it break me.

I started slowly grounding myself in reality. One day I moved my full-length mirror to the middle of my apartment so I'd pass it anytime I changed rooms, and I finally took a really long look in a mirror for the first time since before I had my son. I'd been avoiding the reflection that "disgusted" my ex, and had in turn made me ashamed and disgusted with myself. Burning pink candles on the strawberry moon wouldn't make me beautiful—I had to accept the body in front of me as the vessel that had protected me from violence. Accept that coming back to myself would take years.

I made doctor's appointments, spreadsheets, workout schedules, diet plans, a budget instead of new moon intentions. It all hurt, like falling out of a tree and hitting every branch on the way down—on a cold day, in public, while hungover. I stopped pulling tarot spreads, put the cards in their boxes, and turned them around so the titles of the cards faced the wall. I deleted hundreds of pictures of tarot spreads and "angel number" screenshots, maybe thousands. When I'd see a repeating number, or a stray song popped in my head, or I got any other kind of "sign," I had to intentionally reroute my brain away from any spiritual interpretation, shut down the thought that ancestors were speaking to me. When someone I respected tweeted that they'd muted all the zodiac signs, I uninstalled all my astrology apps, unfollowed astrologers, and stopped preparing for moon phases and transits. And I did one last ritual: a cord cutting.

Above: *A doe that appeared with her fawn on a hike. Griffith Park, February 2022.*

Top right: *A dead deer I encountered on a hike just a few weeks before my marriage ended. Griffith Park, California, spring 2017.*

Right: *A green parrot out of about twenty to thirty in a tree, March 2022.*

Some suicidally hard winter months went by. I was back where I started, maybe worse. By late February I started taking long walks again, especially long ones to ward off making any real plans—this is what I'll do with my books so that my mom and brother don't have to deal with them, I'll make a will tomorrow, etc. Then the strangest things started to happen, far too strange to ignore. The ones I remember:

I. In early March, I was praying out loud on a hike and said, "What am I doing? I don't believe in anything anymore."

Suddenly a young doe appeared in front of my face, maybe fifteen feet away. I didn't move, and she didn't move—we just looked at each other for a beat, then another, and another. Another. Then she took a step, and just when I thought she'd leap away, she settled into a gaze with me, calm, while I held back my dog Rumi. But she was also calm. So when the doe's fawn came out into the open, tender and awkward and brand-new in the purple evening sun, and walked across the trail and into the brush, I could hardly believe what I was seeing. I remembered seeing a nearly intact deer skeleton on a run mere months before my marriage would end, and now here, in front of me, was new life. As the mother doe leapt away, I took out my phone and started recording, hoping I'd catch something, but instead of running off, the doe poked her head out of the brush and just stared at me, blinking, unafraid.

II. I talked to my dad one evening in late March when he told me his childhood friend Perico (Spanish for *parrot*) had died the week before. I asked him the date, and he told me: March 26. I looked up a photo I'd taken on my phone to make sure. And there it was—on March 25, on the eve of Perico's death, on my evening walk with Rumi, I saw about twenty parrots in a tree.

I'm not a bird person, but since living alone in LA, I've had rare wildlife encounters strangely up close, especially with birds. Owls, hummingbirds, hawks, an eagle once. I've never seen parrots, like big green pet-store parrots, in the wild, and certainly not twenty. But there they were, eating berries from this tree.

I took pictures of them because of the sheer oddity of the sight and didn't think of it again. Then, that following week, when Papi told me about Perico's passing, I told my parents about the parrots over Face-Time and sent them the photo. They were silent for a moment, and looked at each other in a kind of shock. "Mami, a lo mejor eres vidente como tu tía Lupe," my mom said. *Maybe you're a seer like your grand-aunt Lupe.* It's tempting to believe.

Later that night, I looked up "wild parrots LA" and learned that feral parakeets are actually a common phenomenon in Southern California—something about the ports and illegal exotic bird trade.

And that's how signs are: something appears before you, too strange a coincidence to not be a sign, and just before you let yourself believe it, almost immediately afterward, there's an explanation that shatters that belief, and on goes the cycle of breaking your own heart with hope.

I wanted to let my dad believe, though—since he's gone blind, it's difficult for him to keep up with old friends, and I hoped the pictures of those parrots helped him believe that, through me, Perico was able to say goodbye to him one last time.

But before I end this book, there is one last sign.

III. The day I stopped believing in magic, I also stopped believing in love. So much, I wrote that as the first sentence of an essay: *The day I stopped believing in magic, I also stopped believing in love.* In the reflection of my screen, two figures. Then I turned around and saw them.

Two mourning doves in near-perfect symmetry, facing each other inside a heart—a symbol a friend would later read as a Sankofa, a coming back for that which you love. I took a photo of the birds as a kind of proof that I wasn't crazy, that the natural world really was in conversation with us all the time. What were these doves here to tell me? For a long time, I interpreted it in the smallest, most simplistic way—*love is real, and it's coming.*

Two mourning doves facing each other inside a heart just outside my front door, June 19, 2022.

Except the sign came to me as I was writing about how magical thinking is a trauma response indicating a wounded psyche—wrong mind, wrong brain, wrong thoughts—and magical realism is a genre haunted by the specter of colonialism, a fabulation narrated from the psychic wound of collective trauma, epigenetic scarring, and dispossession. In the "real" world, the First World, where psychological realism is king, sanity is a state of rational skepticism and disbelief—the more the brain rejects magical thinking, the healthier and more reliable it is.

But as I grounded, I didn't feel healthier. I felt broken, empty, robotic, gray, like the mystery of living had left the world. I longed to believe, longed for some intelligence thrumming beneath the world. And then it dawned on me—my critical emphasis on *the brain* had been my limitation all along. I was still intellectualizing, self-diagnosing, pathologizing, splitting my consciousness into mind over body, reason over emotion, in the classic dualist tradition of Western thought, even as I critiqued that split, that unnatural border in our consciousness, as a colonial wound. This journey hasn't been about coming back to clinical definitions of mental health, or about literary catharsis and epiphany— it's been about reintegrating a deeply and historically fractured self through intuition, restorying, fabulation, ancestral communion, ritual.

Magical realism, as it turns out, is not a way of thinking, or writing, or reasoning. It's not a literary genre or a third-world narrative consciousness or dissociative derealization disorder. And it isn't a mental illness or psychosis or a fantasy. It's not of the human brain at all. Magical realism is of the heart; how the heart sees the world, how the heart thinks, reads, remembers, what it calls out for to stay alive. Magical realism is seeing what the heart believes possible in the real world, even after it's broken. Maybe even especially then.

ACKNOWLEDGMENTS

In order for this book to be possible, I had to be possible, which has always been a collective project. Thank you first and foremost to my agent Amanda Orozco, whose early faith in me has opened doors I never dreamed could open; and to my editor, Pilar Garcia-Brown, whose gifts and patience are vast and generous and deep. Thank you for arranging these disparate shards into a kaleidoscopic vision, and thank you for believing in this book.

Special shout-out to the brilliant production team at Penguin Random House and Dutton Books for their endless patience, and for making such a stunning book on borrowed time: production editors Alice Dalrymple and Erica Rose, designer Daniel Brount, jacket designer Kaitlin Kall, managing editor Melissa Solis, and assistant managing editor Clare Shearer, as well as publicist Sarah Thegeby and marketer Nicole Jarvis. And thank you to Amber Oliver and Phoebe Robinson and Tiny Reparations Books, for taking a chance on me, and all the daughters who dream to be.

There are many friends, family, fellow writers, and colleagues whose brilliant work has inspired my own, and whose mentorship and friendship have been invitations to expansion and possibility—thank you for your pathways. Forever gratitude to queen Carmen Maria Machado, whose video game recommendations via Twitter DM encouraged me to branch out from *Skyrim* and find the witcher in me; thank you to Carmen and to J. Robert Lennon, editors for the *Critical Hits: Writers Playing Video Games* anthology, published by Graywolf Press, who invited me to the table with other writers who were also gamers; thank you to Keith S. Wilson, who guided me toward Thedas, and whose poems and friendship helped me connect many fantasy worlds in the process. Thank you to the magazine editors who took a chance on the essays that formed this book, and guided those early versions to fruition: Danielle Jackson and Noah Britton at *Oxford American*, Andrea Morales and Wendi Thomas of *MLK50*, Jen Gann and Jen Ortiz from *The Cut*, Claire Mueschke for *Pleiades*, Patrycja Humienik for the *On Rivers* anthology for *Seventh Wave*, and Kaitlyn Greenidge from *Harper's Bazaar*.

Thank you to the writers and friends in the real world, some who read these essays at various stages of making and unmaking, and some who guided me through various stages of making and unmaking. Thank you to Muriel Leung, who does homework so that she can talk to me about my fantasy obsessions, and whose care and courage inspire me every day; to Marcelo Hernandez Castillo, heart-sibling and visionary, whose friendship and fatherhood heal me constantly; to oracle poet Carolina Ebeid; to opulent docent poet Derrick Austin; to truth-teller Khadijah Queen; and to my mentor Ruth Ellen Kocher. Thank you also to these writers and friends who have inspired and supported me throughout the writing of this book: Carina del Valle Schorske, Jean Ho, Ashaki Jackson, Kenji Liu, Dan Lau, Vickie Vertiz, Sara Borjas, Soraya Membreno, and SA Smythe. Thank you to writers and mentors who have been friends to my work, minds I've been lucky to commune with during fellowships, residencies, invitations, and readings while in the process of making and unmaking: Natalie Diaz, aracelis girmay, Marcia Douglas, Stephen Graham Jones, Cristina Rivera Garza, Jeff Vandermeer, Ingrid Rojas Contreras, R. O. Kwon, Alex Marzano-Lesnevich, Meredith Talusan, Eve Ewing, Meg Fernandes, Jake Skeets, Talia Lakshmi Kolluri, Nadia Owusu, Dantiel W. Moniz, Melissa Febos, Kaveh Akbar, Camonghne Felix, Lisa Nikolidakis, Cass Donish, Naomi Williams, and Nayomi Munaweera. And to friends who stuck with me from the before-times, from odd jobs and graduate school, and who fondly people many of these memories: Karen Skinner, Monica Koenig, Caroline Davidson.

Thank you to Lance Cleland and A. L. Major, directors of Tin House Workshop, friends of my work and all work crossing borders and in the margins, who let me make coffee at ten p.m. and talk at length about failure, video games, AI, and cumbia, and who guide so many voices out of the dark and onto the stage, both in writing and karaoke—"Kiss from a Rose" crew for life. Thank you to Sarah Audsley at Vermont Studio Center, for inviting me to share ideas from this book in their galaxy-brain stage; thank you to Christian Kiefer and Ashland University Low Residency MFA program, for early faith in the craft talk that shaped this book; thank you to Arizona State University and the Center for Imagination in the Borderlands, for inviting me to share the earliest fragments of ideas that would shape this book alongside Joseph Earl Thomas; and thank you to Michael Taeckens and Whitney Peeling of the Whiting Foundation—Michael, for encouraging me to pitch the Jon Snow essay after hearing me go on and on about him at dinner; and Whitney, for telling me I should write about my matrilineal connection to perfume—thank you for listening, and for believing in my ideas beyond the first book.

I almost wasn't possible at many points in my life, and it is only because of my family that I have survived. To my mother, Silvia Angélica Villarreal, whose hero's journey has built and rebuilt worlds and crossed impossible bridges, who has fought every injustice and monster, and in so doing, has saved our lives every single day of hers; to my father, Gilberto Villarreal, La Máquina de Reynosa, whose roots are deep and song is eternal; to my brother, Gilbert Villarreal, loving protector whose brilliance will be known and whose dreams are destined to come true. Also to Jesse, thank you for helping me pursue an impossible future, and for letting go when I couldn't.

And to Joaquín, the boy from the future who willed himself into existence, and the love of my life: thank you for your make-believe, and for making me believe again. You are who I imagine for.

BIBLIOGRAPHY

The Migrant's Journey

Adapted from Joseph Campbell's diagram of the Hero's Journey narrative structure. In *The Hero with a Thousand Faces*. New York: Pantheon, 1949.

Fram, Alan, and Jonathan Lemire. "Trump: Why Allow Immigrants from 'Shit-Hole Countries'?" AP News, January 11, 2018. https://apnews.com/article/immigration-north-america-donald-trump-ap-top-news-international-news-fdda2ff0b877416c8ae1c1a77a3cc425.

About a Girl

Baudrillard, Jean. *Simulacra and Simulation*. Translated by Sheila Faria Glaser. The Body, in Theory: Histories of Cultural Materialism. Ann Arbor: University of Michigan Press, 1994.

Cri-Cri (Francisco Gabilondo Soler). "El Ropero." *Cri-Cri*. RCA Victor MKE-26, 1953.

Cummins, Jeanine. *American Dirt*. New York: Flatiron Books, 2020.

Febos, Melissa. "In Praise of Navel-Gazing." In *Body Work: The Radical Power of Personal Narrative*. New York: Catapult, 2022.

Million, Dian. "Felt Theory." *American Quarterly* 60, no. 2 (June 2008): 267–72. https://www.jstor.org/stable/40068531.

Morrison, Toni. "The Site of Memory." In *Inventing the Truth: The Art and Craft of Memoir*, ed. William Zinsser, 2nd ed. Boston: Houghton Mifflin, 1995, 83–102.

Online Etymology Dictionary. S.v. "Radical." https://www.etymonline.com /search?q=radical.

Paul, Pamela. "The Long Shadow of 'American Dirt.'" *New York Times*, January 26, 2023. https://www.nytimes.com/2023/01/26/opinion/american-dirt -book-publishing.html.

Said, Edward W. *Orientalism*. Penguin Modern Classics. London: Penguin Classics, 2003.

Sehgal, Parul. "The Case against the Trauma Plot." *New Yorker*, December 27, 2021. https://www.newyorker.com/magazine/2022/01/03/the-case-against-the -trauma-plot.

Shriver, Lionel. "When Diversity Means Uniformity." *Spectator*, June 9, 2018. https://web.archive.org/web/20180611082945/https://www.spectator .co.uk/2018/06/when-diversity-means-uniformity/.

Tolentino, Jia. "Lionel Shriver Puts On a Sombrero." *New Yorker*, September 14, 2016. https://www.newyorker.com/culture/jia-tolentino/lionel-shriver -puts-on-a-sombrero.

All the Atreyus at the Sphinx Gate

Petersen, Wolfgang, dir. *The NeverEnding Story*. Burbank: Warner Bros. Entertainment Inc., 1984.

After the World-Breaking, the World-Building

Archive of Our Own. "AO3 Census: Demographics." 2013. https://archive ofourown.org/works/16988199/chapters/39932349.

Blakinger, Keri. "The Dungeons & Dragons Players of Death Row." *New York Times*, August 31, 2023. https://www.nytimes.com/2023/08/31/magazine/dungeons-dragons-death-row.html.

Hartman, Saidiya. "Venus in Two Acts." *Small Axe* 12, no. 2 (2008): 1–14. https://muse.jhu.edu/article/241115.

Lodge, David. *The Art of Fiction: Illustrated from Classic and Modern Texts*. New York: Viking, 1993.

Morrison, Toni. "The Site of Memory." In *Inventing the Truth: The Art and Craft of Memoir*, ed. William Zinsser, 2nd ed. Boston: Houghton Mifflin, 1995, 82–102.

Narcos. West Hollywood: Gaumont International Television. Streamed on Netflix, 2015–2017.

Rushdie, Salman. "Angel Gabriel." *London Review of Books* 4, no. 17 (September 16, 1982). https://www.lrb.co.uk/the-paper/v04/n17/salman-rushdie/angel-gabriel.

Curanderismo

Berry, Ellen. "Brain Study Suggests Traumatic Memories Are Processed as Present Experience." *New York Times*, November 30, 2023. https://www.nytimes.com/2023/11/30/health/ptsd-memories-brain-trauma.html.

Online Etymology Dictionary. S.v. "Cure (n. 1)." https://www.etymonline.com/word/cure.

Perl, O., et al. "Neural Patterns Differentiate Traumatic from Sad Autobiographical Memories in PTSD." *Nature Neuroscience* 26, no. 12 (2023): 2226–36. https://doi.org/10.1038/s41593-023-01483-5.

En Útero

Kerslake, Kevin, dir. *Nirvana: Live! Tonight! Sold Out!* Los Angeles: Geffen Records, 1994. VHS.

Quintanilla, Selena. Video interview by J. R. Castilleja, 1994. Filmed by Kevin Copeland. YouTube video, 4:13. https://www.youtube.com/watch?v=WaooXSxDqVU. Cited material begins at 1:13.

Memory, a Lacuna

Alatorre, Luis. "Tras 6 años seco, corre agua por el lecho del Río Nazas." *Milenio*, September 9, 2022. https://www.milenio.com/estados/laguna-corre-agua -lecho-seco-rio-nazas.

Derrida, Jacques. *Specters of Marx: The State of the Debt, the Work of Mourning, and the New International*. New York: Routledge, 1994.

Hauser, Christine. "Land O'Lakes Removes Native American Woman from Its Products." *New York Times*, April 17, 2004. https://www.nytimes.com /2020/04/17/business/land-o-lakes-butter.html.

Parker, Morgan. "How to Stay Sane While Black." *New York Times*, November 20, 2016. https://www.nytimes.com/2016/11/20/opinion/sunday/how-to -stay-sane-while-black.html.

Valdes-Perezgasga, Francisco. "Place Where You Live: La Laguna, Mexico." *Orion Magazine*, May 31, 2012. https://www.orionmagazine.org/place/la -laguna-mexico-6888/.

Williams, Patricia J. "Gilded Lilies and Liberal Guilt." In *The Alchemy of Race and Rights*. Cambridge, MA: Harvard University Press, 1991, 15–43.

My Boyfriend's Maid

Bennett, Leslie. "Ben's Open Road." *Vanity Fair*, March 2003. https://archive .vanityfair.com/article/2003/3/bens-open-road.

Dunn, Jancee. "Ben Affleck's Hollywood Ending." *Rolling Stone*, no. 945, April 2004. https://www.rollingstone.com/tv-movies/tv-movie-news/ben -afflecks-hollywood-ending-200904/.

"Jennifer Lopez Plays Italian in The Wedding Planner." *NYPress*, February 16, 2015. https://www.nypress.com/news/jennifer-lopez-plays-italian-in -the-wedding-planner-BVNP1020010207302079999.

Volver, Volver

Fernández, Vicente. "Volver, Volver." Track 8 on *¡Arriba Huentitàn!* Caytronics Records, 1972.

Hernandez Castillo, Marcelo. *Children of the Land*. New York: Harper, 2020.

Knowles-Carter, Beyoncé. "6 Inch." *Lemonade*. Directed/performed by Beyoncé Knowles-Carter, Kahlil Joseph, Dikayl Rimmasch, Todd Tourso, Jonas Åkerlund, Melina Matsoukas, and Mark Romanek. Los Angeles: Parkwood Entertainment. Streamed on HBO, 2016.

In the Shadow of the Wolf

Anti-Defamation League. "White Supremacists Adopt New Slogan: 'You Will Not Replace Us.'" *ADL Blog*, June 9, 2017. https://www.adl.org/resources /blog/white-supremacists-adopt-new-slogan-you-will-not-replace-us.

Assassin's Creed Valhalla. Montreal: Ubisoft, 2020.

Dragon Age: Inquisition. Edmonton, Alberta, Canada: BioWare, 2015.

Gobineau, Arthur de. *Essay on the Inequality of the Human Races*. Translated by Adrian Collins. New York: G. P. Putnam's Sons, 1915.

Hartman, Saidiya. *Scenes of Subjection: Terror, Slavery, and Self-Making in Nineteenth-Century America*. New York: Oxford University Press, 1997.

Jackson, Peter, dir. *The Lord of the Rings: The Fellowship of the Ring*. New Line Cinema, 2001.

Vasconcelos, José. *The Cosmic Race / La raza cósmica*. Translated by Didier T. Jaén. Baltimore: Johns Hopkins University Press, 1997.

The Final Boss

Abraham, Yuval. "'A Mass Assassination Factory': Inside Israel's Calculated Bombing of Gaza." *972 Magazine*, November 30, 2023. https://www .972mag.com/mass-assassination-factory-israel-calculated-bombing -gaza/.

Authors Guild. "The Authors Guild, John Grisham, Jodi Picoult, David Baldacci, George R. R. Martin, and 13 Other Authors File Class-Action Suit Against OpenAI." Press release, September 20, 2023. https://authorsguild.org /news/ag-and-authors-file-class-action-suit-against-openai/.

Bachelard, Gaston. *The Poetics of Space*. Translated by Maria Jolas. London: Penguin Classics, 2014. First published as *La poétique de l'espace* in 1958 by Presses Universitaires de France (Paris).

Beaumont, Hilary. "'Never Sleeps, Never Even Blinks': Hi-Tech Anduril Towers Spreading along the US Border." *Guardian*, September 16, 2022. https://www .theguardian.com/us-news/2022/sep/16/anduril-towers-surveillance-us -mexico-border-migrants.

Cameron, Dell, Shoshana Wodinsky, and Dhruv Mehrotra. "We Found Clearview AI's Shady Face Recognition App." Gizmodo, February 27, 2020. https://gizmodo.com/we-found-clearview-ais-shady-face-recognition -app-1841961772.

DeGeurin, Mack. "'Thirsty' AI: Training ChatGPT Required Enough Water to Fill a Nuclear Reactor's Cooling Tower, Study Finds." Gizmodo, May 10, 2023. https://gizmodo.com/chatgpt-ai-water-185000-gallons-training -nuclear-1850324249.

Drake, Shaw. "A Border Officer Told Me I Couldn't Opt Out of the Face Recognition Scan. They Were Wrong." American Civil Liberties Union. https:// www.aclu.org/news/immigrants-rights/a-border-officer-told-me-i -couldnt-opt-out-of-the-face-recognition-scan-they-were-wrong.

Fossi, Connie. "Miami Police Used Facial Recognition Technology in Protester's Arrest." NBC 6 South Florida, August 17, 2020. https://www.nbcmiami .com/investigations/miami-police-used-facial-recognition-technology -in-protesters-arrest/2278848/.

Franco, Marisa. "Palantir Filed to Go Public. The Firm's Unethical Technology Should Horrify Us." *Guardian*, September 4, 2020. http://www.theguardian .com/commentisfree/2020/sep/04/palantir-ipo-ice-immigration-trump -administration.

Gay, Ross. "A Small Needful Fact." In Split This Rock, The Quarry: A Social Justice Poetry Database, added April 30, 2015. https://www.splitthisrock .org/poetry-database/poem/a-small-needful-fact.

Ghosh, Amitav. "Amitav Ghosh: Where Is the Fiction about Climate Change?" *Guardian*. October 28, 2016. http://www.theguardian.com/books/2016 /oct/28/amitav-ghosh-where-is-the-fiction-about-climate-change-.

Ghosh, Amitav. *The Great Derangement: Climate Change and the Unthinkable.* Chicago: University of Chicago Press, 2016.

BIBLIOGRAPHY

Gil, Yásnaya Elena A. *Ää: Manifiestos sobre la diversidad lingüística* [Ää: Manifestos of linguistic diversity]. Mexico City: Almadia, 2023.

Glissant, Édouard. *Poetics of Relation.* Translated by Betsy Wing. Ann Arbor: University of Michigan Press, 1997.

Hao, Karen. "Training a Single AI Model Can Emit as Much Carbon as Five Cars in Their Lifetimes." *MIT Technology Review,* June 6, 2019. https://www .technologyreview.com/2019/06/06/239031/training-a-single-ai-model -can-emit-as-much-carbon-as-five-cars-in-their-lifetimes/.

Haraway, Donna J. *Staying with the Trouble: Making Kin in the Chthulucene.* Durham, NC: Duke University Press, 2016.

Harwell, Drew. "FBI, ICE Find State Driver's License Photos Are a Gold Mine for Facial Recognition Searches." *Washington Post,* July 7, 2019. https:// www.washingtonpost.com/technology/2019/07/07/fbi-ice-find-state -drivers-license-photos-are-gold-mine-facial-recognition-searches/.

Horizon Zero Dawn. Amsterdam: Guerrilla Games, 2017.

Jackson, Zakiyyah Iman. *Becoming Human.* New York: New York University Press, 2020.

Kapil, Bhanu. *Humanimal.* Berkeley, CA: Kelsey Street Press, 2009.

Lee, Timothy B. "Stable Diffusion Copyright Lawsuits Could Be a Legal Earthquake for AI." *Ars Technica,* April 3, 2023. https://arstechnica.com/tech -policy/2023/04/stable-diffusion-copyright-lawsuits-could-be-a-legal -earthquake-for-ai/.

Long Soldier, Layli. "Obligations 2." In *New Poets of Native Nations,* edited by Heid E. Erdrich. Minneapolis: Graywolf Press, 2018. https://www.poetry foundation.org/poems/149976/obligations-2.

Lyons, Kim. "ICE Just Signed a Contract with Facial Recognition Company Clearview AI." *Verge,* August 14, 2020. https://www.theverge.com /2020/8/14/21368930/clearview-ai-ice-contract-privacy-immigration.

Mac, Ryan, Caroline Haskins, and Logan MacDonald. "Clearview's Facial Recognition App Has Been Used by the Justice Department, ICE, Macy's, Walmart, and the NBA." BuzzFeed News, February 27, 2020. https://www.buzzfeed news.com/article/ryanmac/clearview-ai-fbi-ice-global-law-enforcement.

BIBLIOGRAPHY

McKittrick, Katherine, ed. *Sylvia Wynter: On Being Human as Praxis*. Durham, NC: Duke University Press, 2015.

Mendieta, Ana. "Siluetas Series 1973–78." https://blogs.uoregon.edu/anamendieta/2015/02/20/siluetas-series-1973-78/.

Milmo, Dan. "'Impossible' to Create AI Tools Like ChatGPT without Copyrighted Material, OpenAI Says." *Guardian*, January 8, 2024. https://www.theguardian.com/technology/2024/jan/08/ai-tools-chatgpt-copyrighted-material-openai.

O'Brien, Luke. "The Far-Right Helped Create the World's Most Powerful Facial Recognition Technology." *HuffPost*, April 7, 2020. https://www.huffpost.com/entry/clearview-ai-facial-recognition-alt-right_n_5e7d028bc5b6cb08a92a5c48.

O'Brien, Matt, and Hannah Fingerhut. "Artificial Intelligence Technology behind ChatGPT Was Built in Iowa—with a Lot of Water." AP News, September 9, 2023. https://apnews.com/article/chatgpt-gpt4-iowa-ai-water-consumption-microsoft-f551fde98083d17a7e8d904f8be822c4.

Ongweso, Edward, Jr. "Palantir's CEO Finally Admits to Helping ICE Deport Undocumented Immigrants." *VICE*, January 24, 2020. https://www.vice.com/en/article/pkeg99/palantirs-ceo-finally-admits-to-helping-ice-deport-undocumented-immigrants.

Online Etymology Dictionary. S.v. "Robot (n.)." https://www.etymonline.com/word/robot.

Perrigo, Billy. "Exclusive: OpenAI Used Kenyan Workers on Less Than $2 Per Hour to Make ChatGPT Less Toxic." *TIME*, January 18, 2023. https://time.com/6247678/openai-chatgpt-kenya-workers/.

Philip, M. NourbeSe. *Zong!* Middletown, CT: Wesleyan University Press, 2011.

Plato. "Phaedrus." Project Gutenberg. https://www.gutenberg.org/files/1636/1636-h/1636-h.htm.

Shelley, Percy Bysshe. "Ozymandias." In *Shelley's Poetry and* Prose, edited by Donald H. Reiman and Neil Fraistat. Norton Critical Editions. New York: W. W. Norton, 1977. https://www.poetryfoundation.org/poems/46565/ozymandias.

Villeneuve, Denis, dir. *Arrival*. Paramount Pictures, 2016.

Watercutter, Angela. "The Hollywood Strikes Stopped AI from Taking Your Job. But for How Long?" *WIRED*, December 25, 2023. https://www.wired .com/story/hollywood-saved-your-job-from-ai-2023-will-it-last/.

Xiang, Chloe. "OpenAI Used Kenyan Workers Making $2 an Hour to Filter Traumatic Content from ChatGPT." *VICE*, January 18, 2023. https://www .vice.com/en/article/wxn3kw/openai-used-kenyan-workers-making -dollar2-an-hour-to-filter-traumatic-content-from-chatgpt.

The Uses of Fantasy

Andor. Burbank: Lucasfilm Ltd. Streamed on Disney+, 2022.

Baldur's Gate 3. Ghent, Belgium: Larian Studios, 2023.

Bennett, Eric. *Workshops of Empire*. Iowa City: University of Iowa Press, 2015.

Breznican, Anthony. "*Andor* Star Wars Series: 'What You Know Is Really All Wrong.'" *Vanity Fair*, May 23, 2022. https://www.vanityfair.com/hollywood /2022/05/andor-star-wars-series-diego-luna.

Edwards, Gareth, dir. *Rogue One*. Burbank: Lucasfilm Ltd., Walt Disney Studios Motion Pictures, 2016.

Fisher, Mark. *Capitalist Realism: Is There No Alternative?* Ropley, UK: Zero Books, 2009.

James Cameron's Story of Science Fiction. 6 episodes. Leawood, KS: AMC, 2018.

Johnson, Rian, dir. *Star Wars: The Force Awakens*. Burbank: Lucasfilm Ltd., Bad Robot Productions, Walt Disney Studios Motion Pictures, 2015.

Johnson, Rian, dir. *Star Wars: The Last Jedi*. Burbank: Lucasfilm Ltd., Walt Disney Studios Motion Pictures, 2017.

Lucas, George, dir. *Star Wars Trilogy*. Beverly Hills: Lucasfilm, 20th Century Fox, 1977–1983.

Sontag, Susan. "The Imagination of Disaster." In *Against Interpretation and Other Essays*. New York: Picador, 1961, 20–25.

Whitney, Joel. *Finks: How the C.I.A. Tricked the World's Best Writers*. New York: OR Books, 2017.

MAGICAL REALISM, Or the Wolf Is the Land Is the People Is the Border

Coleman, Jon T. *Vicious: Wolves and Men in America*. New Haven, CT: Yale University Press, 2006.

Voyageurs Wolf Project. "GPS Tracking Shows How Much Wolf Packs Avoid Each Other's Range." Minnesota Senate Committee on Agriculture, Rural Development, and Housing Finance, accessed December 2022. https://www .senate.mn/committees/2019-2020/3088_Committee_on_Agriculture _Rural_Development_and_Housing_Finance/GPS%20Tracking%20 Shows%20How%20Much%20Wolf%20Packs%20Avoid%20Each%20 Other.pdf.

Wolfe, Cary. *Before the Law: Human and Other Animals in a Biopolitical Frame*. Chicago: University of Chicago Press, 2013.

When We All Loved a Show about a Wall

Game of Thrones. New York: HBO Entertainment. Streamed on HBO, 2011–2019.

"Obama Has Deported More People Than Any Other President." ABC News, August 29, 2016, https://abcnews.go.com/Politics/obamas-deportation -policy-numbers/story?id=41715661.

Rankine, Claudia, and Beth Loffreda. "On Whiteness and the Racial Imaginary." *Literary Hub*, April 9, 2015. https://lithub.com/on-whiteness-and -the-racial-imaginary/.

"What You Need to Know About the Violent Animals of MS-13." The White House, May 21, 2018. https://trumpwhitehouse.archives.gov/articles /need-know-violent-animals-ms-13/.

Afterword

"The Moment Kit Harington Said Goodbye to Jon Snow." *Esquire*, April 15, 2019. https://www.esquire.com/entertainment/tv/a27021012/kit-harington -game-of-thrones-season-8-interview-2019/.

ABOUT THE AUTHOR

Vanessa Angélica Villarreal was born in the Rio Grande Valley to Mexican immigrants. She is the author of *Beast Meridian*, which received a Whiting Award, a Kate Tufts Discovery Award nomination, and the Texas Institute of Letters John A. Robertson Award. She was a 2021 National Endowment for the Arts fellow, and her work has appeared in *The New York Times*, *Harper's Bazaar*, *The Paris Review*, and elsewhere. She lives in Los Angeles with her son.